Silent Struggles: When Those Above Them Hurt Leaders

A Survival Guide to Top-Down Workplace Harassment and How Supervisors Can Reclaim Respect

By

Dr Haroon Rashid Khan

Dedication

To every leader who stood firm, even when pulled down from above: to those silenced, sidelined, or made to feel small by the very people who should have had their backs.

You carried on through sabotage, steadied your team through chaos, and stayed committed even when your strength was questioned.

You were never the problem. You are not alone.

To the professionals who, despite being hurt, held onto their integrity instead of giving in, who refused to respond to pain with pain: may this book be your voice, your affirmation, and your guide to reclaiming the respect you deserve.

And to those still quietly fighting behind titles and polite smiles, please remember this: your struggle matters. Your leadership matters. This is for you. You deserved better. You still do.

Table of Content

Part I: Power Plays and Control Tactics

How upper management exerts control or limits autonomy

Part II: Psychological and Emotional Manipulation

Mental tactics that erode confidence and well-being

Part III: Recognition, Rewards, and Career Stagnation
When growth, credit, and fairness are systematically denied

Part IV: Personal Invasions and Professional Boundaries Crossed
When your private life and dignity are no longer respected

Part V: Discrimination and Bias at Work
Discriminatory behaviors based on identity, age, beliefs, or culture

Part VI: Protecting Yourself and Pushing for Change
How to respond, recover, and drive accountability

Acknowledgments

This book would never have come to life without the quiet strength of the supervisors, managers, and mid-level leaders who entrusted me with their stories. Thank you for your honesty, your vulnerability, and your willingness to share experiences that were often painful, personal, and deeply human. Your voices do not just fill these pages; they shape them. Your stories were the heartbeat behind every chapter. It was your unseen courage, your silent endurance, that gave this work its soul. I can only hope I have carried your truth with the care and respect it deserves.

To the readers, many of whom may find this book during a season of uncertainty or exhaustion, thank you for letting these words into your world. If you are here looking for clarity or simply to feel understood, know this: you are not alone. My hope is that what you find in these pages offers more than just answers. May it offer recognition, relief, and maybe even a path forward.

This book is at its heart a tribute to your strength, your integrity, and your refusal to abandon what is right, even when the cost is high. Thank you for leading with heart, even when your own was breaking. Your quiet resilience continues to inspire me more than you know.

Preface

From Silence to Strength: Why This Book Had to Be Written

This book was not born from theory; it was born from lived experience. It emerged from late-night reflections, unspoken frustrations, and the quiet resilience of supervisors caught in one of the most misunderstood roles in the modern workplace.

Supervisors are often seen as the bridge between frontline workers and upper management, tasked with enforcing policies, motivating teams, resolving conflicts, and ensuring smooth operations. They are expected to lead with strength, embody professionalism, and deliver results. On the surface, the role carries influence and authority.

But beneath that surface lies a more complex and often vulnerable reality.

Supervisors are, in many ways, trapped in a paradox. They are held accountable like executives but lack the privileges that come with that status. They are expected to support employees, yet rarely receive adequate support themselves. And most disturbingly, many are subjected to silent and persistent mistreatment, not from their subordinates, but from those above them.

Over the years, I've listened to countless stories, stories shared in whispers, over coffee, or in resignation letters never sent. Stories of being micromanaged into paralysis, praised in public, then sabotaged behind closed doors, or pushed to emotional breaking points with no safe place to turn. These supervisors were not weak or incompetent. They were dedicated professionals placed in impossible situations and made to feel alone.

The harm they endured wasn't always visible. It came in the form of exclusion, manipulation, gaslighting, and strategic sidelining. It came through biased evaluations, denied promotions, and workloads designed to exhaust. And perhaps worst of all, it came with a culture of silence that told them this was "just part of the job."

But leadership should not require quiet suffering.

It's time we dismantle the myth that supervisors are immune to workplace injustice. In truth, their unique position—neither protected like unionized employees nor empowered like executives- makes them especially susceptible to exploitation. With limited recourse and immense pressure, they often absorb the emotional and operational strain of entire teams, all while being quietly disempowered from above.

While the focus is on supervisors, the consequences of this systemic mistreatment ripple outward, lowering team morale, increasing turnover, and weakening the very culture companies strive to build. HR professionals and senior leaders will also find in these pages the insights needed to recognize red flags, address toxic dynamics, and rebuild trust where it has eroded.

This book is more than a call to awareness; it's a companion for those navigating the complex realities of leadership.

Divided into six themed sections, the book explores 45 pressing leadership challenges faced by supervisors and the people who walk beside them. Each section is an invitation: to feel seen, to find language for what's often left unspoken, and to move forward with greater clarity, strength, and dignity. Together, they form a path toward a more compassionate and sustainable culture of leadership.

This book exists to change that narrative.

It offers a voice to the unheard. It names the tactics used to diminish and destabilize. And it challenges the systemic undervaluing of mid-level leaders who serve as the heartbeat of organizational life.

In addition to personal stories and organizational critiques, this book also explores the legal rights of supervisors in the Canadian context, strategies for documentation, and guidance on how to navigate internal power struggles safely.

Whether you are a supervisor battling burnout, an HR professional seeking to improve your organization's culture, or an executive ready to lead differently, this book is for you. It is a mirror to reflect hard truths, a map to guide healing and action, and a rallying cry for justice in leadership.

We can no longer accept silence as the price of leadership.

It's time to acknowledge the invisible wounds, challenge toxic power structures, and demand workplaces where supervisors are not merely tools of compliance, but humans worthy of dignity, support, and fair treatment.

Let this be the beginning of that journey, grounded in awareness, courage, and growth.

Dr. Haroon Rashid Khan

Introduction

The Invisible Burden of Supervisors — And Why It Must Be Acknowledged

Supervisors are the silent engines of most organizations. They are expected to lead teams, meet deadlines, resolve conflicts, and interpret executive decisions. They are caught in the middle—responsible for translating high-level strategy into practical outcomes, while shielding their teams from the inevitable pressures of upper management. Yet, when things go wrong, it is often the supervisor who takes the fall.

What happens when those who are tasked with managing others are themselves being controlled, manipulated, or mistreated?

What happens when a leadership title becomes a trap, not a platform?

This book seeks to answer those questions, without flinching and without apology.

Across six parts and 45 chapters, we examine the many ways supervisors—often overlooked in discussions about workplace abuse—are subjected to systemic harm. From **micromanagement that strips autonomy**, to **emotional abuse that chips away at confidence**, to **discrimination that limits opportunity**, the impact is profound, cumulative, and too often ignored.

But this isn't just a book about what happens **to** supervisors. It's also a book about what supervisors can do in response.

Each section not only reveals a category of harm—such as power manipulation, emotional erosion, denied recognition, personal boundary violations, and identity-based discrimination—but also offers a roadmap for **recovery, resistance, and reclaiming control**.

Why Focus on Supervisors?

Supervisors occupy a unique and often vulnerable position within organizations. They have just enough authority to be held accountable, but not enough to protect themselves when they're targeted. When things go well, credit flows upward. When things go poorly, blame falls squarely on them.

And when supervisors face abuse from upper management, it's rarely seen as abuse at all. It's rebranded as "tough leadership," "business pressure," or "organizational discipline."

This book rejects that narrative.

Leadership abuse is still abuse—no matter who the target is.

Supervisors deserve the same protections, respect, and voice as every other worker. They deserve to be seen not just as doers and fixers, but as people—with mental health needs, boundaries, ambitions, and rights.

Structure of the Book

- **Part I** exposes the structural power plays used by upper management to dominate and diminish supervisory roles—from excessive control to intentional exclusion.
- **Part II** explores the psychological tactics that break down confidence and erode professional identity—gaslighting, public shaming, blame-shifting, and more.
- **Part III** addresses the deep injustice of recognition withheld—unfair evaluations, denied promotions, and the silencing of success.
- **Part IV** tackles personal boundary violations, where work crosses into coercion and control over one's private life.
- **Part V** delves into the realities of identity-based discrimination—racism, sexism, ageism, and cultural exclusion—that many supervisors quietly endure.
- **Part VI** turns the spotlight on action: understanding your rights, seeking support, protecting your mental health, and leading with integrity despite systemic pressures.

Who This Book Is For

- **Supervisors** who feel alone, gaslit, or punished for doing the right thing.
- **Current and aspiring leaders** who want to understand how to lead with humanity, not hierarchy.
- **HR professionals, consultants, and organizational reformers** seeking to create better systems that prevent harm and promote dignity.
- **Executives and board members** willing to confront uncomfortable truths about workplace power dynamics.

A Call to Action

This is not a comfortable book, because the truth it tells is not comfortable.

But comfort has never been the soil in which justice grows.

We must reimagine leadership as a space where strength is defined not by domination, but by **decency, fairness, and courage**. We must hold organizations accountable for the cultures they create. And we must ensure that supervisors, often praised for "holding it all together," are no longer forced to suffer in silence.

If you have ever felt isolated, overlooked, or exhausted by the weight of invisible abuse, this book is for you.

If you've ever wondered whether the way you've been treated is usual, or whether it should be, this book is for you.

And if you're ready to reclaim your strength, protect your dignity, and lead on your own terms, then this book is most definitely for you.

Welcome to a different kind of leadership conversation. One grounded in truth, resilience, and the refusal to stay silent any longer.

Disclaimer:

All case studies, examples, characters, and scenarios presented in this book are either entirely fictional or are composites created for illustrative and educational purposes. Any resemblance to actual individuals, organizations, or events—past or present—is purely coincidental. The intention is not to depict or accuse any specific person or institution, but to shed light on systemic patterns and lived experiences commonly reported across diverse workplaces.

Part I: Power Plays and Control Tactics

How Upper Management exerts control or limits autonomy.

Chapter 1
Micromanaged to the Point of Collapse

"When control replaces trust, burnout isn't far behind."

"When every move is watched, your confidence fades faster than your will."

Micromanagement doesn't just slow progress; it drains initiative, crushes autonomy, and erodes trust. It's often disguised as "attention to detail," but in reality, it's about control. When every decision is questioned, every step monitored, and every idea second-guessed, the message is clear: you're not trusted.

Over time, this constant scrutiny does more than frustrate; it exhausts. You don't just lose time. You lose confidence, energy, and eventually, the will to care. There's a critical difference between leadership and surveillance. Micromanagement falls squarely in the latte, and it's one of the fastest ways to burn out talented people.

Introduction: The Myth of Power in a Supervisory Role

On paper, the role of a supervisor appears to carry influence, responsibility, and autonomy. It is often assumed that supervisors are in control of their teams, equipped with decision-making power, and trusted by senior leadership to carry out the company's goals. But for many supervisors, the reality is very different.

Instead of being empowered to lead, they find themselves scrutinized, second-guessed, and micromanaged; not only by their direct reports, but by those above them. Senior leaders, directors, and executive management often engage in behavior that strips supervisors of their authority and turns them into passive middlemen. The result? Supervisors collapse under the weight of over-control, spiraling morale, and mental exhaustion.

This chapter explores what it means to be micromanaged by upper management, not just as a workplace annoyance, but as a form of systemic dysfunction and psychological harm.

1. What Is Micromanagement from Above?

Micromanagement occurs when a leader excessively monitors, controls, or dictates how others perform their tasks. While it is often discussed in terms of supervisors micromanaging frontline employees, it happens just as frequently in the opposite direction, where senior leaders micromanage supervisors, essentially treating them as powerless functionaries rather than operational leaders.

1.1 Forms of Top-Down Micromanagement

1.1.1 Requiring approval for minor decisions

Micromanagement frequently shows up as senior leaders demanding approval for routine decisions that should fall within a supervisor's domain. For instance, if a supervisor wants to rearrange work shifts to accommodate team needs or approve a small purchase for office supplies, having to wait for permission delays operations and diminishes their autonomy. This excessive need for sign-off implies that supervisors are not trusted to make even basic calls, leading to frustration and inefficiency.

Example: Imagine a supervisor who notices a key employee needs to take a day off urgently due to a family emergency. Instead of making a quick judgment call, they must first seek approval from their manager, who might be unavailable or slow to respond. This delay impacts the employee and the whole team's workflow.

Advice: Supervisors can address this by proactively discussing decision boundaries with their manager. Asking, "Which decisions can I handle independently to speed things up?" can help clarify trust levels and push for greater autonomy.

1.1.2 Overriding the supervisor's instructions to staff

When higher-ups regularly override a supervisor's guidance, it creates confusion and undermines their leadership. For example, a supervisor might assign tasks based on team members' skills, but a senior leader could change these assignments without consulting the supervisor. This action sends a message that the supervisor's judgment isn't valued.

Example: In a weekly team meeting, a supervisor directs the group to prioritize a particular project. Later, a senior manager tells the team to focus on something else without informing the supervisor. Team members are left unsure who to follow.

Advice: To handle this, supervisors should seek to maintain open communication with their senior leaders, ensuring alignment on priorities. If overrides happen publicly, asking for private discussions afterward can help resolve misunderstandings and preserve authority.

1.1.3 Imposing strict protocols that leave no room for discretion

Strict protocols without flexibility can suffocate a supervisor's ability to lead effectively. For instance, if senior management enforces rigid reporting formats or exact scripts for customer interactions, supervisors cannot adapt to their team's unique challenges or use their judgment.

Example: A supervisor tries to customize a customer support script to address specific client needs, but management insists on a fixed script for every situation, making the team sound robotic and ineffective.

Advice: Supervisors can collect data showing how flexibility improves outcomes and present this evidence to senior leaders. Suggesting pilot programs with some discretionary power might help demonstrate the value of adaptability.

1.1.4 Demanding constant updates or reports

Senior leaders who require frequent, detailed updates can overwhelm supervisors with paperwork, taking them away from leading their teams. For example, receiving daily requests for progress reports on all projects, even those tracked in existing systems, creates redundant work and stress.

Example: A supervisor spends hours each day compiling detailed status emails, only for the manager to ask more questions or demand even more data.

Advice: Supervisors might propose consolidating reporting channels or using dashboards that senior leaders can access anytime, reducing repetitive update requests. Clear communication about the time burden can sometimes lead to more trust and less micromanagement.

1.1.5 Monitoring attendance, emails, or team communication excessively

Excessive monitoring of day-to-day activities signals distrust. When senior management tracks emails word-for-word or scrutinizes attendance minutiae, supervisors feel their professionalism is questioned. This can create a tense atmosphere where creativity and open communication suffer.

Example: A supervisor's manager regularly checks internal chats to see if they're responding quickly enough, or reads emails to judge tone, rather than focusing on outcomes.

Advice: Supervisors can request more outcome-focused evaluations. Demonstrating reliability over time and inviting feedback on priorities may help reduce unnecessary surveillance.

1.1.6 Correcting language in emails or instructions, focusing on petty details

When senior leaders fixate on minor wording or tone in emails rather than content, it signals mistrust and can slow communication. This micromanagement undermines the supervisor's professionalism and can cause them to second-guess every message.

Example: A supervisor sends a team email and receives a reply from their manager requesting changes in phrasing to sound "more positive," delaying communication and frustrating the supervisor.

Advice: Supervisors should try to understand what tone or style their manager prefers and adapt accordingly. However, they should also gently remind managers that excessive edits can hinder timely communication.

1.1.7 Publicly reversing decisions the supervisor has made

Publicly undoing a supervisor's decisions is perhaps the most damaging form of micromanagement. It erodes the supervisor's credibility and authority in front of their team and peers, leading to loss of respect and motivation.

Example: During a team meeting, a supervisor announces a new process, only for their manager to interrupt and declare it won't be followed, correcting the supervisor on the spot.

Advice: When public reversals happen, supervisors can request a private follow-up meeting with their manager to clarify expectations and express how the public correction affects team morale. Building a partnership based on mutual respect can reduce these incidents.

While some oversight is necessary, the difference between leadership and micromanagement lies in trust. Supervisors are professionals. When they are not trusted to manage even the fundamental aspects of their role, it sends a message that they are incapable, even if they are succeeding.

2. A Day in the Life: Example of Micromanagement in Action

Consider "Amira," a team supervisor in a mid-sized software company in Toronto. She manages a team of seven developers and reports to a Senior Engineering Manager.

On paper, Amira's responsibilities include managing her team's workload, tracking performance, facilitating communication, and working with HR on hiring or conflict resolution.

But in practice, Amira's every decision must be signed off by her manager, including shift schedules, emails to her team, and even the phrasing of performance feedback. Her manager monitors the team's Slack channel, interrupts stand-up meetings to "clarify" what Amira says, and demands end-of-day written updates on everyone's tasks, even though Amira already tracks these in their project system.

When Amira tried to implement a rotation system for code reviews to balance the workload, her manager reversed it within an hour, saying, "I need to make sure it aligns with how I used to do things." Her credibility with her team was damaged. Morale dropped.

Despite her competence, Amira feels like a puppet. "I'm called a supervisor," she says, "but I can't actually supervise anything."

3. Why Upper Management Micromanages Supervisors

Micromanagement by senior leaders is often a symptom of deeper organizational or personal issues rather than mere managerial style. Understanding these reasons can help supervisors navigate and possibly improve their working relationships with upper management.

3.1 Fear of Losing Control

One of the most common drivers of micromanagement at senior levels is a deep-seated fear of losing control. For some executives, leadership means maintaining tight oversight of every detail, believing that without their direct involvement, things will go wrong. This anxiety can stem from pressure to meet targets, fear of failure, or insecurity about their position within the company hierarchy.

Example:

A Senior Director may insist on approving all budget expenditures, even minor ones, not because they distrust the financial system but because they fear any misstep could reflect poorly on them. They might also hover over project timelines and refuse to delegate decisions, fearing that mistakes could threaten their reputation.

Advice:

Supervisors can help alleviate this fear by providing frequent, transparent updates that demonstrate competence and control. Proactively sharing progress reports, risk assessments, and contingency plans can reassure senior leaders. Building a track record of reliability can gradually reduce the executive's perceived need for control.

3.2 Ego and Identity

For some upper managers, the identity of being "in charge" is a core part of their self-worth. They may enjoy having the final say and being the primary source of information within the company. Relinquishing control to supervisors can feel like losing status or power, threatening their relevance.

Example:

An executive might insist on being cc'd on all team emails or personally intervening in minor disputes, not because it's necessary but because it feeds their desire to feel indispensable and authoritative.

Advice:

Supervisors can try to appeal to the executive's ego by framing delegation as a way to amplify their influence. For example: "If you trust me with this responsibility, it frees you up to focus on higher-level strategic decisions." Also, highlighting the successes achieved under their delegated leadership can help the manager feel valued rather than sidelined.

3.3 Poor Leadership Training

Many senior leaders ascend through ranks due to technical expertise, financial acumen, or sales ability rather than people management skills. Without proper training on how to lead other leaders, they may default to managing through control and instruction rather than coaching and empowerment.

Example:

An executive who was a top engineer might struggle to shift from "doing" to "leading," continuing to provide step-by-step instructions to supervisors as they once did to junior engineers.

Advice:

Organizations can invest in leadership development programs specifically targeting mid- to senior-level managers, emphasizing delegation, coaching, and trust-building. Supervisors might also suggest or request mentorship or training opportunities for their managers, framing it as beneficial for the whole team's success.

3.4 Blame Culture

In workplaces where mistakes are punished harshly and risk-taking is discouraged, senior leaders may feel compelled to control every decision to avoid blame. Micromanagement becomes a defensive tactic to "cover their backs" in case something goes wrong.

Example:

If a product launch fails, a micromanaging executive can point to their involvement in every decision as proof that the failure was not due to negligence or poor judgment.

Advice:

Shifting from a blame culture to a learning culture is critical. Supervisors can help by encouraging open dialogue about risks and failures as opportunities for growth. Documenting decisions and their rationale transparently can protect all parties. Advocating for organizational change that rewards innovation and tolerates calculated risks can also reduce micromanagement driven by fear.

3.5 Lack of Organizational Clarity

When roles, responsibilities, and decision-making authority are not clearly defined or communicated, confusion reigns. Upper management may step into supervisors' duties simply because there is no agreed-upon boundary, or because they feel the need to "fill in" gaps due to unclear expectations.

Example:

In a rapidly growing startup, a senior leader might take over daily team management because the organizational chart hasn't caught up with new hires and promotions, leaving supervisors unsure about their authority.

Advice:

Clear role definitions and organizational structures are essential. Supervisors can request or help develop detailed job descriptions and decision matrices that delineate who is responsible for what. Regular alignment meetings can ensure everyone understands their authority limits and areas of ownership, reducing unnecessary interference.

4. The Human Cost: What Micromanagement Does to Supervisors

Micromanagement is often talked about in terms of inefficiency or poor leadership, but its real toll is much more personal. Supervisors sit in a uniquely challenging position. They are expected to lead, inspire, and deliver results, yet many are denied the autonomy to make decisions or take meaningful action. Over time, this disconnects chips away at more than just productivity; it wears down confidence, mental health, physical well-being, and long-term career potential.

4.1 Emotional and Mental Impacts

Micromanagement may seem like just a frustrating style of leadership, but for supervisors, it becomes an everyday mental burden. It creates a persistent state of anxiety, self-doubt, and even shame, all of which grow quietly and invisibly under the surface.

Anxiety and Self-Doubt

When supervisors are second-guessed at every turn, they begin to doubt their own instincts. Even simple decisions, like approving a schedule change or providing feedback to a team member, can trigger uncertainty. "Will this be reversed later?" "Will I get in trouble for this?" Over time, this constant hesitation leads to decision paralysis, where every action feels like a risk.

Burnout

The day-to-day exhaustion isn't just about being overworked; it's about being undercut. Having to repeat tasks because someone else didn't approve them the first time, explaining your choices over and over, or being asked to lead a team without being trusted is not just an annoyance. It's draining. When a supervisor is stuck in this loop for months or even years, burnout isn't just likely; it's inevitable.

Loss of Confidence

Leadership is built on trust, and that includes trusting yourself. When micromanagement strips away autonomy, supervisors lose the ability to build confidence through experience. Every reversal or contradiction by a higher-up sends a message: *You can't be trusted to lead.* Eventually, that message becomes internalized. Confidence fades, and leadership becomes mechanical rather than inspired.

Reduced Credibility with Staff

Team members are quick to notice when their supervisor doesn't actually have control. If decisions get changed, approvals reversed, or instructions contradicted, employees stop taking their supervisor seriously. This doesn't just create awkwardness; it can lead to open defiance, conflict, or apathy on the floor. The supervisor becomes the face of leadership, but without any real power, and both sides know it.

Isolation and Disconnection

Many supervisors feel caught between two worlds: not quite "management," but no longer "just staff." When they're micromanaged, they often can't be honest with senior leaders, and at the same time, can't fully relate to their team anymore. That in-between space can be incredibly isolating. It's lonely, and worse, it feels like no one understands.

Moral Distress

Perhaps one of the most painful experiences is being forced to enforce policies or decisions you disagree with. When supervisors feel they're acting against their own judgment or values, and can't speak up without risk, it creates deep moral stress. Some compare it to watching your team struggle while your hands are tied behind your back.

4.2 Professional Consequences

The emotional and mental impact of micromanagement is only part of the story. Over time, it also reshapes a supervisor's career, often in damaging and invisible ways.

Stalled Career Growth

When you're constantly being micromanaged, you're rarely given a chance to show initiative or lead independently. That means fewer accomplishments, fewer success stories, and fewer chances to grow into higher roles. Promotions don't just come from showing up; they come from showing leadership. And micromanaged supervisors rarely get that chance.

Increased Turnover

Some supervisors eventually leave their roles simply to escape the stress. Others leave because they've realized they'll never be allowed to lead in their current environment, truly. It's not just a matter of quitting a job; it's often the end of a leadership path they once felt excited about. The result is a steady churn of mid-level talent that organizations can't afford to lose.

Silencing of Innovation

When every suggestion is dismissed or micromanaged out of existence, supervisors stop offering ideas. Why bother proposing a better system if it will just be rejected or ignored? This quiet shutdown of creativity might not be visible right away, but over time, it adds up. A culture that discourages risk also discourages progress.

Damage to Reputation

Ironically, supervisors often get blamed for the very problems micromanagement creates. If a team isn't performing, the supervisor becomes the scapegoat, even if their hands were tied the entire time. This can result in poor performance reviews, a damaged internal reputation, and fewer opportunities in the future. On paper, it looks like they failed, when in reality, they were never given a fair chance to succeed.

4.3 Physical Health Consequences

While the emotional toll of micromanagement is often discussed, the physical side is just as real and frequently overlooked.

Sleep Disruption

Supervisors under constant pressure often struggle to "turn off" at night. Sleep becomes erratic or elusive altogether. Thoughts spin endlessly: What went wrong today? What will I be blamed for tomorrow?

Digestive and Stress-Related Issues

Prolonged stress can wreak havoc on the body. Headaches, acid reflux, ulcers, and chronic fatigue are just a few of the physical symptoms reported by supervisors who feel trapped in high-pressure, low-autonomy roles.

Increased Risk of Long-Term Health Problems

Stress is more than just uncomfortable; it's dangerous. Studies have shown that chronic workplace stress can increase the risk of high blood pressure, heart disease, and even a weakened immune system. The longer the stress lasts, the greater the risk.

5. How to Recognize You're Being Micromanaged by Senior Leadership

Micromanagement from senior leadership can be complex to identify at first, especially for supervisors. It often starts with helpful-sounding "support" and escalates into a slow erosion of trust, authority, and clarity. Recognizing the signs early gives you a chance to protect your role, reassert your leadership, and open up honest dialogue before things spiral.

5.1 You Must Seek Approval for Decisions That Used to Be Yours

What it looks like:

You used to approve overtime, adjust schedules, or handle basic performance feedback; now, you have to email someone first or "check in" before making a move. You may even start hesitating before making simple calls because the chain of approval has become unclear or burdensome.

Why it's a red flag:

Micromanagement often disguises itself as "increased alignment" or "process consistency," but if it strips away autonomy you previously held, it's really a sign of lost trust.

What to do:

- Keep a list of decisions you've historically made independently. If that list is shrinking, ask for clarity:

"Can we revisit what level of decision-making I'm still expected to own? I want to make sure I'm not slowing down the team."

- Offer to pilot a decision-making boundary:

    "For the next two weeks, I'll handle scheduling adjustments directly; we can review outcomes together after that."

5.2 You're Corrected for Tone or Word Choice, Even in Minor Communications

What it looks like:

A senior manager rewrites your emails before sending them, or gives unsolicited feedback like, "That sounded too soft" or "I would've said it differently," even when the message was clear and professional.

Why it's a red flag:

While feedback is normal, persistent interference in your communication style, especially in routine matters, suggests a lack of confidence in your leadership voice.

What to do:

- Ask for **clarity on intent**:

    "I noticed you've edited a few of my messages. Is there a tone or brand standard I should be aligning with?"

- Reframe it as an opportunity to **set guidelines**:

    "If there's a preferred communication template or tone guide, I'm happy to follow it, but I'd also like to maintain ownership of team messages when possible."

5.3 Your Team Stops Coming to You; They Wait for Direction from Someone Higher Up

What it looks like:

Employees start bypassing you. Instead of asking you questions, they email your manager. Or worse, they say things like, "I'll wait to hear from [senior leader] before I do that."

Why it's a red flag:

This signals that others no longer see you as the true decision-maker. It undermines your influence and can fracture team cohesion.

What to do:

- Speak directly to your team, reaffirm your role:

  "Just a reminder, if you have questions about project X or team matters, please come to me first. I'll always escalate if needed."

- Talk to your senior leader privately:

  "I've noticed some confusion about reporting lines. Can we clarify with the team that I'm the first point of contact on operational matters?"

5.4 You're Left Out of Decisions, Then Expected to Execute Them

What it looks like:

You find out about a significant team change or policy shift **after** the announcement, but you're still expected to roll it out, answer questions, and ensure compliance.

Why it's a red flag:

Being excluded from decisions that impact your team signals that your input isn't valued, but being expected to "clean up" or implement them anyway adds insult to injury.

What to do:

- Ask for a seat at the table early:

  "For future rollouts that affect the team directly, could I be looped in earlier? I can help ensure smoother execution."

- Suggest a brief decision-preview process:

  "Would it help if we had a weekly 15-minute check-in for any upcoming changes that I'll be supporting?"

5.5 You're Doing Administrative Reporting That Adds No Value; Only Oversight

What it looks like:

You spend hours creating detailed reports or spreadsheets that no one acts on. The only purpose seems to be to monitor your performance, not improve outcomes.

Why it's a red flag:

Excessive reporting is a classic micromanagement tactic. It creates a false sense of control and wastes time that could be used for actual leadership.

What to do:

- Ask what the report is being used for:
- "Could you help me understand how this report is being used? I'd like to make sure the data is actually supporting decision-making."
- Propose streamlining:
- "Would it make sense to move this to a weekly summary or dashboard format so we can save some admin time?"

5.6 You're Regularly Told, "Don't Worry About That; I'll Handle It Myself."

What it looks like:

You bring up an issue or offer to take on a task, and your manager waves it off. Instead of delegating or discussing, they take control directly.

Why it's a red flag:

This signals a breakdown in trust. Repeatedly being dismissed tells you: You're not needed, and you're not capable. It stunts your growth and leaves you disengaged.

What to do:

- Reassert gently:
- "I'd really like to stay involved in that, even if I'm not leading it. Could I support the rollout or follow-up?"
- Ask for future ownership:
- "If this comes up again, would you feel comfortable having me lead it? I'd like to build experience in that area."

Final Advice:

Micromanagement isn't always about control; sometimes it's about fear. Senior leaders may be under pressure themselves or uncertain about how to delegate effectively. But if you don't advocate for your authority and autonomy, it can quietly disappear.

What you can do overall:

- Stay calm, not defensive.
- Document your responsibilities and wins.
- Communicate proactively, don't wait to be asked.
- Build trust by delivering consistently, even in small things.

- When possible, coach upward; help leaders learn to let go by showing them you've got it handled.

6. What Can Supervisors Do?

Dealing with micromanagement, especially when it comes from your own manager, is never easy. It's frustrating and often feels like you're caught in a no-win situation. Still, there are steps you can take to protect your role, your sanity, and your future. Here's how you can respond thoughtfully and with purpose.

6.1 Keep Track of What's Happening

When you're micromanaged, it can sometimes feel like it's all happening in your head — like you're just being overly sensitive. That's why it's important to write things down. Keep a private record of times when you make decisions but someone above you changes them, or when you spend extra time fixing work because someone second-guessed you.

For example, note down: *"Approved schedule change on Monday; on Tuesday, manager overturned without explanation."* Also, jot down how much extra time this took or how it affected your team. Over time, this log will help you see patterns more clearly. If you ever need to talk to HR or higher-ups, having concrete examples makes your case stronger and easier to understand.

6.2 Set Gentle Boundaries

You don't have to accept micromanagement silently. Sometimes, simply asking questions can help remind your manager that you want to lead and can do so well. Try saying things like, *"I want to take full responsibility for this task, so the team hears one consistent message. Could we agree on where I have decision-making freedom?"* This kind of approach shows you're on the same team but want to do your job thoroughly.

You might also suggest a trial period where you handle things independently, then report back. This opens the door for your manager to see that you can be trusted without feeling threatened.

6.3 Ask for Clear Roles

Often, micromanagement happens because nobody has spelled out exactly who is responsible for what. If that's the case, ask for a clear breakdown of decision-making authority. Bring your job description or past reviews to the conversation so you can show what you've been told your role includes.

You can say, *"I want to make sure I understand which decisions I'm expected to own and which ones I should bring up with you."* Getting this clarity can reduce overlap and confusion, making it easier for everyone to know where their boundaries lie.

6.4 Get Help When Needed

If the micromanagement turns into something more harmful, like bullying, harassment, or constant undermining, it's important to get support. Keep your notes on hand and reach out to HR or your union representative confidentially. Explain what you're experiencing and ask what resources or steps are available to help.

You don't have to face a toxic situation alone. Sometimes just having someone listen and acknowledge the problem makes a big difference, and HR may be able to intervene or offer guidance.

6.5 Know When to Move On

Sometimes, no matter what you do, the environment remains controlling and draining. If micromanagement is part of the company's culture, or your manager won't change, it's okay to think about leaving. Leaving isn't quitting; it's choosing a healthier place to grow.

Start quietly exploring workplaces where leaders trust their teams and encourage autonomy. When you find a better fit, you'll protect your well-being and get the chance to shine as a true leader.

Remember: Micromanagement is tough, but it doesn't have to define your career. By paying attention, speaking up respectfully, and protecting your boundaries, you can keep control over your work and your peace of mind.

Summary:

1. **"Micromanagement Is a Leadership Failure, Not a Supervisor's Weakness"** is a powerful statement that challenges a common misconception. When supervisors face micromanagement, it's easy to assume they're not capable or strong enough. But this section flips that narrative — showing that the real issue lies in the inability of senior leadership to delegate and trust.
2. **Micromanagement Reflects on Senior Leadership:**
3. It signals that those at the top are struggling with a core leadership skill: **delegation**. Delegation isn't just handing off tasks; it's trusting others to make decisions, giving them space to learn and grow, and resisting the urge to control every detail. If senior leaders can't do this, it creates a bottleneck and disempowers supervisors.
4. **Organizational Consequences:**
5. When supervisors are micromanaged, it's not just an individual problem — the whole organization suffers. Innovation dries up because supervisors and teams are too focused on approvals and second-guessing. Morale declines as people feel undervalued and mistrusted. High turnover follows because talented supervisors either burn out or leave for healthier workplaces.
6. **What True Leadership Looks Like:**

7. Effective leaders **build leaders**, not followers. They cultivate environments where supervisors feel supported, have clarity on their roles, and are respected for their expertise. This leads to stronger teams, better performance, and a healthier work culture.
8. **The Need for Support Instead of Oversight:**
9. The conclusion emphasizes that what supervisors need isn't more rules or check-ins, but more **support** — including training, clear expectations, resources, and encouragement. Respecting supervisors' autonomy shows trust and boosts confidence.

Chapter 2
Overloaded with Unrealistic Work & Expectations

"Burnout isn't a badge of honor, it's a warning sign."

Workplace overload often masquerades as dedication, but there's a fine line between being committed and being crushed. When expectations consistently exceed what's humanly possible, stress becomes a daily condition, not a temporary challenge.

Being stretched too thin doesn't just affect productivity; it chips away at morale, health, and clarity. Supervisors and professionals under pressure often carry the unspoken belief that saying "yes" proves worth. But chronic overwork isn't sustainable. Eventually, it leads to resentment, fatigue, and disengagement, not success.

Introduction: The Hidden Struggle of Supervisors Under Unrelenting Pressure

Supervisors are often seen as the glue holding organizations together. Positioned between frontline workers and upper management, they translate strategic objectives into everyday actions, solve unexpected problems, and keep teams motivated. Yet, the role is frequently misunderstood and underestimated, especially regarding the sheer volume of work they're tasked with managing.

Across industries, supervisors report being overwhelmed by unrealistic workloads assigned by upper management. Unlike frontline employees, supervisors don't just execute tasks; they also bear accountability for team performance, compliance, and morale. When upper management piles on excessive responsibilities without providing adequate resources or support, supervisors can become trapped in a cycle of chronic stress, declining performance, and burnout.

This chapter explores in depth the causes, effects, and real-life manifestations of supervisors overloaded with unrealistic work. It also offers practical strategies supervisors and organizations can adopt to restore balance and foster healthier work environments.

What Does "Unrealistic Workload" Look Like for Supervisors?

When it comes to supervisory roles, it's not just about how many tasks are on your list — it's about **how complex they are**, how much **emotional energy** they demand, how many **conflicting priorities** you're juggling, and whether you have the **tools, time, and authority** to actually get them done.

In manufacturing, these challenges can be magnified by production deadlines, safety compliance, union relations, machinery issues, and a non-stop pace that leaves no room for error.

Here's what an unrealistic workload *really* looks like — in any industry, and especially on the factory floor.

1. Managing More Employees Than Is Practically Possible

What it looks like:

You're responsible for 20+ operators, technicians, or assemblers — each with their own shift issues, training gaps, or performance concerns. You're expected to keep output high while also maintaining quality and safety.

In manufacturing:

On a production floor, too many direct reports means **missed quality checks**, overlooked safety violations, and a reactive, rather than proactive, management style.

Advice:

Push for a more reasonable span of control — around 8–12 direct reports is manageable depending on complexity. Back up your case with data (e.g., error rates, incident reports, or absenteeism trends).

2. Overseeing Multiple High-Stakes Projects at Once

What it looks like:

You're simultaneously overseeing a machine upgrade, leading a lean manufacturing initiative, and preparing for an ISO audit — all with tight, overlapping deadlines.

Why it's a problem:

Each project pulls your focus and drains your energy. You can't give each the attention it deserves, so **everything gets done halfway**, and you're the one left apologizing.

In manufacturing:

Delays in one area (like equipment calibration) can halt entire production lines, making these overlapping projects even more critical and stressful.

3. Constantly Switching Between Urgent Priorities with Conflicting Deadlines

What it looks like:

You're dealing with a safety incident, a supplier delay, a staffing shortage, and corporate asking for KPI updates — all before your second cup of coffee.

Why it's a problem:

The constant switching creates mental overload and decision fatigue. You start reacting to everything instead of leading intentionally.

In manufacturing:

Unplanned downtime and "firefighting" become the norm. You're constantly pulled off strategic work to fix immediate issues on the line.

Advice:

Build a tiered escalation system. Not every issue should land on your plate first. Train leads or shift supervisors to triage problems.

4. Performing Administrative Duties That Should Be Handled by Clerical Staff

What it looks like:

You're entering vacation requests, printing training sign-in sheets, and tracking PPE inventory — while your production targets go unmet.

In manufacturing:

Time spent on clerical tasks is time *not* spent monitoring line efficiency, engaging with operators, or preventing errors.

Advice:

Document how much time you're spending on admin work, then make a case for a shared administrative resource or automation tools.

5. Handling Disciplinary Issues and Performance Management Without Proper Support

What it looks like:

You're expected to correct behavior, manage underperformance, and write up disciplinary actions — all without HR guidance, coaching skills, or confidence.

In manufacturing:

Disciplinary issues might involve safety violations, insubordination, or attendance — all sensitive and high-stakes. One misstep and you could face grievances or union disputes.

Advice:

Request formal HR training or "just-in-time" coaching when tough situations arise. Don't wing it — that puts both you and the company at risk.

6. Rolling Out New Company Initiatives Without Enough Time or Resources

What it looks like:

You're told to implement a new safety protocol, digital tracking system, or 5S initiative "by end of week" — but there's no training, no budget, and no input from frontline staff.

In manufacturing:

If the rollout isn't done carefully, you risk **confusion, resistance, or accidents.** You're stuck between trying to "make it happen" and keeping morale intact.

Advice:

Push for phased rollouts, pilot testing, or at least **a clear plan with milestones.** Document barriers early to protect yourself from blame later.

So, What Happens When All These Stack Up?

If one or two of these issues hit at once, most supervisors can push through. But when they **all hit at the same time** (and they often do), things become unmanageable:

• There's no time to coach your team

• You can't finish your own tasks

• You start missing small things, then big things

• You go home exhausted and wake up dreading work

And worst of all, you start to wonder if it's you who's failing. In reality, it's the system that's failing you.

Especially in Manufacturing: The Stakes Are Higher

In industries like tech or marketing, a missed deadline may lead to an apology email.

In **manufacturing**, it could mean:

- A product recall
- A safety incident
- A production shutdown
- A failed audit
- Or worse, a team member getting hurt

Supervisors are the pressure valve. When the system ignores its limits, something gives. It is often safety, quality, or retention.

Final Thoughts: What Can Be Done?

Unrealistic workloads don't just burn out supervisors — they weaken entire teams. If we want supervisors to lead, not just survive, we have to:

- **Design roles that are doable**, not superhuman
- **Provide tools and training**, not just tasks
- **Give decision-making power**, not just responsibility
- **Normalize asking for help**, not glorify suffering in silence

If you're a supervisor carrying too much, remember this: **It's not a weakness to speak up; it's leadership.**

The Story of Sarah: A Supervisor Overwhelmed by Growth

Sarah's story is a fictionalized account, drawn from patterns and experiences shared by many supervisors across industries. While the specifics may vary, the underlying challenges are very real.

After a major restructuring, Sarah's responsibilities nearly doubled overnight. Where she once managed a team of 10 agents, she now had 20, with no additional staffing, tools, or time. On top of that, she was tasked with leading the rollout of a new software system, expected to train her team, report progress, and troubleshoot issues, all while still maintaining her daily output.

Despite clearly communicating to upper management that the workload was unsustainable, the only response she received was vague encouragement: "Just do your best." There were no deadline adjustments, no additional resources, and no recognition of the complexity she was now managing.

What made Sarah's situation especially difficult wasn't just the workload; it was the **lack of acknowledgment and support**. Her capacity was treated as limitless, and her concerns as mere complaints. Over time, the weight of unrealistic expectations took a toll. She became exhausted, emotionally drained, and disconnected from the work she once enjoyed.

Eventually, Sarah made the difficult decision to leave. Her departure wasn't due to a lack of commitment or ability; it was a response to a system that **valued output over well-being** and refused to recalibrate even when the signs of burnout were clear.

Why Her Story Matters

Sarah's experience is not unique. In countless workplaces — particularly during times of rapid change — supervisors are expected to absorb more and more without the time, tools, or authority to manage it. Stories like hers remind us that **even the most capable leaders have limits**, and when those limits are ignored, organizations risk losing the very people holding everything together.

Why Do Upper Management Overload Supervisors?

1. Cost Pressures and Budget Constraints

Organizations constantly juggle budgets. In efforts to save costs, companies reduce staffing or increase spans of control without recalibrating expectations. A supervisor who once managed 10 staff might suddenly be responsible for 20, but paid and supported for 10.

2. Misaligned Expectations

Executives sometimes lack insight into frontline realities. Goals are set with optimism or political motives, but the operational feasibility is overlooked. The phrase "Just get it done" masks the disconnect between vision and resources.

3. Communication Gaps and Poor Planning

When multiple departments assign tasks without coordination, supervisors can receive conflicting demands — for example, marketing wants a campaign launched by next week, while IT needs new software training immediately. This results in supervisors juggling impossible priorities.

4. Authority Without Power

Supervisors often lack authority to make critical decisions — like hiring temporary help or extending deadlines — yet are held responsible for outcomes. This mismatch between responsibility and authority intensifies pressure.

5. Cultural Norms that Reward Overwork

In many workplaces, a culture of "hustle" glorifies long hours and heavy workloads. Requests for help may be stigmatized as weakness, pressuring supervisors to take on more than they can reasonably handle.

The Emotional and Physical Toll on Supervisors

When supervisors are pushed beyond their limits, the effects don't just stay on their calendars or to-do lists — they show up in their **bodies, minds, and relationships**, and often ripple out to their teams. While the pressure may seem invisible from the outside, the personal cost is anything but.

Let's take a closer look at what this toll really feels like:

1. Chronic Stress and Anxiety

Supervisors often operate in a near-constant state of tension. The pressure to meet unrealistic goals, juggle competing priorities, and keep their teams afloat — all while being the buffer between staff and upper management — creates a slow-building but relentless form of stress.

What it feels like:

You wake up already behind. There's a pit in your stomach as you check your email. Your brain runs a mile a minute even when you're off the clock.

Why it matters:

This kind of stress doesn't just affect productivity — it erodes confidence, patience, and mental clarity. Over time, it can lead to anxiety that bleeds into every part of life, even outside work.

2. Burnout

Burnout isn't just being tired — it's a deep emotional depletion. It's what happens when you care deeply about your work, but the demands never let up, and nothing you do seems like enough.

Signs include:

- Feeling emotionally numb or cynical
- Dreading interactions with others
- Struggling to feel proud of your accomplishments

Real talk:

You may still show up. You may still hit deadlines. But inside, the spark is gone — and that disconnection can be devastating.

3. Sleep Disruption

It starts innocently — a late night finishing reports. Then it becomes habitual: checking your phone before bed, tossing and turning as your brain replays the day's chaos.

What happens next:

Lack of sleep dulls focus, increases irritability, and makes emotional regulation harder — which, ironically, makes the next workday even tougher.

Cycle alert:

Sleep deprivation feeds stress, and stress prevents restful sleep. It becomes a loop that's hard to escape without boundaries and recovery time.

4. Physical Health Decline

The body keeps the score. When stress becomes chronic, physical health often declines. Common issues include:

- Headaches and migraines
- Stomach problems
- Weakened immune response
- High blood pressure and heart strain

In manufacturing or physically demanding roles, this can also mean a higher risk of injury due to fatigue or decreased alertness.

Why it's serious:

Supervisors are often so focused on keeping things running, they don't realize their own health is slipping — until something forces them to stop.

5. Decreased Job Satisfaction

It's hard to enjoy your work when you're constantly underwater. Things you used to love — mentoring, problem-solving, team wins — start to feel like just another task on an endless list.

What you may notice:

- Loss of motivation
- Irritability with your team
- Wondering, "Why am I still doing this?"

This is often the first quiet red flag before burnout fully sets in. Left unaddressed, it can lead to disengagement — and eventually, resignation.

6. Career Stagnation

Ironically, supervisors who are overloaded often end up looking like they're underperforming. Not because they lack skills or drive, but because:

- They're too overwhelmed to take on growth projects
- They don't have time to network or upskill
- Their results suffer from having too much on their plate

The result:

They get stuck — passed over for promotions, viewed as "struggling" when in reality, they've been **propping up a broken system**.

Final Thought

When we expect supervisors to do more than is humanly possible — and we do nothing to help — we aren't just risking turnover. We're risking people's health, fulfillment, and futures.

Recognizing the emotional and physical toll isn't about making excuses. It's about finally telling the truth: **Overload comes at a cost, and it's often paid by the people who care the most.**

Case Study: Marco's Manufacturing Nightmare

Marco's story is a fictionalized case drawn from real challenges supervisors often face in manufacturing environments, especially during periods of high demand.

At a manufacturing plant in Ontario, Marco was responsible for overseeing multiple production lines, managing quality assurance, and ensuring safety compliance — all without additional staff or resources during a surge in production.

The expectations were overwhelming. With no backup and an ever-growing workload, Marco began to experience operational breakdowns: safety incidents increased, product quality suffered, and employee morale took a nosedive. Despite raising these concerns with upper management, his appeals were brushed aside in favor of "keeping up with targets."

Marco's case illustrates the **danger of overburdening supervisors** without recalibrating expectations or providing support. When management fails to recognize and act on workload stressors, the consequences affect not just one person but the entire operation.

Practical Strategies for Supervisors Facing Overload

While organizational change is ideal, supervisors can adopt coping and advocacy strategies:

1. Prioritize Effectively

Identify the tasks that have the greatest impact on organizational goals. Communicate these priorities clearly to your team and management.

Example: If a project deadline conflicts with an ongoing quality audit, discuss which delivers more immediate value and negotiate timelines accordingly.

2. Set Boundaries

Politely but firmly communicate capacity limits. For example, "I want to deliver excellent results on X, but with the current workload, Y may need to be postponed or delegated."

3. Delegate Wisely

Empower capable team members to assume responsibilities where possible. Delegation not only lightens your load but also develops your team's skills.

4. Document Workload and Time Use

Keep detailed records of tasks, hours worked, and impacts on deadlines. This can support requests for additional resources or deadline extensions.

5. Communicate Upward Regularly

Provide factual status reports that include workload assessments. Frame these reports to demonstrate commitment while highlighting capacity constraints.

6. Seek Support

Engage HR, employee assistance programs, or mentors to manage stress and advocate for change.

7. Self-Care and Work-Life Balance

Maintain boundaries between work and personal life. Regular exercise, sleep hygiene, and social support are essential.

What Organizations Can Do to Prevent Supervisor Overload

When supervisors are overloaded, it's not just their problem — it's a red flag for the whole organization. Fixing this means real change at the company level. Here's what workplaces can do to help supervisors thrive instead of just survive:

1. Conduct Regular Workload Assessments

Organizations need to **check in regularly** to see if supervisors are drowning or managing well. This means gathering real data — not just guessing — and listening to supervisors themselves.

For example, surveys, one-on-one interviews, or even time-tracking can reveal when the workload is becoming unmanageable before it leads to burnout or errors. Catching problems early means solutions can be put in place before things spiral out of control.

2. Invest in Staffing and Technology

Supervisors shouldn't have to do clerical work or struggle with outdated tools. Investing in enough staff — like administrative assistants — and modern technology can make a huge difference.

Imagine a supervisor who spends hours each week manually compiling reports when software could automate that work. Giving supervisors the right tools and people to support them frees up their time to focus on leadership, problem-solving, and coaching their teams.

3. Clarify Roles and Authority

It's incredibly frustrating to be held responsible for outcomes but not have the power to make key decisions. Organizations should make sure supervisors' authority **matches their responsibilities**.

For example, if a supervisor is responsible for meeting tight deadlines but can't approve overtime or hire temporary help, they're set up to fail. Giving supervisors clear decision-making power means they can respond quickly and effectively to challenges, without endless red tape.

4. Encourage a Culture of Realistic Expectations

Culture starts at the top. When senior leaders model reasonable workloads, respect work-life balance, and reward quality over quantity, it sets a powerful tone.

If the message is always "work harder, longer," supervisors feel pressured to overextend themselves just to keep up. But when leaders show they value sustainable work practices, supervisors are more likely to feel safe setting boundaries and asking for support.

5. Provide Leadership Training

Supervisors aren't born with all the skills they need. Training is essential — not just on technical skills, but on **managing workload, delegating effectively, and communicating up and down the chain**.

Good training helps supervisors feel more confident and capable, which reduces stress and improves team performance. It also signals that the organization is invested in their growth and success.

6. Act on Feedback

It's one thing to ask supervisors how they're doing, but it's another to actually respond and make changes based on what they say.

Organizations should have systems in place to collect supervisor feedback and then take meaningful action. When supervisors see their concerns lead to real improvements — whether that's hiring extra help, adjusting deadlines, or updating policies — it builds trust and morale.

Final Thought

Preventing supervisor overload isn't a quick fix — it's an ongoing commitment. But organizations that prioritize these actions don't just help their supervisors; they create healthier, more productive workplaces where everyone can succeed.

Conclusion: Balancing the Scales for Supervisors

Supervisors are the connective tissue of any workplace — they translate big-picture goals into everyday action, support their teams through chaos and change, and carry the emotional weight of people management that's invisible on paper. They're often the first in and the last out, the ones quietly holding everything together.

But too often, they're also the ones asked to do the impossible.

When supervisors are burdened with unrealistic workloads, the results aren't just late projects or missed KPIs. The cost shows up in **burnout, turnover, stress-related health issues, and a quiet erosion of workplace trust**. And it doesn't just harm the supervisor — it hurts the whole team, and eventually, the whole organization.

Real change doesn't come from slogans or surface-level wellness programs. It comes from **honest, ongoing dialogue** — where supervisors can safely voice their realities, and where leadership truly listens. It comes from **rethinking systems** that reward exhaustion instead of effectiveness, and from **building cultures** that support people as human beings, not just job titles.

One supervisor once said, "I don't mind hard work. I mind being invisible."

That sentiment speaks volumes.

When supervisors are heard, respected, and given the tools they need to succeed, everything changes. They become more than just middle managers — they become empowered leaders who can drive growth, foster strong teams, and help create workplaces people are proud to be part of.

Call to Action for Organizations:

- Make supervisor wellbeing a strategic priority — not a personal problem to solve alone.
- Ask your supervisors what's working and what isn't — and **believe them**.
- Regularly assess workloads, not just outcomes.
- Back up responsibilities with real resources, real support, and real trust.

Call to Action for Supervisors:

- Speak up. Advocate for what you need — your voice matters more than you think.
- Prioritize your health and set boundaries, even if the culture around you hasn't caught up yet.
- Remember, asking for help isn't weakness — it's leadership.

Balancing the scales for supervisors is not just an act of fairness — it's an investment in the future of work. Because when we take care of the people who take care of others, **every part of the organization gets stronger.**

Chapter 3
Undermined in Front of Your Team

"Public doubt is a silent dismissal."

Being undermined in front of your team doesn't just bruise your ego — it fractures your credibility. When a supervisor is corrected, dismissed, or contradicted publicly by higher-ups, it sends a clear message: your authority doesn't count.

This kind of behavior erodes trust, not only between you and your leadership but also between you and your team. It creates confusion about who's in charge, undercuts your ability to lead effectively, and leaves you feeling exposed and powerless. Respect behind closed doors means little if you're discredited in the open.

1. Introduction: The Fragile Authority of Supervisors

In any workplace, supervisors are the linchpin that holds teams and operations together. They bridge the gap between upper management's strategic goals and frontline employees' daily work. To succeed, supervisors need something vital: authority. Authority isn't just about having a title or giving orders. It's about the trust and respect of both their team and their own managers.

However, this authority is delicate and can be undermined—sometimes publicly, sometimes subtly—by upper management. When a supervisor's decisions or leadership are questioned or overridden in front of their team, it sends a damaging message. It not only diminishes the supervisor's role but also shakes the confidence of the team and disrupts the workflow.

Being undermined in front of your team is more than an embarrassing moment. It's a serious issue that affects morale, productivity, and mental health. Yet, it is often overlooked or normalized in workplace cultures that tolerate power imbalances and poor communication.

This chapter explores this challenging dynamic: what it means, why it happens, how it impacts supervisors and teams, and most importantly, what can be done to prevent and address it.

2. What Does "Being Undermined" Really Mean?

Being undermined as a supervisor doesn't always come in loud, obvious moments. Sometimes, it's a quiet series of actions that chip away at your authority — and your confidence — little by little.

When a supervisor is undermined, it sends a message to the team: "This person isn't really in charge." That can destroy trust, create confusion, and make leadership feel like a losing battle.

Here are some of the most common — and frustrating — ways supervisors get undermined at work:

1. Contradicting or Overriding Decisions in Front of the Team

Imagine this: You're running a team meeting and assigning responsibilities. Everything's going smoothly — until your own manager suddenly jumps in, cancels your decisions, and gives their own orders.

What does that do? It instantly tells the team that your voice doesn't carry weight. It makes you look powerless, even if you're doing your best to lead fairly and effectively.

- *How it feels:* Embarrassing, frustrating, and deeply demoralizing.
- *Why it matters:* It creates confusion about who's in charge — and fractures the trust your team has in your leadership.

2. Public Criticism in Front of Staff

No one likes being called out in front of others — especially not by their boss. When a manager questions a supervisor's judgment, decisions, or competence in front of the team, it's not just uncomfortable — it's damaging.

- *Example:* "I don't know why you approved that — that's not how we do things," said loudly in a team meeting.
- *Impact:* It sows doubt. Team members start second-guessing their supervisor, and the supervisor may start second-guessing themselves, too.

3. Ignoring a Supervisor's Input in Meetings

Sometimes the undermining isn't loud — it's silent. A supervisor shares an idea, a progress update, or a concern in a meeting, and leadership simply talks over it or moves on like nothing was said.

- *How it feels:* Invisible.
- *Why it matters:* Consistently disregarding a supervisor's input sends a message to others that what they say doesn't matter — which kills morale and stifles initiative.

4. Bypassing Supervisors in Communication

This happens when upper management talks directly to team members — giving them tasks, guidance, or even feedback — without involving the supervisor.

- *Why it's harmful:* It cuts the supervisor out of the loop. It creates mixed messages and makes it nearly impossible for them to manage effectively.
- *How it plays out:* The team stops checking in with the supervisor because they're getting answers from "above." The supervisor loses visibility — and eventually, authority.

5. Taking Over Leadership Tasks Without Consultation

Leadership should be about trust and delegation. But some managers don't let go — they step in to lead meetings, take over projects, or issue orders, even when it's clearly the supervisor's role.

- *What these signals:* "I don't believe you can handle this."
- *The result:* The supervisor feels sidelined, and the team starts to mirror that belief — looking to the manager instead of the person meant to be leading them day-to-day.

Why This Matters

Being undermined isn't just about bruised egos. It's about **eroded trust**, **lost credibility**, and **diminished effectiveness**. When supervisors are sidelined or second-guessed too often, they can't lead their teams well — and over time, they may stop trying.

To build strong supervisors, organizations need to **respect and reinforce their authority**, not undercut it. That means alignment between managers and supervisors, trust in the chain of command, and private feedback when course correction is needed — not public takedowns.

Example: Mark's Public Undermining

Mark worked as a shift supervisor at a large warehouse in Toronto. One afternoon, during a regular team briefing, he outlined the day's priorities and assigned duties based on staff availability and workload. Suddenly, his regional manager joined the meeting.

Instead of supporting Mark's plan, the manager said, "That won't work. Here's what we're doing instead," and proceeded to give new instructions to the team.

Mark felt blindsided and humiliated. His team was confused about whose instructions to follow, and his credibility suffered. Over the following weeks, the manager repeatedly contradicted Mark in similar ways, steadily eroding his authority.

3. Why Do Managers Undermine Supervisors?

Undermining is rarely random or accidental. It stems from a combination of psychological, organizational, and cultural factors that influence how managers relate to their supervisors. Understanding these root causes is crucial to addressing the problem effectively.

Power Struggles and Control

At its core, undermining often reflects a power struggle. Supervisors hold a unique position—they must manage teams and daily operations, but they also report to higher management. This middle-ground role can create tension, especially when managers feel their own authority is challenged or diluted.

In some cases, managers undermine supervisors to reassert their dominance. By publicly contradicting decisions or taking control in front of the team, they send a clear message: **"I'm the one in charge here."** This need for control may stem from insecurity, fear of losing influence, or a desire to maintain a strict hierarchical order.

Consider the example of David, a sales supervisor at a mid-sized company. His regional manager frequently overruled his client assignment decisions during team meetings, often without prior discussion. David later learned that his manager feared losing control of sales targets and wanted to ensure directives came directly from the top, even if it created confusion among the sales team.

This behavior breeds distrust and resentment. Supervisors feel disempowered, while teams become confused about whom to follow. Over time, such power struggles degrade collaboration and stifle initiative.

Lack of Trust or Respect

Undermining also signals a deeper issue: a lack of trust or respect. When managers doubt a supervisor's competence, judgment, or commitment, they may publicly question or override their decisions as a way to "correct" perceived mistakes.

This distrust may be based on real performance issues, but it can also arise from biases or poor interpersonal relationships. For instance, a manager may unconsciously undermine supervisors who come from different cultural backgrounds, genders, or age groups, reflecting implicit prejudices rather than objective assessments.

Jessica, a young female supervisor at a manufacturing plant, experienced this firsthand. Her manager often dismissed her proposals in meetings, favoring ideas from older male colleagues. Jessica's input was frequently sidelined, and her decisions were second-guessed in front of her team. This lack of respect made her hesitant to speak up and diminished her confidence.

Lack of respect harms not only the individual supervisor but also the entire work environment, as it sets a tone of disrespect and unequal treatment.

Miscommunication and Micromanagement Culture

Sometimes undermining arises less from intent and more from poor communication or organizational culture. In companies where micromanagement is prevalent, managers may habitually insert themselves into daily operations, bypassing supervisors as a matter of course.

Such managers might believe they are helping by providing direct instructions, but this often has the opposite effect. Without clear communication channels and role boundaries, managers may unintentionally contradict supervisors, making them appear ineffective.

In one manufacturing company, the production supervisor, Alan, noticed that the plant manager frequently issued instructions directly to operators on the floor, especially during busy shifts. The plant manager's goal was to speed up problem-solving, but by doing so, he undermined Alan's authority and confused the operators about the chain of command.

This reflects a micromanagement culture where supervisors are viewed as mere conduits for orders, rather than empowered leaders. The result is diminished autonomy, increased stress, and a fractured leadership structure.

Organizational Politics

Undermining can also be a tool in organizational politics—used strategically to gain favor, advance careers, or shift blame.

In highly political workplaces, managers may publicly question or override supervisors to showcase their own expertise or to align themselves with senior executives. Undermining can serve as a way to discredit supervisors who are seen as rivals or obstacles.

For example, in a large tech company, a department manager regularly second-guessed the project supervisor's decisions during team meetings. Colleagues speculated that the manager aimed to position himself as the "real" leader ahead of the upcoming corporate restructuring.

Moreover, when problems arise, undermining can be a form of scapegoating. Managers may blame supervisors publicly for failures to deflect responsibility, preserving their own reputation at the expense of others.

This political undermining corrodes trust and collaboration, turning workplaces into battlegrounds instead of cooperative environments.

Case Study: Nadia's Hospital Experience

Nadia was a nursing supervisor in a busy urban hospital, known for her steady leadership and the strong rapport she had built with her team. She took pride in advocating for patient-centered care and creating a supportive work environment for her nurses.

But when a new department director arrived, things started to unravel.

During staff meetings, Nadia would introduce updated protocols or propose schedule adjustments to better meet patient needs. Before she could finish explaining, the director would step in — questioning her approach and directing staff to follow a different plan instead. These moments, often in front of the entire team, left everyone confused.

At first, Nadia tried to brush it off. But the pattern continued. Week after week, the director contradicted her publicly, eroding her credibility. Nurses didn't know whose instructions to follow. Some even started skipping Nadia and going straight to the director.

Why Did This Happen?

Several dynamics contributed to the breakdown:

- The new director, still finding her footing, felt the need to assert authority quickly — and misinterpreted Nadia's confidence as resistance.
- Their roles and decision-making boundaries were never clearly defined.
- The hospital's culture tended to favor top-down command structures over collaborative leadership.
- Nadia's ideas, though forward-thinking, often challenged traditional practices, creating tension with the director's more conservative style.

The Consequences

The impact was swift and painful. Nadia's team began to lose trust in her leadership. Morale dropped. Nurses resigned. Even patient care began to suffer as miscommunication increased and consistency in procedures declined.

Nadia, feeling demoralized and micromanaged, began to question her future at the hospital.

The Turning Point

Eventually, HR intervened. A series of facilitated conversations helped uncover the root of the conflict. Through leadership coaching and structured communication agreements, Nadia and the director began to rebuild trust.

They clarified roles, established communication protocols, and agreed on a shared approach to decision-making. Slowly, Nadia regained authority with her team, and the director learned how to provide oversight without undermining her.

The culture of the unit began to shift — from one of hierarchy and tension to one of mutual respect.

Final Thoughts

This story shows how easily a supervisor's authority can be undercut — and how much it matters. But it also reminds us that with support, self-awareness, and dialogue, repair is possible. When leaders at all levels commit to respecting roles and lifting each other up, the ripple effect benefits everyone — staff, patients, and the organization alike.

Summary

Supervisors aren't undermined in a vacuum — the reasons are often complex. Sometimes it's about a manager's need for control, a lack of trust, poor communication, or internal politics. Regardless of the cause, the impact is real: it damages relationships, erodes confidence, and weakens the entire organization.

Understanding these root causes is the first step toward change. When leaders commit to self-awareness, clarity, and respect, they create the conditions for supervisors to lead with confidence — and for teams to truly thrive.

4. The Consequences of Being Undermined

Being undermined isn't just an uncomfortable moment in a meeting or an awkward misstep in communication — it's something deeper, more damaging, and often long-lasting. When a supervisor is repeatedly dismissed, contradicted, or bypassed by upper management, the consequences ripple far beyond that one moment.

It affects **how they see themselves**, **how their team sees them**, and **how well the organization functions as a whole**.

1. Personal Confidence Takes a Hit

When a supervisor is undermined — especially in front of their team — it chips away at their self-trust. They may start second-guessing their decisions, hesitating to speak up, or avoiding leadership responsibilities out of fear of being shut down again.

"Why bother making a plan if it's going to be overruled?"

It's demoralizing. People who once felt proud of their leadership role begin to feel invisible or even dispensable.

2. Authority Erodes in the Eyes of the Team

Supervisors are the bridge between leadership and frontline staff. When that bridge is weakened, it creates confusion and doubt. Team members start to wonder: *"Who's really in charge here?"*

Even if it's unintentional, when a higher-up overrides or questions a supervisor in public, it signals to the team that the supervisor's voice doesn't matter. Over time, employees may stop going to them altogether — which only deepens the problem.

3. Team Morale and Trust Decline

Teams thrive when they have stable, trusted leaders. But when they see their supervisor being undermined — especially by someone higher up — it creates anxiety. They may fear speaking up, worry about internal conflict, or feel unsure about the direction of their work.

It also sets a dangerous example: *"If my supervisor isn't respected, what chance do I have?"*

4. Increased Turnover and Burnout

No one wants to stay in a role where they feel powerless or unsupported — and that includes supervisors. When they're constantly undermined, many start thinking about leaving. Some transfer out. Some burn out quietly. Others quit altogether.

And it doesn't stop there. Teams that witness this dysfunction are more likely to disengage or leave, too, especially if they feel stuck in the middle of tension between leaders.

5. Organizational Performance Suffers

Undermining may feel like a personal conflict — but it has real business consequences. When roles are unclear and authority is constantly in question, **execution slows down**. Decisions are delayed, mistakes increase, and alignment disappears.

Leaders start pulling in different directions. Projects stall. Culture suffers. And what could have been resolved with respectful communication becomes a systemic problem.

Bottom Line

Undermining a supervisor isn't a minor interpersonal issue — it's a leadership breakdown. And the longer it goes unaddressed, the more damage it causes.

But the good news? It's also preventable.

With **clear boundaries**, **mutual respect**, and a culture that values open, honest leadership, supervisors can be empowered to lead effectively — and organizations can grow stronger from the inside out.

Psychological Impacts: Confidence, Stress, and Burnout

When supervisors are repeatedly undermined, the psychological toll can be severe. Authority is tied closely to identity and self-worth in leadership roles. Publicly having decisions questioned or overridden chips away at confidence.

Take Sarah, a team supervisor at a large customer service center. After several instances where her manager contradicted her in front of the team, Sarah began doubting her own judgment. "I started to question every decision I made, even those I was sure about," she recalls. This self-doubt made her hesitant, less decisive, and anxious.

Research supports these experiences. A 2019 study published in the *Journal of Occupational Health Psychology* found that workplace undermining is strongly associated with increased anxiety, lowered self-esteem, and reduced job satisfaction among managers and supervisors (Liu et al., 2019).

The stress from undermining isn't just mental—it can manifest physically. Chronic stress raises cortisol levels, disrupts sleep, and can lead to health problems such as hypertension and depression. When supervisors feel powerless or disrespected, burnout becomes a real risk.

Burnout—a state of emotional exhaustion, depersonalization, and reduced personal accomplishment—is a leading cause of supervisor turnover. A Gallup poll in 2021 indicated that 52% of employees cited feeling burned out due to workplace stressors, including conflicts with management (Gallup, 2021).

Effects on Team Dynamics: Morale, Productivity, and Trust

The consequences of undermining don't stop at the supervisor—they ripple outward to affect the entire team. Supervisors act as the team's leader, role model, and primary source of guidance. When their authority is weakened, the team's morale suffers.

Imagine a sports team where the captain's decisions are constantly questioned by the coach in front of the players. The team's unity breaks down as players become confused about whom to follow. The same happens in workplaces.

Lower morale leads to reduced motivation. Team members may withdraw effort or become cynical if they perceive inconsistent leadership. The productivity of the team declines as confusion or conflict increases.

Trust is particularly vulnerable. Trust is the cornerstone of effective teamwork, and it depends on clear, consistent leadership. When a supervisor is undermined, team members may lose confidence not only in the supervisor but in the organization itself.

For example, in a mid-sized tech firm, a project manager named Ravi found that after his manager publicly questioned his technical decisions, his team started bypassing him, going directly to upper management for approvals. Ravi felt sidelined, and the team's cohesion fractured. The project timeline suffered, and client satisfaction dropped.

This aligns with research by Dr. Amy Edmondson of Harvard Business School, who stresses the importance of psychological safety in teams—the shared belief that it is safe to take interpersonal risks (Edmondson, 2019). Undermining destroys psychological safety, making teams less innovative, less collaborative, and less effective.

Impact on Organizational Culture and Retention

When undermining is systemic or tolerated, it contributes to a toxic organizational culture. Cultures that allow public disrespect and power struggles foster fear and disengagement, rather than collaboration and trust.

Employees at all levels observe how supervisors are treated. If leadership models undermine middle managers, frontline workers notice. This trickle-down effect can lead to widespread dissatisfaction and cynicism about the company's values.

Retention becomes a significant challenge. Talented supervisors who feel undervalued or disrespected are more likely to leave. The costs of turnover—recruitment, training, lost knowledge—are substantial.

Consider a healthcare organization where hospital administrators regularly undermined nurse supervisors. A staff survey revealed that 40% of supervisors were considering leaving within a year due to stress and lack of support. Patient care quality also declined, highlighting how undermining affects even core business outcomes.

Expert Perspectives and Research Findings

Leadership experts highlight the critical dangers of undermining:

- **John Maxwell**, a renowned leadership coach, states, "Leadership is not about titles or positions—it's about influence. Undermining erodes influence and therefore destroys leadership."
- According to **Brene Brown**, a researcher on vulnerability and leadership, "Respect is a key ingredient in creating trust. When leaders publicly disrespect others, it breaks down trust and creates barriers to connection."
- The *Harvard Business Review* warns that undermining behavior contributes to what they call "toxic leadership," which results in disengaged employees and poor performance (Harvard Business Review, 2020).

Summary: Why Undermining Can't Be Ignored

Being undermined isn't just an awkward moment or a bruised ego — it cuts much deeper. When a supervisor's authority is constantly dismissed or contradicted, it shakes their confidence at the core. Over time, what starts as public embarrassment often grows into something heavier: chronic stress, self-doubt, and eventually, burnout.

But the impact doesn't stop with one person.

The whole team feels it. When staff see their supervisor being disrespected or sidelined, it sends a message that leadership isn't consistent or trustworthy. Morale drops. Productivity suffers. People become disengaged, and some start looking for the exit.

Left unchecked, undermining behaviors can quietly poison a workplace culture. They create division, miscommunication, and turnover — all of which cost time, trust, and money.

That's why this issue can't be brushed off as "just a personality clash" or "how things work around here." It's a leadership problem, and it demands a leadership solution.

Organizations that take these impacts seriously — and commit to building cultures of respect, communication, and shared leadership — don't just protect their supervisors. They build stronger teams, healthier workplaces, and more resilient businesses.

Reflection Prompts for Deeper Understanding

To help you connect these ideas to your own experience and workplace, here are some guided reflections:

1. Recognizing Unrealistic Workload

- Have you ever faced a workload that felt impossible to manage? What made it so overwhelming—too many tasks, pressure, or lack of support?
- What could have helped you regain control or feel supported?

2. Feeling the Emotional and Physical Toll

- Think about a time your job affected your health or personal life. What signs did you notice — stress, exhaustion, frustration?
- What changes could your workplace make to better support wellbeing?

3. Experiencing or Witnessing Undermining

- Have you had your decisions challenged or dismissed in front of others? How did it affect your confidence and leadership?
- How could senior leaders better support supervisors in such situations?

4. Consequences for Teams and Culture

- Have you seen someone else being undermined? What happened to the team dynamics and trust?
- What might have prevented those negative effects?

5. Practical Coping Strategies

- Which coping strategies—like prioritizing, setting boundaries, or delegating—seem doable for you right now?
- What keeps you from asking for help, and how might you change that?

6. Organizational Solutions

- Does your workplace assess workloads or leadership strain? If not, how could you encourage this conversation?
- If you were a senior leader, what would you do to prevent supervisor overload?

Take a moment to reflect on these questions. Your insights are the first step toward healthier leadership and stronger teams.

5. Strategies for Supervisors Facing Undermining

When supervisors get undermined by their own managers, it can feel like an invisible weight holding them down. It's frustrating, confusing, and often lonely—like no one's got your back. You might question yourself, wonder if you're doing something wrong, or feel stuck in a no-win situation.

But the good news is, there are real, practical steps you can take to protect yourself and push back in a way that's professional and effective. It's not about confrontation for the sake of arguing; it's about standing your ground, rebuilding trust, and creating clearer boundaries.

Some key strategies include:

- **Clear Communication:** Being open and assertive about your role, your decisions, and your priorities helps set expectations. When others see you communicating confidently, it boosts your credibility.
- **Building Your Credibility:** Keep delivering consistent, quality results. When your team and upper management recognize your competence, it's harder for undermining behaviors to stick.
- **Documenting Everything:** Keep a record of conversations, decisions, and incidents of undermining. This can be a powerful tool if you need to escalate the issue or seek support.
- **Seeking Allies and Support:** Don't try to handle it alone. Whether it's HR, a mentor, or trusted colleagues, having people who understand and back you up makes a big difference.

By taking these steps, supervisors can start to regain a sense of control, protect their authority, and help shift the workplace culture toward one of respect and collaboration. It's about turning a tough situation into an opportunity to strengthen your leadership and your team.

Private Conversations and Setting Boundaries

The first line of defense against undermining is direct communication. When a manager publicly questions or contradicts you, it can feel humiliating and confusing. However, addressing these issues privately and professionally can often defuse tension before it escalates.

Setting clear boundaries is essential. This involves calmly expressing your perspective and clarifying your role. For example, after a meeting where your manager publicly overrules your decision, request a private discussion:

"I'd like to understand your concerns about my decision and discuss how we can present a united front to the team."

This opens a channel for dialogue rather than confrontation.

In her book *Crucial Conversations*, Patterson et al. (2012) emphasize the power of addressing difficult conversations early and privately to prevent misunderstandings and build mutual respect.

Consider the case of Marcus, a logistics supervisor whose director frequently bypassed him to give instructions directly to staff. Marcus requested a private meeting, where he respectfully outlined how this undermined his authority and confused the team. The director hadn't realized the impact and agreed to communicate through Marcus from now on.

Private conversations also allow supervisors to understand whether undermining stems from miscommunication, insecurity, or organizational issues—information that's critical for choosing the correct response.

Strengthening Credibility with Your Team

Your authority rests largely on your team's trust and confidence. When upper management undermines you, reinforcing your credibility and leadership with your team can act as a buffer against negative impacts.

Consistency is key. Always follow through on commitments, communicate clearly, and be transparent about decisions. When team members see you as reliable and fair, they're less likely to be swayed by contradictory messages from above.

Another tactic is **increasing visibility and engagement** with your team. Regular check-ins, one-on-one meetings, and collaborative problem-solving foster strong relationships and loyalty.

Take the example of Lisa, a retail supervisor whose manager publicly questioned her staffing decisions. Lisa responded by holding weekly team huddles where she shared updates, acknowledged challenges, and solicited feedback. Over time, the team's respect for her grew, making management's undermining less effective.

According to Kouzes and Posner's *The Leadership Challenge* (2017), leaders who model integrity and build trust create resilient teams that can withstand external pressures.

Additionally, **educating your team** on organizational structures can help. When staff understand that sometimes messages come from different levels and aren't personal, it reduces confusion and aligns loyalty.

Documentation and Escalating Concerns

When undermining becomes persistent or severe, documentation is a powerful tool. Keep a detailed record of incidents, including dates, what was said or done, witnesses, and the impact on your work or team.

Documentation serves multiple purposes:

- It provides concrete evidence when raising concerns with HR or higher leadership.
- It helps you identify patterns that might not be obvious in isolated incidents.
- It reinforces your professionalism and seriousness when addressing the issue.

For example, Kevin, a manufacturing supervisor, maintained a log of every meeting where his manager contradicted or dismissed his decisions. When he escalated the issue to HR, the documentation made a compelling case, prompting an internal review.

When escalating, approach the process methodically:

1. Begin with your immediate manager or HR representative in a calm, factual manner.
2. Share your documentation and describe how the undermining affects your role and team.
3. Request clear steps for resolution, such as mediation, training, or role clarification.

Organizations like the Society for Human Resource Management (SHRM) recommend formal escalation when informal conversations fail to resolve undermining (SHRM, 2022).

Seeking Support: HR, Mentors, Counseling

Facing undermining alone can be overwhelming. Supervisors should seek external support systems to navigate the emotional and practical challenges.

Human Resources (HR) can offer mediation, conflict resolution, and guidance on company policies. Engaging HR early can prevent escalation and promote organizational accountability.

Mentors and peer networks provide valuable perspectives and advice. Experienced supervisors who have navigated similar challenges can share strategies, validate experiences, and provide encouragement.

For instance, Anne, a finance supervisor, found that joining a professional supervisors' association connected her with mentors who helped her build confidence and develop tactics for handling difficult managers.

Counseling or coaching can address the emotional toll. Talking with a counselor helps manage stress, build resilience, and develop assertiveness skills. Executive coaches can work on communication and leadership strategies to better navigate complex power dynamics.

The American Psychological Association highlights that social support is a critical factor in reducing workplace stress and preventing burnout (APA, 2020).

Examples of Successful Interventions

Real-world success stories illustrate how supervisors can overcome undermining:

- **The Manufacturing Supervisor:** David faced repeated public criticism from his director. After documenting incidents, he requested a mediated session involving HR. Through facilitated dialogue, boundaries were set, and David's role clarified. The director agreed to discuss concerns privately, and David's confidence was restored. Productivity improved as team trust was rebuilt.

- **The Hospital Nurse Manager:** Nadia's case (see Chapter 3) demonstrates the power of leadership coaching combined with HR support. The intervention not only addressed immediate conflicts but also fostered a more collaborative culture that benefited patient care.
- **The Tech Team Leader:** When Ravi's decisions were overridden, he increased transparency by holding team Q&A sessions and circulating clear written protocols. This strengthened his position and reduced contradictory directives from management.

Additional Examples of Successful Interventions

Case Study: Handling Undermining with HR Mediation

Jessica, a marketing supervisor, was often contradicted by her manager during client meetings, causing embarrassment and loss of team confidence. After months of private conversations with little change, Jessica documented incidents and approached HR. The company arranged a mediation session where Jessica and her manager openly discussed their concerns with a neutral facilitator. They established ground rules for communication and agreed that the manager would provide feedback privately rather than in front of clients. Jessica's confidence grew, and the team's morale improved.

Case Study: Building Team Loyalty as a Buffer

Tom, a production supervisor, found that his director often gave orders directly to line workers, bypassing him. To counteract this, Tom initiated daily briefings where he shared updates and gathered input, making himself the central communication point. He also started recognizing workers publicly for their achievements. His team's loyalty strengthened, making external messages less disruptive. Over time, the director recognized Tom's leadership role and adjusted his behavior.

Summary

Undermining by upper management is a serious challenge for supervisors, but it is not insurmountable. Key strategies include initiating private conversations and setting clear boundaries, reinforcing credibility with teams, meticulously documenting incidents, escalating concerns through formal channels, and seeking support from HR, mentors, and counseling resources.

Implementing these approaches requires patience, professionalism, and courage. Yet, as the examples show, supervisors who take proactive steps can restore their authority, improve their work environment, and continue to lead effectively despite challenges.

6. What Organizations Must Do

Creating a workplace where supervisors are respected and empowered is essential—not only for the well-being of those supervisors but for the health and success of the entire organization.

Undermining behavior from upper management can cripple supervisory roles, disrupt team dynamics, and ultimately impair organizational performance. It is the responsibility of organizations to proactively build structures, policies, and cultures that prevent such behavior and provide effective tools to address it when it occurs.

Training and Policies for Managers

The foundation of preventing undermining behavior lies in thorough training and clear policies aimed at managers and executives. Organizations must recognize that leadership is not just about authority—it's about responsible use of that authority to foster collaboration, respect, and accountability.

Leadership training programs should emphasize emotional intelligence, communication skills, and conflict resolution. Managers must learn how to provide feedback constructively, support their supervisors, and manage power dynamics ethically. Training that includes role-playing scenarios can prepare managers for difficult conversations and illustrate the damaging effects of undermining behaviors.

For example, **Google's Manager Development Program** includes modules on effective communication and coaching, which focus on empowering mid-level managers and preventing toxic leadership dynamics (Garvin, 2013). Companies like Google report higher employee engagement and lower turnover when managers receive such focused training.

Policies should clearly define unacceptable behaviors, including undermining, public criticism, and exclusion from decision-making. These policies must be communicated transparently and enforced consistently. A well-crafted **anti-harassment and workplace respect policy** not only protects employees but sets expectations for managerial conduct.

Moreover, performance evaluations of managers should include **360-degree feedback**, incorporating input from supervisors and their teams. This ensures that those in leadership roles are held accountable for their behavior and treatment of subordinates.

Building a Respectful Workplace Culture

Policies and training alone are not enough without a genuine culture of respect and trust. Organizations must cultivate an environment where respect is the norm and open communication is encouraged.

A respectful culture empowers supervisors to voice concerns without fear of retaliation. Organizations should encourage **psychological safety**—the belief that it's safe to take interpersonal risks at work. Studies from Harvard Business School show that teams with high psychological safety are more innovative and productive (Edmondson, 2019).

To build this culture, organizations can:

- Promote **transparent communication** across all levels

- Recognize and reward leaders who demonstrate supportive behaviors
- Regularly assess workplace climate through surveys and feedback channels
- Encourage collaboration rather than competition among management tiers

A practical example is **Patagonia**, the outdoor apparel company, renowned for its inclusive culture and strong ethical leadership. Patagonia actively promotes open dialogue and holds leadership accountable for maintaining respectful relationships (Chouinard & Stanley, 2012). Such companies demonstrate that respect and profitability are not mutually exclusive.

Tools for Monitoring and Addressing Undermining Behavior

To address undermining effectively, organizations need reliable tools to monitor workplace interactions and respond proactively.

Anonymous reporting systems allow supervisors and employees to report undermining or other harmful behaviors safely. Platforms such as **Ethics Point** or **Whispli** provide confidential channels for raising concerns without fear of reprisal.

Regular **climate surveys** and **360-degree feedback tools** provide quantitative and qualitative data on managerial behavior and workplace culture. Analyzing these results helps leadership identify problem areas and intervene early.

Additionally, organizations should establish **clear, accessible procedures for conflict resolution and mediation**. Having trained mediators or ombudspersons on staff facilitates fair investigations and supports conflict resolution without escalating to formal disciplinary action unnecessarily.

Technology can also assist. Some companies employ AI-driven sentiment analysis tools to monitor internal communications for signs of toxic interactions or stress, allowing HR teams to intervene before issues worsen (Fisher & Cortina, 2021).

Examples of Companies with Strong Leadership Cultures

Several organizations stand out for their proactive approaches to leadership development and workplace respect.

- **Microsoft,** under CEO Satya Nadella, transformed its culture by emphasizing empathy, growth mindset, and collaborative leadership (Nadella & Shaw, 2017). Microsoft's focus on inclusive leadership training has helped reduce hierarchical undermining and fostered greater innovation.
- **Zappos** is famous for its core value of "Deliver WOW Through Service," which extends to how leaders treat their teams. Their **holacracy model** distributes authority more evenly, reducing top-down undermining and promoting empowerment (Robertson, 2015).
- **Salesforce** prioritizes **equality and transparency** in leadership, with programs designed to support managers and supervisors in building trust and collaboration across teams.

Salesforce's regular employee feedback cycles help identify leadership gaps and address undermining behaviors promptly (Benioff & Adler, 2019).

Conclusion

When supervisors get undermined, it's not just a personal problem—it's a clear sign that something bigger is going wrong in the organization. It's like a warning light flashing about deeper issues that, if ignored, slowly chip away at team morale, hurt productivity, and drive good people away.

That's why organizations can't just brush this off or hope it goes away. They need to step up with real, consistent action: training leaders to communicate and collaborate better, setting clear policies that protect supervisors' roles, building a culture where respect is the norm, and keeping a close eye on how things are going over time.

Investing in this kind of supportive leadership isn't just about avoiding problems—it's about helping everyone thrive. When supervisors feel respected and equipped to handle challenges, they can lead their teams with confidence and energy. That positive ripple effect strengthens the whole organization and helps it reach its full potential.

In the end, protecting supervisors from undermining isn't just good for them—it's good for business and for the people who make the business run every day.

7. Conclusion: Restoring Respect and Building Trust

As we conclude this exploration into the challenges supervisors face when undermined by upper management, it is vital to reflect on the core message: respect and trust are not just ideals—they are the foundation of effective leadership and healthy workplaces.

Throughout this book, we have seen how behaviors such as micromanagement, public criticism, exclusion from key decisions, and other forms of undermining can damage not only a supervisor's confidence but also team morale and organizational success. The toll is real—manifesting as stress, burnout, fractured team dynamics, and costly turnover.

Yet, the path forward is equally clear and hopeful. Supervisors can reclaim their authority and resilience by setting boundaries, building strong connections with their teams, carefully documenting issues, and seeking support from human resources and trusted mentors. These individual strategies are crucial first steps in restoring a sense of agency and dignity at work.

Equally important is the role organizations must play. No supervisor should have to endure undermining behaviors silently or alone. Companies committed to long-term success must invest in training managers to lead with empathy and integrity, implement clear policies that define and prevent harmful conduct, and foster a culture where open communication and respect are non-negotiable. Monitoring tools, anonymous reporting, and conflict resolution mechanisms must be accessible and effective.

When respect is restored between layers of management, trust naturally follows. This trust fuels collaboration, innovation, and engagement—the very elements that propel organizations forward in competitive, ever-changing markets.

For supervisors who find themselves facing these struggles, know that your experience is shared by many and that resources and allies exist. Your role is vital; your voice matters. Taking proactive steps to protect your well-being and professional standing is not only courageous—it is necessary.

For leaders and organizations, the call to action is clear: prioritize respect in every decision and interaction. By doing so, you build workplaces where everyone—from executives to frontline supervisors—can thrive.

In the end, restoring respect and building trust is not a single event but an ongoing commitment. It requires vigilance, compassion, and a willingness to learn and adapt. When both supervisors and organizations embrace this commitment, the result is a healthier, more productive workplace—one where people feel valued, empowered, and ready to succeed together.

Chapter 4
Excluded from Decision-Making Processes

"Exclusion speaks louder than silence."

Being left out of decisions that affect your work isn't just frustrating — it's disempowering. When you're sidelined or ignored, it sends a message that your voice doesn't matter.

This kind of exclusion damages collaboration and stifles innovation. It creates gaps in communication, undermines your confidence, and disconnects you from the very outcomes you're responsible for. Inclusion isn't just a courtesy — it's essential for effective leadership and team success.

Introduction

Supervisors are the unsung heroes of any organization. They're the vital link between the big-picture plans from upper management and the everyday work done by frontline employees. They take broad strategies and turn them into real actions that keep things running smoothly.

But what happens when supervisors get left out of important decisions? When they're not included at the table where key choices are made, it sends a message—not just to them, but to their teams—that their input doesn't matter. This can seriously weaken their authority and make it harder for the whole organization to succeed.

In this chapter, we'll dig into why supervisors sometimes get sidelined, what that means for them and their teams, and most importantly, how to push back against it. The goal is to help organizations understand the value of including supervisors in decision-making—and to give supervisors tools to reclaim their voice and influence.

1. The Role of Supervisors in Decision-Making

Before we talk about what happens when supervisors are left out, it's important to remember why their involvement really matters.

Supervisors are the ones who keep daily operations on track. They're on the front lines, working closely with employees every day, so they have a deep understanding of how things actually get done — and where the real challenges lie.

When supervisors are part of decision-making, several good things happen:

- **Decisions make sense on the ground.** They reflect the real conditions and challenges that teams face, not just what looks good on paper.

- **Teams get clear directions.** Because supervisors understand the plan fully, they can communicate it consistently and effectively to their people.
- **Problems get spotted early.** Supervisors can flag issues before decisions are rolled out, saving time and frustration down the line.
- **Employees feel supported.** When their supervisor is involved and informed, team members feel more connected and confident about changes.

Research backs this up, showing that when middle managers and supervisors have a real voice in decisions, projects tend to go smoother and employees are more motivated (Floyd & Wooldridge, 1997). It's no surprise — people trust leaders who've been part of the process and who understand their work firsthand.

In short, supervisors aren't just messengers — they're essential partners in making smart, workable decisions that help everyone succeed.

2. What Does Exclusion Look Like?

Exclusion from decision-making doesn't always involve being told "you're not part of this." More often, it's quiet and subtle — showing up in small, repeated actions that eventually chip away at a supervisor's role, authority, and dignity. Let's break down the most common ways this happens in a workplace:

2.1. Not Being Invited to Meetings Where Critical Decisions Are Made

One of the clearest signs a supervisor is being excluded is when they're consistently left out of meetings where important changes or strategies are discussed. These aren't casual get-togethers — they're meetings where decisions are made about staffing, budgets, project priorities, or department shifts. When supervisors are not present, their voice isn't heard, and their team's needs go unrepresented.

Imagine a logistics supervisor not being included in a meeting where delivery schedules and warehouse processes are being overhauled. When asked to implement changes, the supervisor is blindsided. Not only does this make them look uninformed, but it also strips them of the opportunity to share practical insight that could improve the decision itself.

Being excluded from the room sends a clear message: "We don't see you as part of the decision-making team."

2.2 Lack of Consultation Before Changes Impacting the Team Are Implemented

It's one thing to be told about a change after it's decided. It's another not to ask for input before decisions that directly impact your team are made.

Supervisors are the ones who understand the daily realities of their departments — workload, morale, who's excelling, and who's burning out. When leadership introduces new goals, technologies, or workflows without asking the supervisor for feedback first, they miss out on crucial context.

Take, for example, a healthcare supervisor who isn't consulted before a new patient intake procedure is implemented. Without their insight, the plan overlooks scheduling bottlenecks and staff availability. The result? Confusion, inefficiency, and rising frustration.

Consultation shows respect. Ignoring it shows the opposite.

2.3. Decisions Communicated as *Fait Accompli*, Without Prior Discussion

Fait accompli is a fancy term, but the feeling it creates is familiar and frustrating. It means being presented with a decision as if it's final and already done — no questions asked, no room to weigh in.

A retail supervisor might open an email that says, "Effective immediately, all stores will close an hour earlier on weekdays." No explanation. No warning. No time to prepare the team or adjust customer expectations.

This approach turns supervisors into messengers, not leaders. They become the face of decisions they had no part in making, and this undermines both their credibility and their control. Over time, it can make a supervisor feel like their only role is to carry out orders — not to lead or contribute.

2.4. Directives Bypassing the Supervisor and Going Straight to Frontline Employees

In healthy organizations, communication flows through the proper channels. When a company wants to inform a team of changes or expectations, the supervisor should be looped in — if not leading the conversation themselves.

But sometimes, senior leaders or departments bypass the supervisor entirely. They might send an update directly to frontline employees or announce changes in a group chat without copying the supervisor. This may seem small, but the impact is significant.

For instance, if frontline staff are told directly by upper management to start using new software, and the supervisor isn't even aware, they're left looking incompetent. Even worse, staff may begin bypassing the supervisor regularly, knowing they can get direction from higher up.

This behavior devalues the supervisor's role. It tells the team: *"You don't need your supervisor. We're in charge."*

2.4a. Misusing the "Open-Door Policy" to Bypass Supervisors

In some organizations, employees are given the freedom to bypass their immediate supervisors or managers and go directly to senior leadership. While this may seem like a well-intentioned effort to promote transparency and accessibility, it can undermine the chain of command and diminish the authority of frontline leaders. When used improperly, this approach can leave supervisors feeling sidelined and devalued in their roles.

The "open-door policy" may sound progressive and inclusive, but its misuse can have serious consequences. The true intent of an open-door policy is not to encourage employees to skip over their managers at the first sign of concern. Rather, it should serve as a last resort—an option when attempts to address issues with immediate supervisors have failed or been ignored. When this boundary is not respected, it disrupts leadership dynamics, weakens team cohesion, and erodes trust between managers and their teams.

Spotlight: When Exclusion Becomes Undermining

Supervisors are sometimes actively undermined by upper management when they are excluded from critical decision-making processes. For example, a lead hand may be chosen to interview candidates for both lead hand and operator positions, while the supervisor is left out entirely.

This not only diminishes the supervisor's authority but also creates confusion around roles and responsibilities within the team.

In some cases, supervisors also grapple with biased performance reviews, unequal opportunities for advancement, or invasive monitoring that crosses the line from accountability into personal invasion. These issues are real, widespread, and deeply impactful—affecting not only a supervisor's ability to lead but also their mental health, confidence, and long-term career prospects.

2.5. Information Withheld or Delayed That Impairs the Supervisor's Ability to Prepare the Team

Supervisors rely on timely, accurate information to support their teams, manage workloads, and prepare for changes. But when they're not given information early enough — or at all — they're left trying to lead in the dark.

Let's say there's a new policy starting next Monday. HR knows. Senior leadership knows. But the supervisor only finds out late Friday afternoon, with no time to explain it to staff, answer questions, or prepare documentation.

It's not just inconvenient — it's damaging. It forces supervisors into a reactive posture, always playing catch-up. It also makes it difficult for them to earn the trust of their teams. After all, how can employees rely on someone who always seems to be the last to know?

The Deeper Message

Each of these examples may seem like a one-off — a forgotten invite, a missed email, a decision that needed to be made quickly. But when these moments pile up, they tell a deeper story.

They tell supervisors they aren't trusted.

They tell supervisors they aren't important.

They tell supervisors they're just there to execute, not contribute.

This isn't just frustrating — it's demoralizing. It takes away the supervisor's ability to lead effectively. It puts them in an impossible position: responsible for outcomes they had no power to influence.

And the ripple effects don't stop there. When supervisors are consistently excluded, their teams suffer. Confusion increases, morale drops, and organizational trust begins to unravel.

3. Why Do Organizations Exclude Supervisors?

Understanding the reasons behind supervisors' being excluded from decision-making sheds light on organizational dynamics and helps pinpoint solutions. The causes are often complex, involving human behavior, organizational culture, and structural factors.

3.1 Power and Control

One of the primary reasons supervisors are sidelined is that upper management seeks to consolidate power. Decision-making is a form of influence, and by centralizing it, senior leaders maintain tight control over the organization's direction. In some cases, this is driven by insecurity or fear of losing authority.

For example, a regional manager might deliberately avoid including supervisors in strategic planning to prevent challenges or dissent. This exclusion serves to minimize debate or feedback that could complicate or slow decision-making.

3.2 Lack of Trust or Confidence

Sometimes, supervisors are excluded because upper management doubts their abilities or judgment. This lack of trust may stem from previous mistakes, perceived incompetence, or simply not understanding the supervisor's role fully.

In a retail chain, for example, a district manager might exclude floor supervisors from marketing discussions, assuming they lack strategic insight. This results in supervisors feeling undervalued and isolated.

3.3 Communication Breakdown

In larger organizations or those with siloed departments, information flow is often inconsistent. Supervisors can be unintentionally left out of conversations simply because communication channels are unclear or poorly maintained.

For instance, in a multinational corporation, time zone differences and hierarchical layers can result in supervisors missing key updates, even when no one deliberately excludes them.

3.4 Organizational Politics

Workplace politics also play a role. Exclusion can be a tactic used in power struggles, favoritism, or personal conflicts. Supervisors who don't "fit in" with the dominant group or who challenge the status quo may be deliberately marginalized.

An example is an IT supervisor who frequently questions management's tech investments and subsequently finds themselves excluded from planning meetings as a subtle form of retaliation.

4. Real-World Examples

Case Study 1: Manufacturing Firm's Plant Supervisor

Jane, a plant supervisor at a mid-sized manufacturing company, found herself excluded from strategic meetings regarding production schedule changes. Management would send directives to her workers without involving her in planning or explaining the rationale. As a result, Jane's team struggled with unrealistic deadlines, leading to missed targets and low morale.

After Jane raised concerns with HR, the company initiated monthly planning meetings, including supervisors, which significantly improved communication and efficiency.

Case Study 2: Hospital Unit Manager

In a hospital setting, Mark, a unit manager, was often left out of discussions about new patient care protocols. These decisions were made by top administrators and disseminated via emails, bypassing Mark's input. This caused confusion among nurses and impacted patient care quality. Mark advocated for inclusion through union channels, leading to the establishment of a supervisory advisory board.

5. Consequences of Exclusion

Being left out of decision-making processes has wide-ranging effects not only on supervisors but on their teams and the entire organization.

5.1 Impact on Supervisors

- **Reduced Authority:** Supervisors lose credibility with their teams when decisions are made without their input. Employees sense their leader's limited control, which undermines respect.
- **Lower Job Satisfaction:** Feeling sidelined creates frustration and decreases motivation. A survey by Gallup (2022) found that employees who felt excluded from decisions were 50% more likely to report low job satisfaction.

- **Increased Stress:** The pressure to implement decisions they had no part in crafting can cause supervisors to feel overwhelmed, leading to burnout.

5.2 Impact on Teams

- **Mixed Messages:** If supervisors are unaware of key decisions, conflicting instructions may reach employees, causing confusion and reduced productivity.
- **Confusion and Errors:** Without supervisors' practical insights during decision-making, plans may not consider on-the-ground realities, resulting in costly mistakes.
- **Decreased Morale:** Teams often pick up on tension between supervisors and upper management, creating a toxic atmosphere.

5.3 Impact on Organizations

- **Inefficiency:** Decision-making without frontline input can lead to strategies that are difficult to implement, wasting time and resources.
- **High Turnover:** When supervisors and employees feel undervalued, turnover rates increase. The Center for American Progress estimates that replacing an employee costs about 20% of their salary.
- **Damage to Culture:** Persistent exclusion fosters distrust, discourages open communication, and impedes collaboration.

6. Legal and Ethical Considerations

While exclusion from decision-making is not always illegal, it raises ethical concerns and may sometimes infringe on workplace rights.

6.1 Discrimination Risks

If exclusion disproportionately affects supervisors based on protected characteristics such as gender, race, age, or disability, it could constitute discrimination under human rights laws in Canada and elsewhere. For instance, a study by Catalyst (2020) highlighted that women managers were often excluded from leadership conversations, limiting career progression.

6.2 Hostile Work Environment

Repeated exclusion can contribute to a hostile work environment, especially if it is combined with other forms of harassment or bullying. Organizations have a legal and ethical obligation to provide a respectful workplace.

6.3 Duty to Accommodate

Supervisors with disabilities have rights to accommodations, which may include inclusion in decision-making processes to ensure effective management of their teams.

Organizations ignoring these responsibilities risk legal consequences, damaged reputations, and reduced employee trust.

7. Strategies for Supervisors to Combat Exclusion

Feeling left out of important decisions can be really tough. But supervisors don't have to just accept it — there are practical ways to step up, show your value, and make sure your voice is heard.

7.1 Proactive Communication

Don't wait for invitations—take the initiative to connect. Reach out to your managers regularly and express your interest in being part of planning and decision-making. Setting up one-on-one chats or asking to join key meetings shows that you're engaged and ready to contribute.

Example: Sarah, a construction supervisor, started sending monthly progress reports to her regional manager. She also asked for feedback on her team's performance. Over time, this opened the door for her to join quarterly strategy meetings — opportunities she didn't have before.

7.2 Building Relationships

Sometimes, it's about who you know. Taking time to build genuine relationships with senior leaders can make a big difference. Casual conversations over coffee or participating in company events can help build trust and keep you on their radar.

Example: Carlos, a sales supervisor, volunteered to help with projects that involved other departments. This gave him a chance to work alongside executives and build connections beyond his immediate team.

7.3 Demonstrating Competence

Actions speak louder than words. When you consistently deliver results, solve problems, and communicate clearly, it becomes hard for managers to ignore your value. Bringing data or clear examples to the table helps reinforce your expertise.

Example: Priya, an IT supervisor, created a detailed report showing where the workflow was getting stuck. Her insights impressed leadership, leading to an invitation to participate in important budget discussions.

7.4 Escalating Concerns

If you've tried the above and still find yourself excluded, don't hesitate to raise the issue through formal channels. Talk to HR, employee committees, or union reps if you have them. Keeping a record of when and how you were excluded will help make your case clear.

Example: After being repeatedly sidelined, Tom, a production supervisor, filed a formal complaint explaining how it hurt his ability to lead effectively. HR took his concerns seriously and reviewed the company's meeting and communication policies.

8. What Organizations Can Do to Include Supervisors

When supervisors feel included in decision-making, everyone wins — teams work better, communication flows more smoothly, and the whole organization becomes stronger. But this doesn't happen by accident. It takes thoughtful, deliberate effort from the top down.

8.1 Structured Communication Channels

Organizations can create regular, predictable spaces where supervisors and upper management come together. This could be weekly check-ins, monthly strategy sessions, or cross-level team meetings. Having these set routines ensures supervisors stay informed and have a chance to share their frontline insights. It also avoids surprises that can throw teams off balance.

8.2 Transparency

An open culture where decisions are explained clearly and quickly helps build trust. When supervisors understand *why* changes are happening, they can communicate more effectively with their teams and feel more confident in their leadership. This openness cuts down on rumors and frustration, making the workplace feel safer and more collaborative.

8.3 Leadership Training

Managers don't always know how to include supervisors well — but they can learn. Training programs focused on inclusive leadership teach managers to see supervisors as partners rather than just "middle managers." For example, one tech company ran leadership workshops that helped managers better engage their supervisors. As a result, supervisor satisfaction scores jumped by 30% (Corporate Leadership Council, 2021). When leaders learn to listen and include, it makes a huge difference.

8.4 Feedback Mechanisms

Organizations should ask supervisors regularly how they're experiencing communication and involvement. Using surveys, focus groups, or anonymous tools lets supervisors share honestly without fear. The key is not just gathering feedback but acting on it — showing supervisors their voices lead to real change.

In summary:

Excluding supervisors from decision-making doesn't just hurt them personally — it ripples through teams and the entire organization, creating confusion, low morale, and missed opportunities. But when organizations recognize the problem, listen carefully, and commit to inclusive practices, they build workplaces where respect, trust, and success grow naturally.

9. Conclusion: Reclaiming the Seat at the Table

Excluding supervisors from decision-making isn't just a procedural oversight—it's a deeper cultural misstep that sends a clear, albeit often unspoken, message: "Your voice doesn't matter." When supervisors are left out of conversations that directly affect the teams they lead, it undermines not just their role but the very structure of trust that good leadership is built on.

A supervisor is more than a messenger or task distributor. They are the pulse of a department, the translator between high-level strategy and daily execution, and often the first line of emotional support for team members. To treat their perspective as optional is to rob the organization of insight, adaptability, and accountability at one of its most crucial levels.

Throughout this chapter, we've seen the many reasons supervisors get excluded—power plays, poor communication, even unconscious bias—and we've also explored the damaging consequences. Supervisors lose confidence. Teams lose direction. Organizations lose efficiency, loyalty, and sometimes even reputation.

But there is a different path. When supervisors are included in decision-making processes—when their knowledge is respected and their insight welcomed—they flourish. Their teams become more engaged—upper management benefits from real-time feedback. And the organization, as a whole, becomes more resilient, collaborative, and responsive.

Inclusion doesn't require complex systems or costly restructuring. It starts with simple, consistent acts: inviting supervisors to planning meetings, asking for their input before rolling out major changes, and treating their insight as necessary rather than optional. It's about building a workplace culture where leadership is not defined solely by title, but by contribution.

For supervisors reading this: your role matters. Your experience on the ground holds value that no executive dashboard can replace. Don't be afraid to speak up, seek inclusion, and advocate for the voice of your team.

And for leaders and organizations: reflect deeply on your current practices. Ask yourself, "Are we really listening to those closest to the work?" Because the health of your organization depends not just on big-picture strategy, but on the day-to-day decisions made by those you've entrusted to lead at every level.

Inclusion isn't just the right thing to do—it's the smart thing to do. It builds stronger supervisors, better teams, and ultimately, a workplace where people feel seen, heard, and respected.

Reflection: The Quiet Cost of Exclusion

Exclusion may not leave a bruise, but it leaves a scar. When those closest to the work are kept furthest from the table, we lose more than ideas—we lose trust, dignity, and connection.

Leadership isn't about control; it's about conversation. And supervisors are not just task managers—they're the interpreters of vision, the stabilizers in change, the steady voice when the ground shifts. When we listen to them, we lead better. When we include them, we grow stronger.

Let the measure of a healthy organization be this: *No one feels invisible in a role built on responsibility.*

Quote to Close the Chapter

"People support what they help create. If they're not in the room, they won't be in the solution."

— **Margaret J. Wheatley**, leadership author and organizational thinker

Reflection & Discussion Questions

1. **Have you ever experienced being left out of a decision that directly affected your role or team?**
2. How did it make you feel—and how did it impact your ability to lead or contribute?
3. **What are some subtle ways exclusion shows up in your current organization?**
4. Think about meetings, communication practices, or who's "in the loop."
5. **Why do you think upper management might exclude supervisors from certain decisions?**
6. Is it always intentional—or could it be a symptom of organizational culture or habits?
7. **How might the inclusion of supervisors in decision-making strengthen a team's trust, performance, and morale?**
8. What would change if supervisors felt more heard and involved?
9. **If you're a supervisor, what's one small step you can take this week to build a bridge—either upward to your leaders or downward to your team?**
10. If you're in senior leadership, what's one way you could *invite* a supervisor's voice into an upcoming decision?

Optional Call-to-Action:

Challenge: In your next team or leadership meeting, make it a point to invite at least one person who isn't usually in the room. Let their insight surprise you.

Chapter 5
Sabotaged: Projects Delayed or Derailed

"When support disappears, success becomes impossible."

Sabotage doesn't always come with fanfare. Sometimes, it's subtle delays, withheld approvals, or sudden resource cuts that stop your projects in their tracks. These obstacles aren't accidents — they're barriers placed to undermine your efforts.

When projects are derailed, it's not just your work that suffers; your reputation and morale take a hit, too. Recognizing sabotage is the first step toward reclaiming control and pushing back against these hidden attacks.

Introduction: When Support Disappears

Supervisors are often the spark plugs of innovation and improvement in organizations. They see where things can be better—whether that's streamlining a process, boosting team spirit, or saving costs—and they bring those ideas forward with hope and enthusiasm. But what happens when, instead of getting support and collaboration, their efforts are quietly blocked or ignored?

This kind of obstruction isn't always loud or obvious. It can be subtle and slow, wearing supervisors down over time. When projects get delayed without explanation, budgets stall, or decisions suddenly change, supervisors don't just lose momentum—they lose credibility with their teams and peers. Worse, the people they lead start doubting change altogether, and that skepticism spreads through the workplace.

What Does "Sabotage" Look Like?

Sabotage by upper management doesn't usually mean open conflict or shouting matches. More often, it's these quiet tactics that chip away at a supervisor's ability to lead and innovate:

- **Silent Delays:** A project gets approved, but then quietly put on hold with no updates. It's like being told "go" and then sitting still without knowing why.
- **Shifting Priorities:** One day, a project is the priority; the next, it's off the table. These sudden changes leave supervisors scrambling to explain the flip-flop to their teams.
- **Dragging Feet on Approvals:** Budgets might be signed off on, but then procurement moves slowly, or key decision-makers become unreachable, stalling progress.
- **Last-Minute Reversals:** Plans that seemed set suddenly get pulled back, leaving supervisors embarrassed or confused in front of their teams.
- **Reassigning Credit or Blame:** Even if a project succeeds, the supervisor's role gets downplayed. Or if things go wrong, the supervisor takes the fall, regardless of the real cause.

Each of these behaviors chips away at motivation and authority, making supervisors question their own impact—and making it harder for their teams to stay engaged.

Real-Life Examples

Example 1: The Lean Manufacturing Pilot

Maria, a plant supervisor passionate about improving efficiency, launched a pilot program to reduce waste. She had the data, the approval, and the drive. But halfway through, the budget was quietly pulled, procurement delayed key equipment, and a new executive pushed a different approach. Maria's team went from excited to frustrated and confused. Maria found herself apologizing for setbacks she couldn't control. The end result? Her team stopped trusting new initiatives, and her own motivation took a hit.

Example 2: The Software Rollout Reversal

Tony, an IT supervisor, worked hard to introduce a new workflow platform to speed up ticket handling. Management greenlit the plan and budget, and the team was ready to go. Then, just before launch, an executive raised concerns about vendor risk, and Tony was told to "pause for more research." That pause dragged on for months. The team's enthusiasm faded, and they went back to old, clunky methods. Tony felt stuck—he wanted to push innovation forward, but every step seemed blocked without explanation.

This kind of hidden obstruction doesn't just hurt supervisors—it slows down progress across the entire organization. When support disappears like this, it creates confusion, frustration, and lost trust that's hard to rebuild.

Why Does Upper Management Sometimes Get in the Way of Projects?

It's frustrating when you have a great project idea, but somehow, the higher-ups block it or let it fail. Understanding *why* this happens can help you handle it better.

1. Fear of Change or Risk Aversion

Big bosses often worry about what could go wrong. If they don't fully get the new idea, it feels safer to say "no" than to take a chance. It's like sticking to what you know because the unknown seems scary.

2. Office Politics and Turf Wars

Sometimes a new project shakes up who's in charge of what. If the project means another department gets more attention or resources, people who currently hold power might try to stop it. It's less about the project and more about protecting their territory.

3. Not Being on the Same Page Strategically

Managers might be focused on day-to-day improvements, while executives are thinking about big-picture goals. If the project doesn't clearly fit the company's bigger plans, it can get pushed aside—even if it would be helpful.

4. Poor Planning or Communication

If someone doesn't clearly own a project or if its benefits aren't explained well to the top brass, it's easy for it to get ignored or rejected. Sometimes the problem isn't the project itself, but how it's presented.

What Happens When Projects Get Sabotaged?

For Supervisors:

- You lose credibility because you can't deliver what you promised.
- Your team's morale drops—everyone gets discouraged when their hard work is blocked.
- Over time, you stop suggesting new ideas, afraid they'll just get shot down.

For Teams:

- Mixed messages from leadership cause confusion about what to focus on.
- After a few setbacks, people stop believing in new initiatives.
- Staff feel like their effort isn't valued, which leads to frustration.

For the Organization:

- Money and time get wasted on projects that never take off.
- Innovation suffers because people are scared to try new things.
- Good employees might quit, looking for places where their work is supported.

Research from Harvard Business School shows that companies where leaders constantly change direction or override projects tend to have less innovation and more burned-out middle managers. So, it's not just annoying—it actually hurts the whole company.

How Supervisors Can Respond

While being blocked isn't easy to reverse, supervisors can take steps to protect their work and their team:

1. **Clarify Priorities and Stakeholder Roles**
2. Early in the project, agree on who the decision-makers are and what authorities are required for each stage.
3. **Build Cross-Level Alliances**
4. Involve key stakeholders from other functions—finance, legal, operations—so initiatives feel less "owned" by one person or department.
5. **Create Demonstrable Value Quickly**

6. Launch small-scale pilots that deliver visible benefits. Tangible wins build credibility and reduce the risk perceived by upper management.
7. **Develop a Communication Plan**
8. Map out who needs to know what, and when. If priorities shift, report the delay honestly and transparently.
9. **Keep Momentum Alive During Delays**
10. Even if the project is paused, organize updates or side tasks that retain engagement and show a good-faith effort.
11. **Document Decisions and Follow Up**
12. Record when approvals shift or timelines change. This clarity helps prevent undue blame if time or scope gets extended.

Successful Interventions

Lean Piloted, Wait, But Persevered

Maria returned to management after the delay with revised data, aligning her pilot with a new sustainability initiative. The second presentation was welcomed, and with fresh approval, the pilot was completed. Now implemented plant-wide, her methods are recognized as best practice.

Tony's Change Proposal Handbook

Tony formalized a small "playbook": outlining project goals, key milestones, stakeholder sign-offs, benefits, and rollback criteria. His next pilot was approved smoothly, and he earned a promotion.

These cases show that well-prepared supervisors who anchor their work in data, alignment, and transparency can reclaim their initiatives—even after sabotage.

Conclusion

Projects blocked or pulled by upper management aren't just inconvenient—they undermine trust, kill motivation, and damage credibility. But they can be countered.

Supervisors who anticipate resistance, build alliances, and maintain openness and documentation stand a better chance of pushing their ideas forward. Even when projects stall, the act of steering them thoughtfully shows leadership.

Remember: innovation isn't just about new ideas—it's about navigating complexity, aligning stakeholders, and above all, hanging on to your vision long enough for it to be seen. And that's true leadership—supervisor-level leadership at its best.

Chapter 6
Input Ignored or Dismissed

"Silencing your voice is a quiet form of control."

When your ideas, feedback, or concerns are routinely ignored or dismissed, it's more than frustrating — it's a message that you don't matter. Being unheard chips away at your confidence and sense of belonging.

Ignoring input stalls progress and breeds resentment. True leadership listens — and when your voice is silenced, the whole team suffers. This chapter explores how to recognize dismissal and reclaim your space at the table.

Introduction: The Silent Shutdown of Supervisor Voice

You know the feeling—when you speak up with a good idea or real concern, and it goes nowhere. No feedback, no acknowledgment… nothing. It's not just frustrating. It's demoralizing.

Supervisors sit in a unique position. You're the bridge between strategy and reality. You see what's working, what's breaking, and what could be better—*every single day.* But when your voice gets ignored, the whole organization loses. And over time, so do you.

When that input is shut down—intentionally or just out of habit—innovation dries up. Engagement fades. People stop trying.

What Being Ignored Looks Like at Work

It's not always some big, dramatic dismissal. More often, it's quiet. Subtle. But no less damaging:

- You speak up in a meeting—and the conversation moves on like you never said a word.
- Your idea gets used later… under someone else's name.
- You send a thoughtful email—and get radio silence.
- You flag real risks around timelines or workloads—and leadership waves them off.

All of this sends one clear message: **"Your input doesn't matter here."**

Real Stories, Real Impact

Scenario 1: The Overlooked Product Insight

Emma, a product planning supervisor, noticed a gap. She suggested bringing customer support into launch planning earlier, so usability issues could be flagged before new features hit the market. She was thoughtful, clear, and persistent.

But no one really listened. Her point barely registered in meetings, and planning moved on without change.

Six months later? A key feature was launched with major usability problems. Customers were frustrated. Support lines were flooded. Loyalty took a hit.

Now leadership was ready to listen—but it was too late. Emma's insight, while correct, had been *ignored* when it mattered most.

Scenario 2: The Ignored Safety Warning

Raj, a night-shift supervisor in manufacturing, noticed his team was burning out. He raised a flag: stacking three-night shifts in a row was a safety risk. Exhaustion was building, and accidents felt inevitable.

His manager brushed it off: *"It'll be fine. We'll manage."*

It wasn't fine.

A few weeks later, fatigue led to a series of minor incidents—and one serious one. The response? Raj didn't get thanked for his earlier warning. He got *blamed* for the fallout.

No one circled back. No one asked what could have been done differently. His voice was never part of the solution—just pushed aside until there was a problem.

These aren't rare cases. They happen in organizations every day. And the cost isn't just one frustrated employee. It's missed insights, avoidable problems, and a culture that slowly teaches people to stay quiet.

And when supervisors go quiet, the organization loses its eyes and ears on the ground.

Why Does Supervisor Input Get Ignored?

Let's be honest—it's not always malice. More often, it's habits, blind spots, and unspoken dynamics that keep supervisor voices from being heard. Here's how it plays out:

1. Habitual Delegation: "I've Got This" Syndrome

Some managers are just used to leading from the front. They're comfortable driving the ship, making the calls, and setting direction—often based on their own ideas.

The problem? They don't stop to look around and ask, *"Who knows more about this on the ground?"*

When supervisors are closest to the work, ignoring their input is like trying to steer with your eyes closed.

2. Strategy vs. Reality: The Disconnect

Leaders often operate at the 30,000-foot view. They're thinking about vision, growth, and long-term strategy. Meanwhile, supervisors are focused on today's challenges—the actual stuff that keeps the business running.

So when a supervisor raises a concern or makes a suggestion, it can be heard... but not *felt*.

Leaders might nod, but then pivot back to the big picture—missing out on real-time insights that could actually make strategy work better.

3. Bias and Power Dynamics: Who Gets Heard

Let's face it: some voices get more airtime than others.

Managers may naturally gravitate toward people who think like them, talk like them, or have a similar background. And when someone challenges the status quo—especially from a different perspective—it can make leaders uncomfortable.

So instead of leaning in, they tune out.

The result? Diversity of experience fades into the background, and valuable insights get lost just because they don't come in the "right package."

4. Communication Gaps: "Did Anyone Even Hear That?"

Sometimes, input gets shared… and then disappears into the void.

Maybe you dropped an idea in an email that never got read. Perhaps you spoke up in a meeting, but there was no space built in for real discussion. Maybe the format itself—rushed agendas, dominant voices—made it hard to be heard.

Whatever the case, the message is the same: *Your input never made it into the room where decisions get made.*

Bottom Line:

Ignoring supervisor input isn't always intentional—but it's always costly. Organizations that want to stay sharp and responsive need to do more than just "allow" feedback. They need to create space for it actively.

The Human and Organizational Toll of Being Ignored

Impact on Supervisors

- **Decreased Confidence:** Time and again, ideas stall. When your contributions are dismissed, you begin to question your own value.
- **Frustration and Fatigue:** It's draining to voice concerns that disappear without action.
- **Silencing Yourself:** After getting overlooked enough, many supervisors simply stop speaking up, retreating into passive compliance.

Impact on Teams

- **Disengagement:** Teams see their leader's value diminished, which in turn affects team morale and buy-in.
- **Repetition of Errors:** When on-the-ground insights aren't integrated, the organization misses issues that are obvious to insiders.
- **Erosion of Innovation:** If fresh perspectives are ignored, novel ideas dry up—teams learn not to think critically.

Impact on the Organization

- **Lost Opportunities:** Great ideas from supervisors rarely emerge from boardrooms; they come from lived experience.
- **Open Doors for Crisis:** When warning signs are ignored, things can escalate—and often do—leading to higher costs or emergency fixes.
- **Culture of Disempowerment:** When voices get silenced, confidence erodes across levels, and leadership becomes top-down and brittle.

What the Experts Say

- **Peter Senge** in *The Fifth Discipline* (1990, Doubleday) emphasizes learning organizations valuing every voice as a catalyst for renewal.
- **Daniel Pink** in *Drive* (2009, Riverhead) argues autonomy, mastery, and purpose fuel motivation—none of which are possible if input is ignored.
- **Harvard Business Review** has stated: "To lead is to listen" (2015). Listening isn't passive—it's the foundation of adaptive, resilient leadership.

How to Be Heard—and Stay Heard

Getting your voice into the conversation and keeping it there can feel like a battle. But there *are* ways to break through the noise. These strategies don't guarantee instant results, but they help shift the dynamic—and over time, they build credibility, visibility, and influence.

1. Frame Your Ideas Around What Matters Most

Instead of just throwing out a suggestion, tie it to the bigger picture.

Try something like:

"Here's what I'm seeing on the ground, and how I think it connects to our goals. Would you be open to me sharing a possible approach?"

This kind of framing shows you're not just thinking about your corner of the world—you're thinking about *the business*. And that makes leaders more likely to listen.

2. Use Both Data and Storytelling

People respond to facts. But they *remember* stories.

When you pair evidence with real human impact—like Emma did by sharing user frustration data *and* a real customer story—it's much harder to ignore. You're not just making a point, you're painting a picture.

3. Stay Calm. Stay Respectful. Stay Persistent.

You might not get heard the first—or third—time. That doesn't mean you're wrong or unwelcome.

Keep showing up. Keep offering value. Volunteer to help make things happen. When you stay respectful and consistent, it starts to shift how you're seen. Over time, you go from "the person with opinions" to "the person we rely on for insight."

4. Build Quiet Supporters

You don't have to go it alone.

Talk to your peers. Connect with others who are seeing the same problems or opportunities. When multiple voices echo a concern or idea, it gets harder to ignore. Internal momentum matters—and allies help build it.

5. Don't Be Afraid to Ask for a Seat

Sometimes, all it takes is asking.

Saying something like:

"I'd love to be included in that meeting," or

"Would you mind adding me to that email thread?"

—can open the door.

Asking for inclusion isn't pushy—it's proactive. And it signals that you're invested in contributing at a higher level.

Final Thought:

Being heard isn't always about speaking louder—it's about speaking *smarter, together, and consistently.* Change takes time. But every time you speak up with clarity, purpose, and respect, you're nudging the system in the right direction.

Case in Point: From Silence to Solutions

At an Environmental Services firm, a maintenance supervisor, Luis, flagged long-term issues with equipment fatigue in a weekly email. For weeks, nothing changed. He persisted—drafting a short whitepaper covering costs, risks, and alternatives. When leadership saw the potential savings and safety benefits, they allocated funds to the fix. Luis's persistence not only resolved a problem but also earned him a seat at quarterly planning meetings.

Conclusion

When a supervisor's voice is ignored, the organization loses more than one viewpoint—it loses its capacity to learn, adapt, and innovate. Too often, frontline experience is the first casualty when leaders are fast-paced or distracted.

But it shouldn't be that way. With thoughtful preparation, honest persistence, and the right communication, supervisors can reclaim space, earn respect, and help their organizations thrive.

Training Toolkit: Turning Insight into Action

1. Reflection Exercise: Your Voice, Your Value

Purpose: To help supervisors reflect on when their input was ignored and how it impacted them.

Instructions:

- Think of a time when you shared a suggestion or warning that was dismissed or ignored.
- Write briefly:
    o What was the suggestion?
    o How was it handled?
    o How did it affect your confidence or performance?
    o What do you wish had happened instead?

Group Debrief (optional):

- Share your story with a partner or small group.
- Discuss: What patterns do we see? What emotional effects linger?

2. Role-Play Scenario: The Supervisor's Warning

Scenario Setup:

You are a supervisor who has noticed that a new scheduling policy will cause understaffing during peak hours. You raise this in a meeting, but it's brushed aside. Now you must bring it up again.

Roles:

- Supervisor (you)
- Manager (resistant but not hostile)
- Observer (provides feedback)

Your Goals:

- Frame your input to align with company goals.
- Use calm, assertive language.
- Stay professional even if the other person is dismissive.

Observer Feedback Prompts:

- Did the supervisor stay calm and clear?
- Was the message solution-focused?
- Did they reframe their input to be more persuasive?

3. Group Brainstorm: Ways to Be Heard Without Conflict

Instructions:

- Break into small groups.
- List 5–7 ways supervisors can make their voices heard when facing resistance or indifference.
- Share tips that worked in your real workplace.
- Each group presents one "golden tip" to the whole room.

Examples:

- Use data to support your point.
- Find a champion or ally who will repeat your idea in meetings.
- Send a follow-up summary email after speaking up.

4. Self-Advocacy Checklist: Before You Speak Up

Use this checklist to prepare before making a suggestion or raising a concern:

Preparation Step

Have I clearly defined the issue or idea?

Do I understand the broader goals this aligns with?

Can I provide data or examples to support my input?

Preparation Step

Am I choosing the right time and audience to speak up?

Can I present this in a calm, non-confrontational tone?

Have I considered who else might support this?

Do I have a backup plan if my input is dismissed?

Pro Tip: Practice saying your input aloud beforehand. Speaking with confidence increases your chance of being heard.

5. Conversation Script: Pushing Through Dismissal

Here's a sample phrase supervisors can practice:

"I understand we have a lot going on, and I respect the decisions being made. But I'd like to revisit my earlier point. I believe this issue could impact our delivery timeline, and I'd appreciate a few minutes to explain why. May I share a quick summary with the group or in a follow-up email?"

This type of phrasing signals respect and persistence—without sounding confrontational.

Bonus Reflection Prompt (Great for Chapter Closing):

"What's one thing you've been holding back from saying at work—because you've felt it wouldn't matter? What's one small way you could say it differently… or say it anyway?"

Chapter 7
Denied Critical Resources or Support

"Without the right tools, even the best efforts fall short."

Being denied the resources or support you need isn't just inconvenient — it's a deliberate barrier to success. When equipment, budget, or personnel are withheld, your ability to deliver quality work suffers.

This lack of support sends a clear message: your success isn't a priority. Recognizing these obstacles helps you push back and advocate for what you truly need to thrive.

Introduction: The Hidden Barrier to Success

For supervisors, managing a team effectively hinges not just on leadership skills but on having the right resources—whether it's tools, budget, staff, or training. When upper management arbitrarily withholds these essentials, supervisors face an uphill battle. This subtle but powerful form of control undermines their ability to meet goals and sows frustration and resentment. Denying resources without a clear justification can cripple a supervisor's role and disrupt the entire team's performance.

What Does Resource Denial Look Like?

Resource denial can manifest in many ways, often cloaked in vague explanations or promises that never materialize:

- **Budget cuts or refusals for new hires, even when workload increases**
- **Delays or denials in purchasing necessary equipment or software**
- **Withholding training or professional development opportunities**
- **Restricting access to data or decision-making tools needed for team oversight**
- **Ignoring repeated requests for support personnel or technical assistance**

For example, consider James, a production supervisor at a pharmaceutical manufacturing facility. As demand for a new drug increased, he repeatedly requested updated equipment and additional technicians to meet tighter production schedules and ensure quality standards. Despite raising the issue multiple times, management responded with vague promises and delays. The outdated machinery kept breaking down, and his team struggled to keep up with batch targets. Minor issues began to pile up, increasing the risk of compliance violations and production delays. James was doing everything he could, but without the necessary support, both morale and performance on the floor began to slip.

Why Do Organizations Deny Resources Without a Clear Reason?

It can be incredibly frustrating when supervisors are denied the tools or support they need—especially when there's no apparent reason behind it. But looking a little deeper, there are often underlying patterns or power dynamics at play. Here are some of the most common reasons why upper management might hold back resources:

1. **Cost-Cutting Comes First**
2. Sometimes leadership is laser-focused on saving money, even if it means cutting corners operationally. In some cases, it's part of a long-term strategy. In others, it's a knee-jerk reaction with little communication or regard for frontline impact.
3. **Maintaining Control**
4. Withholding resources can be a subtle way to keep supervisors in check. If managers don't have what they need to act independently, they stay dependent on higher-ups—making it easier to control decisions and direction.
5. **Lack of Trust**
6. When leadership doesn't fully trust a supervisor's judgment or ability, they may be hesitant to grant additional resources. It's often unspoken, but the concern is that resources will be wasted or mismanaged.
7. **Communication Breakdowns**
8. In some cases, it's not about intent at all—just poor communication. Requests get buried in inboxes, priorities shift, or there's no straightforward process for following up. As a result, important needs fall through the cracks.

The Fallout: How Resource Denial Affects Everyone

Denying resources doesn't just inconvenience supervisors—it creates a ripple effect across the entire organization.

Impact on Supervisors

- **Stress and Burnout:** Fighting for basic support while trying to lead a team wears people down.
- **Ineffectiveness:** Even the most skilled supervisor can't perform well without the tools, people, or training they need.
- **Damaged Reputation:** When goals aren't met, others may see it as a leadership failure—even if the real issue was a lack of support.

Impact on Teams

- **Low Morale:** Teams quickly pick up on the lack of support. It sends the message that their work isn't valued.
- **Reduced Productivity:** Outdated tools and short staffing slow everything down.
- **High Turnover:** Talented people don't stick around long in environments where they're set up to fail.

Impact on the Organization

- **Missed Growth Opportunities:** Without proper resourcing, teams can't innovate or respond to new challenges.
- **Increased Risk of Mistakes:** Overloaded teams using inadequate systems are more likely to make costly errors.
- **Weakened Culture:** When resource denial becomes the norm, it fosters distrust, disengagement, and a "why bother?" mentality.

Case Study: Denied Resources, Delayed Growth

At a mid-sized manufacturing company, supervisor Jake noticed safety hazards emerging from worn-out machinery. He urgently requested budget approval for replacements. Senior management delayed the decision repeatedly, citing financial caution.

Over time, a minor accident occurred, causing injuries and a costly shutdown. Investigations revealed that the denied resources directly contributed to the incident. Not only was the company liable for damages, but Jake's leadership was unfairly questioned because his warnings were ignored.

What Research Tells Us

Harvard Business Review notes that authority alone doesn't guarantee managerial effectiveness: "You need more than people's simple compliance… You must win their commitment by winning over their heads and hearts."

— Linda A. Hill & Kent Lineback, *Being the Boss*, Harvard Business Review Press

Practical Tips for Supervisors Facing Resource Denial

1. Keep a Clear Record

Whenever you ask for resources—whether it's more staff, equipment, or training—write down the details. Note the date, what you requested, and any response you get. This helps if you need to follow up or escalate the issue later.

2. Show the Impact with Data

Numbers can make your case stronger than just opinions. Track how a lack of resources affects things like your team's productivity, customer satisfaction, or safety. When you present concrete evidence, it's harder for decision-makers to ignore the problem.

3. Suggest Workable Alternatives

If full funding isn't possible right away, propose smaller steps or cheaper solutions that can still make a difference. Showing flexibility demonstrates you're committed to solving the problem, not just complaining.

4. Team Up with Others

You're probably not the only one facing these challenges. Connect with other supervisors or departments in the same boat. Together, your voices carry more weight when asking for support.

5. Bring in HR or Senior Leaders

If your requests keep getting stalled, it might be time to involve HR or higher-level management. Frame the conversation around how resource shortages threaten the organization's goals—this helps keep the focus on business priorities.

Conclusion

Resource denial is often a quiet, overlooked challenge that can seriously hinder supervisors and their teams. When essential tools, staffing, or support are withheld without clear reasons, it creates frustration, lowers morale, and ultimately impacts the entire organization's performance. Supervisors are left struggling to meet expectations without the means to succeed, and teams can become disengaged or burn out.

Recognizing resource denial as a real problem—not just an inconvenience—is the first step toward change. By documenting requests, presenting precise data, building alliances, and engaging higher management when necessary, supervisors can advocate effectively for what their teams need. Addressing this issue head-on not only restores trust but also fosters a culture of support, leading to stronger performance and a healthier workplace overall.

Chapter 8
Key Information Withheld Deliberately

"Knowledge is power — withholding it is a tactic of control."

When vital information is kept from you, your ability to make decisions and lead effectively is compromised. Deliberate withholding creates confusion, mistakes, and missed opportunities.

This silent sabotage undermines trust and hampers your success. Understanding how and why information is blocked is the first step to breaking through these barriers.

Introduction: The Silent Sabotage

Supervisors are expected to lead with confidence, make smart decisions, and keep their teams aligned and productive. But what happens when the very information they rely on is deliberately withheld?

Information is the lifeblood of effective supervision. From scheduling and staffing data to policy updates, performance metrics, and strategic plans—supervisors need accurate, timely, and complete information to do their jobs well. When that flow is interrupted, so is their ability to lead.

In some workplaces, this disruption isn't accidental. It comes in the form of selective updates, vague directives, or critical data being withheld without explanation. This quiet, often invisible tactic—intentional information hoarding by upper management—amounts to a subtle but powerful form of sabotage.

Unlike open conflict or clear resistance, this kind of obstruction is harder to spot and even harder to call out. Yet its impact is significant: supervisors are left in the dark, unable to provide clarity to their teams or act with authority. Over time, this erodes trust, slows down progress, and breeds frustration on the front lines.

The silent sabotage of withholding information doesn't just make a supervisor's job harder—it actively undermines their leadership. And when leaders are undermined, the entire team feels the ripple effects.

What Does Intentional Information Withholding Look Like?

Information withholding takes many forms, often subtle and disguised as oversights or administrative delays. Common examples include:

- **Critical updates about policy or procedural changes communicated too late** to allow supervisors to adjust their plans.

82

- **Excluding supervisors from emails or meetings** where key decisions or updates are shared.
- **Delayed sharing of data or reports** that supervisors need to monitor performance or identify problems.
- **Selective communication**, where only partial or sanitized information is provided to supervisors.
- **Withholding feedback or complaints** about the supervisor's team until problems escalate.

For instance, Tom, a supervisor at a logistics company, was not informed promptly about a change in shipping regulations. When his team failed to comply due to a lack of awareness, he faced reprimands from senior management—even though the communication delay was not his fault.

Real-World Example: The Supervisor Left Out

Consider Priya, a production supervisor in a pharmaceutical manufacturing facility. Her team is responsible for meeting strict daily output targets tied to regulatory compliance. One week, without warning, upper management shifts production priorities due to a new client order. However, no one informs Priya. She only finds out when a quality assurance manager questions why her team is still working on the old schedule. Embarrassed and frustrated, Priya scrambles to adjust, knowing her team will now miss both timelines.

The problem? She wasn't given the information she needed—information that leadership assumed "wasn't relevant to her level."

Strategies for Supervisors Facing Information Withholding

1. Proactively Request Updates

Don't wait for information to trickle down. Set up regular check-ins with leadership, and ask direct, specific questions about changes that could affect your team. Frame your questions around operational needs and outcomes.

Instead of: "Anything I should know?"

Try: "Are there any changes to our production priorities or client orders that will affect this week's output targets?"

2. Build Internal Information Channels

Foster informal networks with peers in other departments. Sometimes your colleagues may hear updates before you do. Staying connected can help fill the gaps when top-down communication fails.

3. Document Information Gaps

Keep a record of key decisions or changes that weren't communicated in time. Include how it affected your team's performance. This isn't about blaming—it's about building a case for better communication systems.

4. Communicate the Impact Upward

When information gaps cause problems, make sure leadership understands the consequences. Use facts, not emotion: missed deadlines, confusion, safety risks, or client dissatisfaction all show why timely information matters.

5. Encourage Transparency Culture

If possible, advocate for a more open communication environment. Suggest shared dashboards, project briefs, or regular cross-team meetings where updates are shared in real time.

The Bigger Picture

Withholding information might not always be malicious—but the result is the same: supervisors are left unprepared and their teams pay the price. By staying proactive, documenting gaps, and building support systems, supervisors can reduce the damage of this "silent sabotage." Over time, small shifts in communication can create big improvements in clarity, trust, and team effectiveness.

Why Do Managers Withhold Information?

Understanding the motives behind withholding information helps frame the problem clearly:

1. Control and Power Dynamics

Keeping supervisors out of the loop is a way to maintain top-down control. When information flows only upward or is tightly controlled, management retains power and can manage perceptions.

2. Lack of Trust

Managers may doubt a supervisor's ability to handle sensitive or complex information, fearing leaks or mismanagement. This mistrust leads to information being restricted "for their own good."

3. Poor Communication Culture

Organizations without transparent communication norms or clear channels are prone to accidental or intentional information silos.

4. Avoiding Accountability

By withholding information, managers can avoid blame for negative developments. If supervisors are uninformed, responsibility shifts upward.

The Consequences of Withholding Information

The damage caused by intentional information withholding extends beyond immediate operational issues.

For Supervisors

- **Impaired decision-making:** Supervisors make uninformed or reactive decisions, reducing effectiveness.
- **Loss of credibility:** When teams learn that supervisors lacked vital information, trust erodes.
- **Increased stress and frustration:** Feeling kept in the dark fosters anxiety and disengagement.

For Teams

- **Confusion and inefficiency:** Without clear guidance, teams may duplicate efforts or work at cross-purposes.
- **Decreased morale:** Perceived lack of leadership clarity causes frustration and disengagement.

For Organizations

- **Operational risks:** Missed deadlines, compliance failures, and customer dissatisfaction increase.
- **Toxic culture:** A culture of secrecy undermines collaboration and innovation.

Case Study: The Hidden Email Chain

At a mid-sized tech firm, a product supervisor, Lena, was routinely excluded from email threads discussing product updates and client feedback. When her team was criticized for delayed responses, Lena was blamed, even though she was not informed about the changes.

Lena documented these exclusions and escalated the issue to HR. An internal audit revealed a pattern of intentional exclusion by a project manager who felt threatened by Lena's leadership. The company implemented new communication protocols, ensuring all supervisors are included in relevant information flows, improving transparency and performance.

What the Research Shows

Effective communication is strongly correlated with positive workplace outcomes. According to a study published in the *Journal of Business Communication* (Men, 2015), withholding critical information negatively impacts employee engagement and increases turnover intentions. Moreover, research from the *Harvard Business Review* (2019) stresses that transparent communication fosters trust and accountability at all organizational levels.

How Supervisors Can Respond

1. Proactively Seek Information

When communication gaps exist, supervisors can regularly check in with key contacts, ask clarifying questions, and request updates.

2. Build Strong Networks

Develop relationships across departments to access informal channels of information.

3. Document Communication Breakdowns

Keep records of instances where critical information was withheld, noting dates and impacts for possible escalation.

4. Address Issues Constructively

Use private, respectful conversations to raise concerns about information gaps with managers or HR.

5. Promote a Culture of Transparency

Advocate for clearer communication policies and regular briefings.

Conclusion

Intentionally withholding information from supervisors is a subtle form of workplace obstruction with serious consequences for individuals and organizations alike. Recognizing this issue and taking proactive steps to foster open, inclusive communication can empower supervisors, strengthen teams, and improve organizational effectiveness.

Strategies for Organizations to Prevent Information Withholding

1. Establish Clear Communication Policies

Organizations must create and enforce policies that define who needs to be informed about what, and when. Transparent guidelines help reduce ambiguity, ensuring supervisors receive all relevant information promptly.

Example: A multinational company implemented a "Communication Accountability Framework," where every project update must include supervisors on email threads and meeting invitations. This reduced information gaps by 40% within six months.

2. Foster a Culture of Openness and Trust

Leadership should model transparent communication and encourage a culture where sharing information is the norm, not the exception. Open-door policies, regular town halls, and informal check-ins can build trust and reduce gatekeeping.

Example: At a healthcare organization, senior leaders hold monthly "Ask Me Anything" sessions where supervisors can raise concerns or ask about upcoming changes, strengthening trust and collaboration.

3. Use Collaborative Technology

Adopting collaborative platforms (e.g., Slack, Microsoft Teams, project management tools) ensures information is accessible in real-time to relevant parties. Transparent digital records reduce the chances of exclusion or delay.

Example: A software firm switched from siloed emails to a shared project workspace where all supervisors can track progress and receive instant updates, improving decision-making speed and accuracy.

4. Train Managers on Inclusive Communication

Many communication breakdowns arise from a lack of awareness. Training managers on the importance of including supervisors in key communications and the negative impacts of exclusion can shift behaviors.

Example: An international retailer introduced mandatory leadership workshops emphasizing inclusive communication practices, resulting in higher supervisor satisfaction scores.

5. Implement Feedback and Reporting Mechanisms

Create anonymous channels or regular surveys where supervisors can report information-blocking behaviors without fear of reprisal. This allows organizations to identify and address communication bottlenecks proactively.

Tools for Supervisors to Monitor Communication Flow

1. Communication Logs

Supervisors can maintain logs of emails, meeting invites, and important updates received. This documentation highlights patterns of exclusion and supports formal escalation if needed.

2. Regular Team Briefings

Holding frequent team briefings helps supervisors confirm they have all the necessary information and identify any missing pieces by comparing notes with team members.

3. Network Mapping

Building a map of key contacts and communication channels across departments helps supervisors identify potential information sources and gaps.

4. Use of Shared Calendars and Platforms

Supervisors should encourage the use of shared calendars and project management tools, increasing transparency about scheduled meetings, deadlines, and updates.

5. Scheduled Check-Ins with Management

Regular, scheduled one-on-one meetings with higher-ups create consistent opportunities to receive updates and raise questions before information gaps become problems.

Final Thought

Preventing the withholding of information requires both organizational commitment and supervisor proactivity. Together, clear policies, open culture, technology, and attentive supervisors can ensure that vital information flows freely—empowering supervisors to lead effectively and teams to thrive.

Part II: Psychological & Emotional Manipulation

Mental Tactics that erode confidence and well-being

Chapter 9
Public Shaming and Private Belittlement

"Humiliation in public wounds deeper than words."

Being shamed in front of others or belittled behind closed doors isn't just a matter of disrespect — it's a method of control. Whether it damages your public image or erodes your private confidence, this form of abuse creates a toxic workplace where fear replaces trust.

Introduction

In today's workplace, supervisors are expected to lead with confidence, inspire their teams, and navigate increasingly complex organizational demands. However, many are forced to do so while enduring a toxic, often invisible, form of psychological abuse: public shaming and private disrespect.

These behaviors, frequently employed by upper management or peers in positions of influence, are more than poor leadership practices — they are strategic forms of emotional manipulation. Public shaming undermines a supervisor's credibility, authority, and standing among their team. Private belittlement, meanwhile, targets the individual directly, eroding their self-confidence and sense of professional worth in isolation.

For supervisors caught in this cycle, the damage is profound. They may begin to second-guess their decisions, avoid taking initiative, or disengage altogether. The organizational culture suffers, too, as fear stifles innovation and trust disintegrates.

This chapter delves into the dynamics of public and private forms of disrespect in the workplace — examining their psychological impact, providing real-world examples, and offering actionable strategies for recognizing, responding to, and ultimately preventing these behaviors. It aims to equip readers with tools not only to defend against such insidious conduct but also to preserve their professional integrity, personal dignity, and leadership presence. Protecting one's dignity isn't just an individual concern — it's essential to fostering a resilient, healthy workplace culture.

Understanding Public Shaming in the Workplace

Public shaming in the workplace isn't about accountability — it's about control. It happens when someone in a position of power criticizes or humiliates a supervisor in front of others, often under the guise of "holding them responsible." But the intent isn't to coach or correct — it's to discredit, embarrass, or assert dominance. And the damage it causes runs deep.

This kind of behavior doesn't just sting in the moment; it sends a clear message to everyone watching: *This person isn't respected, and you shouldn't respect them either.* Over time, public shaming chips away at the authority of the supervisor and undermines trust within the team. It creates confusion about leadership roles and encourages a culture where fear and silence replace openness and collaboration.

Here are a few common ways public shaming shows up in professional environments — and why each one is so harmful:

1. Calling Out Mistakes in Meetings

Example: A senior leader harshly criticizes a supervisor in front of the team, mocking their decision or pointing out an error with sarcasm or condescension.

When this happens, the supervisor's credibility takes a hit — not because they made a mistake, but because they weren't treated with basic respect. Everyone makes errors; it's how leaders respond that sets the tone. Public takedowns don't motivate — they humiliate. Team members watching this unfold may lose confidence in their leader, or worse, start to fear they could be next.

2. Embarrassing Emails with a Wide Audience

Example: An email is sent highlighting a supervisor's oversight, copied to multiple people who didn't need to be involved.

There's a big difference between keeping people informed and putting someone on display. These types of emails often carry a tone of blame or passive-aggressive superiority. They don't solve problems — they create resentment. Worse, they leave a written trail that can resurface again and again, reinforcing the damage long after the initial message was sent.

3. Undermining in Public Discussions

Example: A supervisor is interrupted or dismissed in front of a group, their input, brushed aside, or spoken over by someone higher up.

This form of shaming is subtle but powerful. It sends the signal that the supervisor's voice doesn't carry weight — not just to them, but to everyone in the room. Repeated enough, these moments silence valuable perspectives and discourage participation, not only from the person being dismissed but from others who fear the same treatment.

Why It Matters

When leaders publicly shame supervisors, they don't just hurt one person — they damage the integrity of the entire team. These behaviors create a ripple effect: trust breaks down, collaboration dries up, and people begin to focus more on avoiding blame than doing their best work. In these environments, supervisors feel isolated, demoralized, and less likely to take initiative or lead with confidence.

Psychological safety — the feeling that it's okay to speak up, ask questions, or make mistakes without fear of embarrassment — is essential to a healthy workplace. Public shaming does the exact opposite. It replaces safety with anxiety, curiosity with caution, and creativity with compliance.

A Real-World Example: *"The Meeting That Changed Everything"*

Marissa had been a team supervisor for nearly three years. She was respected by her team, hit her performance targets consistently, and was known for her calm, steady leadership. But during one all-hands meeting, her manager blindsided her.

In front of thirty people — peers, executives, and even junior staff — he tore apart one of her recent decisions, calling it "short-sighted" and "irresponsible." Marissa had no warning. She hadn't even been told there was a problem. She sat frozen, trying to remain composed while the room went silent.

After the meeting, no one said much. People avoided eye contact. Some team members started going directly to her manager for approvals, bypassing her entirely. Within a few weeks, her authority was weakened. Confidence — both in herself and from her team — had taken a hit. She later described the experience not just as embarrassing, but destabilizing. "It didn't just make me question my decision," she said. "It made me question whether I belonged here at all."

Private Disrespect: The Quiet Undermining

While public shaming is visible and overt, **private disrespect** is often subtle but equally harmful. It includes behaviors like:

- Ignoring a supervisor's contributions or requests during one-on-one meetings.
- Using condescending language or dismissive tones when speaking privately.
- Failing to acknowledge a supervisor's achievements or ideas.
- Making sarcastic or belittling remarks behind closed doors.

These micro-aggressions accumulate over time, eroding the supervisor's self-esteem and increasing feelings of isolation and frustration. Private disrespect often goes unnoticed by others, making it harder for the supervisor to find support or validation.

Why Do Managers Engage in Public Shaming and Private Disrespect?

Most people don't enter leadership roles intending to humiliate or hurt others. But when public shaming and private disrespect show up consistently, it's usually not random. These behaviors often stem from deeper issues — either within the individual manager or the culture around them. Let's take a closer look at what drives this kind of damaging conduct.

1. Power and Control

Some managers use public shaming as a way to **reinforce the hierarchy** — to remind others who's in charge.

They may not say it out loud, but the message is clear: *"I control the room. I control you."*

This often happens when a supervisor starts gaining influence — maybe their team is thriving, or they've built strong internal relationships. Instead of feeling proud or supportive, a controlling manager may respond with fear masked as dominance. Public criticism becomes a performance — not for the person being corrected, but for everyone watching. It sends a signal: *"Don't step out of line."*

Over time, these power plays erode trust and create a climate of anxiety rather than accountability.

2. Insecurity

Ironically, the most toxic managers are often the ones who feel the **most threatened**.

When a supervisor is confident, capable, and respected by others, it can trigger deep insecurities in a manager who's unsure of their own value.

Rather than deal with their own self-doubt, they may lash out — nitpicking small mistakes, excluding supervisors from decisions, or undermining them in front of others. It's not about performance; it's about protecting their ego. These managers might not even realize they're doing it, but the impact is the same: capable leaders are silenced or pushed down, just so someone else can feel taller.

3. Poor Emotional Intelligence

Not all harm is calculated — sometimes it's the result of **emotional clumsiness**.

Some managers simply haven't developed the self-awareness or empathy needed to lead with emotional maturity.

They might react to pressure with frustration, take things personally, or project their stress onto others. Instead of pausing to consider how their words land, they blurt out criticism in front of a group. Instead of asking questions, they assign blame. It's not always malicious — but it *is* damaging.

Emotional intelligence isn't just a "soft skill." It's a leadership essential. Without it, even well-meaning managers can cause harm they don't fully see.

4. Organizational Culture

Sometimes the problem isn't one person — it's **the environment they operate in**.

If public shaming and private disrespect are common, it's usually because the culture allows it — or even rewards it.

In some workplaces, tough talk is mistaken for strong leadership. "We don't coddle people here" becomes an excuse for verbal aggression. Or worse, managers who dominate others may be seen as decisive and effective — when in reality, they're just loud.

When bad behavior isn't challenged — or when it's quietly encouraged — it becomes part of the norm. And in that kind of environment, even good people can fall into bad habits.

Final Thought

None of these reasons justify the behavior — but understanding them is the first step toward changing it. Whether it comes from fear, ego, or culture, public shaming and private disrespect have no place in a healthy workplace. The more we recognize the roots, the better we can hold people accountable — and help leaders grow into the kind of managers people want to follow.

Reflection & Action: What to Do With This Awareness

Recognizing toxic leadership behaviors — especially subtle ones like public shaming or private disrespect — can be uncomfortable. Whether you've witnessed it, been on the receiving end, or realized you've engaged in it yourself, the next step is what matters most.

Here are a few questions to reflect on:

If you're a manager or team leader:

- Have I ever corrected or criticized someone in front of others when it could've been done privately?
- Do I ever feel threatened by strong team members, and how do I handle that feeling?
- When I'm frustrated or under pressure, how do I tend to communicate?
- How open am I to feedback — not just from my boss, but from those who report to me?

If you're observing this behavior in someone else:

- Is this a pattern, or a one-off moment under stress?
- Does the workplace culture tolerate or even reward this kind of behavior?
- Are there safe channels to raise concerns or offer feedback?
- Can I support the person being disrespected — even in small, quiet ways?

Small Actions, Big Impact

- **Model what respect looks like.** A calm correction in private, a genuine apology in public, or a kind word after a harsh meeting can go further than you think.
- **Speak up when you can.** Silence often reinforces bad behavior. A well-timed question like *"Was that the right time for that feedback?"* can disrupt the pattern.

- **Seek support.** If you're experiencing public shaming or ongoing disrespect, you don't have to navigate it alone. HR, mentors, or trusted peers can offer perspective and options.

Self-awareness is a leadership skill. The more we reflect on how power, ego, and emotion show up in our roles, the more intentionally we can lead. Respect isn't a luxury in the workplace — it's a foundation.

Real-World Example: Carla's Story

Carla, a sales supervisor at a mid-sized firm, experienced public shaming during weekly sales meetings. Her regional manager would repeatedly point out her team's missed targets with a sarcastic tone and interrupt Carla when she tried to explain mitigating factors. Privately, the manager dismissed Carla's concerns and failed to acknowledge her successful client relationships.

This double-edged abuse led Carla to doubt her abilities and withdraw from proactive leadership. The team's morale dropped, turnover increased, and Carla eventually sought support from HR and external counseling.

Psychological Impact

Research shows that public humiliation and private disrespect contribute significantly to workplace stress and mental health issues. According to a study published in the *Journal of Occupational Health Psychology* (Smith et al., 2018), employees subjected to workplace humiliation experience increased anxiety, depression, and reduced job satisfaction.

For supervisors, who must project strength and stability, such abuse can cause:

- **Loss of confidence:** Doubting their competence and decisions.
- **Burnout:** Chronic stress leading to exhaustion and disengagement.
- **Isolation:** Feeling unsupported by management and peers.
- **Reduced effectiveness:** Impaired ability to lead teams or make decisions.

Effects on Team and Organizational Culture

When supervisors are publicly shamed or privately disrespected, the ripple effects harm the entire organization:

- **Team morale suffers:** Witnessing leaders being demeaned reduces employee engagement and loyalty.
- **Trust erodes:** Teams question leadership stability and fairness.
- **Productivity declines:** Distracted and demoralized supervisors and teams perform poorly.
- **Talent drains:** Skilled supervisors may leave, unwilling to endure toxic treatment.

Addressing and Preventing Public Shaming and Private Disrespect

Dealing with public shaming and private disrespect isn't just about reacting in the moment — it's about creating systems, habits, and cultures that prevent these behaviors from taking root in the first place. Both organizations and individual supervisors have a role to play.

For Organizations

• Establish Clear Anti-Harassment Policies

Make it clear that public shaming, passive-aggressive behavior, and subtle disrespect are unacceptable — not just physical or legal forms of harassment. If it causes emotional harm or undermines someone's role, it needs to be addressed. Policies should name these behaviors explicitly and define consequences to prevent gray areas.

• Train Managers on Emotional Intelligence and Communication

Many harmful behaviors stem from a lack of self-awareness or empathy. Leadership training should include emotional intelligence, respectful communication, and how to give constructive feedback. These aren't "nice to haves" — they're essential leadership tools.

• Create Safe Reporting Channels

People won't speak up if they fear backlash. Organizations must provide simple, confidential, and trusted ways to report disrespectful behavior — especially when it comes from higher up the ladder.

• Model Respect from the Top

Culture trickles down. If senior leaders interrupt, shame, or dismiss others — even subtly — that behavior spreads. On the flip side, respectful leadership sets a powerful tone. People follow what's modeled, not just what's mandated.

For Supervisors

• Keep a Factual Record

If disrespect or public shaming becomes a pattern, start documenting it. Note dates, times, what happened, who was present, and how it affected your work or team. This not only helps with clarity — it also protects you if formal action is needed later.

• Speak Privately, When Safe to Do So

Some managers may not realize the harm they're causing. If it feels safe, request a private conversation to share your perspective. Use "I" statements, like:

"I felt discouraged when my input was dismissed during the meeting."

This approach avoids blame while creating space for productive dialogue.

• Use HR or Mediation When Necessary

If direct communication doesn't help — or isn't safe — involve HR or ask for mediation. You're not making a scene; you're protecting your right to work in a respectful environment.

• Build Peer Support

Supervisors often feel caught between frontline staff and senior leadership. A few trusted peers can make a world of difference — people to talk to, vent with, and feel seen by. Support counteracts isolation and helps maintain your confidence.

• Take Care of Your Mental Health

Ongoing disrespect is draining. Whether through counseling, coaching, or simply taking a step back to breathe, prioritize your mental well-being. Leadership takes energy, and protecting your peace is not a luxury — it's what helps you show up strong.

Practical Communication Tips for Challenging Moments

Sometimes disrespect happens in real-time — in front of others, under pressure, or unexpectedly. These moments are challenging, but how you respond can shape the outcome and preserve your professional presence.

1. Stay Calm in the Moment

Your first instinct may be to defend yourself or shut down. Try instead to:

- Take a breath.
- Keep your tone neutral.
- Maintain composed body language.
- Say, "Let's revisit this privately," if the conversation gets heated.

Example:

If your manager criticizes you in a meeting, reply:

"I hear you — let's find time after this to walk through it in more detail."

This signals openness without surrendering your dignity.

2. Follow Up Privately

Once the situation has cooled, request a respectful, one-on-one conversation. Share how the moment affected you and how you'd prefer to handle feedback in the future. This model reinforces boundaries and promotes emotional intelligence.

3. Keep Records

As mentioned earlier, documenting incidents is key — especially if patterns emerge. Stick to facts. Don't embellish or assume motive. Just log what happened, when, and who was present.

4. Seek Guidance and Support

Don't go through this alone. You have options:

- HR can clarify policies and handle formal complaints.
- Mentors can offer perspective and validation.
- Therapists or coaches can help you process the emotional impact and plan your next move.

5. Reinforce Your Leadership with Your Team

If your credibility was challenged publicly, your team may feel unsure. Rebuild trust by:

- Communicating openly — without gossip or blame.
- Acknowledging the situation if appropriate.
- Staying steady, fair, and focused on outcomes.

Your response becomes part of your leadership brand.

6. Escalate if Needed

If the behavior continues despite your efforts, take formal action:

- Submit a written complaint with documentation.
- Request third-party mediation.
- Elevate the issue to higher leadership if HR is ineffective.

Know your rights. Psychological harassment is a workplace health issue, not just a bad day.

7. Prioritize Recovery and Resilience

Even when things improve, the emotional toll can linger. Recharging isn't a weakness — it's a repair.

- Create work-life boundaries.
- Take mental health days if needed.
- Practice stress-reducing routines: journaling, walking, and time offline.

Conclusion

Public shaming and private disrespect aren't just unpleasant experiences — they are corrosive forces that weaken leadership, damage culture, and harm mental health. But by naming them, responding with clarity, and creating environments that don't tolerate emotional harm, both organizations and individuals can shift the workplace into a space where respect isn't optional — it's expected.

Closing Thought

Remember, you deserve to be treated with respect and dignity at work. By responding thoughtfully, documenting carefully, seeking support, and advocating for yourself, you can navigate the rugged terrain of public shaming and private disrespect while preserving your integrity and mental well-being.

Chapter 10
Gaslighting and Mental Manipulation

"When your reality is questioned, your confidence crumbles."

Gaslighting is a cruel tactic that twists facts and sows doubt, making you question your own memory, perception, and sanity. Mental manipulation isn't just confusing — it's a form of psychological control that can leave lasting damage.

Recognizing gaslighting is the first step to reclaiming your truth and standing firm against manipulation.

Introduction

Gaslighting and mental manipulation are insidious psychological tactics that some managers may use to control, confuse, and undermine supervisors. These covert abuses are especially damaging because they attack a supervisor's sense of reality and self-worth, making it difficult to recognize the problem or defend against it.

This chapter explores what gaslighting and mental manipulation look like in supervisory roles, the impact on individuals and teams, real-life examples, and strategies to identify and counteract these toxic behaviors.

What Is Gaslighting?

The term *gaslighting* originates from the 1944 film *Gaslight*, where a husband manipulates his wife into doubting her perceptions and sanity. In the workplace, gaslighting involves deliberate distortion or denial of facts by a manager or colleague, aimed at making the supervisor question their memory, judgment, or competence.

Common Forms of Gaslighting and Mental Manipulation at Work

Supervisors may encounter gaslighting through:

- **Denial of Facts:** A manager denies having made a request or decision, despite clear evidence.
- **Minimizing Concerns:** Dismissing legitimate issues as overreactions or misunderstandings.
- **Blaming the Victim:** Turning the blame onto the supervisor for problems caused by the manager.
- **Withholding Information:** Intentionally keeping the supervisor uninformed to cause confusion or mistakes.

- **Contradicting Memories:** Insisting that events happened differently than the supervisor recalls.
- **Setting Impossible Expectations:** Creating goals that are unrealistic and then blaming the supervisor for failing to meet them.

How Gaslighting Differs from Simple Miscommunication

It's important to distinguish gaslighting from genuine misunderstandings. Gaslighting is intentional and repeated, with the goal of control or sabotage. Miscommunication is usually accidental and can be resolved with clear dialogue.

The Impact of Gaslighting on Supervisors

Gaslighting is a form of psychological manipulation where someone tries to make you doubt your own perceptions, memories, or judgment. For supervisors, experiencing gaslighting isn't just frustrating—it can seriously damage mental health and how well they perform their jobs. The American Psychological Association points out that ongoing gaslighting can trigger anxiety, depression, confusion, and a drop in self-confidence.

Here's how this plays out for supervisors specifically:

- **Self-Doubt:**
- Gaslighting chips away at your confidence by making you question your own decisions and memory. You might start wondering, "Did I really say that?" or "Am I overreacting?" This constant self-questioning undermines your ability to trust yourself, which is crucial for effective leadership.
- **Increased Stress:**
- When you're constantly second-guessing your actions or anticipating being undermined, it wears you down emotionally and physically. The mental load of trying to prove yourself right or remember events accurately can lead to chronic stress and burnout.
- **Reduced Assertiveness:**
- A supervisor who's been gaslighted may hesitate to speak up, challenge ideas, or make bold decisions. They might fear being dismissed, ridiculed, or told they're "wrong" even when they're right. This silence can hurt team morale and stall progress.
- **Isolation:**
- Gaslighting often makes people feel alone because it's subtle and confusing. Supervisors might think that others don't understand what they're going through or that they can't trust their colleagues or higher-ups. This sense of isolation can deepen feelings of helplessness.
- **Poor Job Performance:**
- When your mental energy is drained by confusion and stress, it's harder to stay focused, organize your team, or meet goals. Gaslighting can make even straightforward tasks seem overwhelming, resulting in slipping performance and frustration for both you and your team.

Supporting Supervisors Facing Gaslighting

Gaslighting can be deeply damaging, but with the right strategies and support, supervisors can rebuild their confidence and regain control. Here's how both individuals and organizations can help:

For Supervisors:

- **Trust Your Reality**
- Keep a journal or log of important conversations, decisions, and events. Writing things down helps you anchor your memory and provides evidence if you need to clarify what actually happened. When your mind doubts itself, having facts on paper can be empowering.
- **Seek Trusted Allies**
- Find colleagues, mentors, or friends who can listen without judgment and help validate your experiences. Just knowing someone believes you can break the isolation gaslighting creates.
- **Practice Self-Compassion**
- Remember that gaslighting is about manipulation — it's not a reflection of your abilities or worth. Be gentle with yourself when feelings of doubt or confusion arise. Treat yourself like you would a friend going through a tough time.
- **Set Boundaries**
- Where possible, limit your exposure to people who gaslight you or create toxic situations. If you can't avoid them altogether, be clear about what behavior you will not accept and stick to those boundaries firmly.
- **Use Professional Support**
- Therapists, counselors, or coaches experienced with workplace stress and manipulation can help you process your feelings, develop coping strategies, and rebuild self-esteem.
- **Build Assertiveness Skills**
- Practice ways to calmly and clearly communicate your views, needs, and boundaries. Role-playing scenarios with a coach or trusted peer can make it easier to speak up confidently when it matters.

For Organizations:

- **Educate Leadership and Staff**
- Provide training about gaslighting, psychological safety, and respectful communication. When everyone understands what gaslighting looks like, it's easier to spot and stop it early.
- **Create Clear Reporting Mechanisms**
- Make sure supervisors can report manipulative or undermining behavior confidentially and without fear of retaliation. A trustworthy HR process encourages people to come forward before issues escalate.
- **Promote a Culture of Transparency and Respect**
- Encourage open dialogue, feedback, and accountability at all levels. When leaders model honesty and respect, it reduces the power dynamics that allow gaslighting to flourish.
- **Provide Access to Support Resources**

- Offer employee assistance programs, mental health resources, or coaching services that supervisors can access confidentially. Supporting mental well-being should be part of workplace care.
- **Regular Check-ins**
- Managers and HR should regularly check in with supervisors to gauge their workload, stress, and overall morale. Early detection of issues helps intervene before gaslighting severely impacts mental health or job performance.

By combining personal strategies with organizational support, supervisors can protect themselves against the harmful effects of gaslighting, restore their confidence, and lead effectively in healthier work environments.

Real-World Example: Michael's Experience

Michael, a logistics supervisor, began noticing patterns in his interactions with his new director. The director frequently told him he never submitted certain reports, though Michael had emails proving otherwise. When Michael raised concerns about shipment delays, the director labeled him "too sensitive" and accused him of poor leadership.

Over months, Michael started doubting his memory and feared for his job. His confidence eroded, and his team noticed his withdrawal. Eventually, Michael sought advice from HR and a workplace counselor, who helped him identify the gaslighting and develop coping strategies.

Conclusion

Gaslighting and mental manipulation are deeply toxic behaviors that erode supervisors' authority, confidence, and overall well-being. Recognizing these tactics, trusting your own perceptions, and building strong support networks are essential steps to resisting and recovering from such abuse. At the same time, organizations play a crucial role in creating transparent, respectful, and accountable workplaces where supervisors can lead with clarity, confidence, and dignity. Cultivating these environments not only protects individuals but also strengthens leadership and the organization as a whole.

Recognizing Early Signs of Gaslighting: A Supervisor's Guide

Gaslighting rarely happens overnight. It usually starts subtly—small comments, overlooked efforts, or questionable denials that, over time, chip away at a supervisor's confidence and clarity. Spotting these early warning signs is essential to protect yourself, your team, and your professional standing before the manipulation deepens.

1. You Begin to Doubt Your Memory or Judgment

One of the first indicators of gaslighting is a creeping sense of uncertainty about your own recollections. If you find yourself frequently questioning whether you actually said or did something because your manager insists otherwise, this is a red flag.

Example: Imagine you clearly remember submitting a report by the deadline, but your manager repeatedly claims it was late or never received. This inconsistency should raise concern.

2. You Feel Like You're 'Walking on Eggshells'

If you constantly adjust your words or actions to avoid upsetting your manager—fearing any disagreement could lead to conflict or punishment—you may be experiencing emotional manipulation.

Example: A supervisor who carefully crafts every email or avoids bringing up problems in meetings because previous attempts were met with hostility or dismissal.

3. Your Concerns Are Dismissed or Minimized

When legitimate issues or feedback you share are brushed aside as "overreactions," "misunderstandings," or "not a big deal," it may be a way to invalidate your perspective and silence you.

Example: Reporting a safety concern and being told you're "making things worse" instead of being heard and supported.

4. You're Given Conflicting Information or Changed Expectations

Gaslighters often shift the goalposts, providing different instructions or expectations without acknowledgment, making you question your competence.

Example: Being assigned a project with clear parameters, only to have those changed midstream, with blame placed on you for not meeting the "original" goals.

5. You Notice Patterns of Isolation or Exclusion

If you're frequently left out of meaningful conversations or decisions, or critical information is not shared with you, it can be a sign of deliberate withholding to confuse or marginalize you.

Example: Discovering after the fact that key decisions affecting your team were made without your input.

6. You Experience Frequent Criticism Coupled with Mixed Messages

Gaslighting often involves alternating between praise and harsh criticism, keeping you off balance and uncertain about your standing.

Example: A manager praising you in private but publicly undermining you or vice versa, leaving you unsure how to act.

7. You Feel Increasingly Anxious or Depressed at Work

Emotional manipulation erodes mental well-being. If your work environment causes you to dread coming to work or you experience physical symptoms like sleeplessness or headaches, take this seriously.

Why Early Recognition Matters

Catching these signs early allows you to take proactive steps to document, seek support, and set boundaries before your sense of self and leadership authority erodes. It empowers you to regain control and protect your mental health, as well as your team's stability.

Quick Checklist: Early Gaslighting Signs

- Doubting your memory or judgment frequently
- Feeling anxious or stressed over minor interactions
- Receiving conflicting instructions without clarity
- Concerns or feedback ignored or trivialized
- Being excluded from key decisions or information
- Experiencing mixed messages from your manager
- Feeling isolated or unsupported

Coping Strategies for Supervisors Facing Gaslighting and Mental Manipulation

When you recognize the early signs of gaslighting, it's crucial to respond thoughtfully and protect both your well-being and professional effectiveness. While dealing with manipulative managers can be deeply challenging, practical strategies can help you maintain your confidence, clarify reality, and reclaim your leadership power.

1. Keep Detailed Records

Documentation is your strongest ally against gaslighting. Keep thorough, dated records of emails, meeting notes, requests, and any communications with your manager. This paper trail not only helps confirm your memory but also provides evidence if you need to escalate the issue.

Example: If your manager denies giving you a task, you can refer to the exact email or meeting minutes showing the assignment.

2. Seek Support and External Validation

Talk to trusted colleagues, mentors, or HR representatives who can provide objective perspectives. Sharing your experience helps confirm that your perceptions are valid and not distorted.

Example: A peer might have witnessed interactions or be able to help you strategize a response.

3. Practice Assertive Communication

When confronting manipulative behavior, calmly and clearly state your observations and concerns. Use "I" statements to avoid sounding accusatory but stand firm on facts.

Example: "I understand you said the report was late, but here's the email I sent last week confirming the submission."

4. Set Boundaries Politely but Firmly

You have the right to protect your mental space. If conversations become manipulative or hostile, it's okay to disengage respectfully and revisit the issue later when emotions are lower.

Example: "I want to discuss this when we can focus calmly. Let's schedule a time to talk."

5. Prioritize Your Mental Health

Recognize when the situation is affecting your well-being. Don't hesitate to seek professional counseling or employee assistance programs. Taking care of your mental health strengthens your resilience and leadership capacity.

6. Focus on Your Team and Role

Keep your attention on what you can control—your team's performance, morale, and support. Building a strong, trusting relationship with your team can buffer the adverse effects of gaslighting from above.

7. Know When to Escalate

If gaslighting persists despite your efforts, consider escalating through formal channels like HR or higher management. Use your documentation to present a clear case.

Real-Life Example: Sarah's Turnaround

Sarah, a retail supervisor, faced constant denial from her district manager about the schedules she had created. Initially, she doubted her own notes. After documenting each interaction and consulting with a mentor, she confidently presented her evidence to HR. With support, Sarah's situation improved, and the toxic behavior was addressed.

Organizational Responsibilities: Preventing and Addressing Gaslighting in the Workplace

While individual supervisors can take steps to protect themselves, the responsibility to prevent and address gaslighting also lies with the organization as a whole. A healthy workplace culture actively discourages manipulative behaviors and fosters psychological safety, where every employee, including supervisors, feels respected and supported.

1. Training Leaders on Psychological Safety and Respect

Organizations must train all managers and leaders on what constitutes healthy leadership behavior versus manipulation or emotional abuse. This training should highlight the signs and consequences of gaslighting, emphasizing the importance of trust, transparency, and accountability.

Example: Companies like Google and Zappos have integrated psychological safety training into leadership programs to promote open communication and respect.

2. Clear, Confidential Reporting Channels

Supervisors experiencing gaslighting need safe avenues to report abuse without fear of retaliation. Organizations should establish confidential reporting mechanisms—such as anonymous hotlines or trusted HR contacts—that encourage early intervention.

3. Regular Well-Being Check-ins

HR and senior leaders should routinely check in with supervisors, especially in high-stress departments, to monitor for signs of psychological distress or manipulation. These proactive conversations can uncover issues before they escalate.

Example: Some organizations use pulse surveys or one-on-one meetings to gauge workplace climate and supervisor support.

4. Zero-Tolerance Policies for Emotional Abuse

To deter gaslighting and related behaviors, companies must have clear policies that define unacceptable conduct and the consequences for managers who engage in manipulation or abuse. These policies must be communicated clearly and enforced consistently.

5. Promote a Culture of Transparency and Accountability

Gaslighting thrives in environments where secrecy and blame-shifting are common. Organizations should promote transparent decision-making, open feedback loops, and collective responsibility to create a culture where manipulative tactics are less likely to occur.

6. Support Programs and Resources

Providing access to employee assistance programs, counseling, and mentoring supports supervisors' mental health and leadership development. Offering these resources sends a message that the organization values their well-being and growth.

Example of Positive Leadership Culture

Patagonia is often cited for its transparent, people-first approach. Their leadership training includes emotional intelligence and communication skills, encouraging managers to foster trust and respect, which significantly reduces toxic power dynamics like gaslighting.

Conclusion: A Shared Responsibility

Preventing gaslighting requires commitment from every level of the organization. When companies invest in respectful leadership, clear policies, and support systems, they not only protect supervisors but also enhance overall workplace morale and productivity.

Chapter Summary: Recognizing and Resisting Gaslighting

Gaslighting is a subtle but deeply damaging form of manipulation that targets a supervisor's confidence, clarity, and mental health. It's not just about misunderstandings—it's a deliberate attempt to control and confuse, often leaving supervisors isolated and doubting their own perceptions.

Recognizing the early signs—such as denial of facts, minimizing concerns, or contradictory memories—is the first crucial step toward protecting yourself. Documenting interactions, seeking trusted support, and communicating assertively can help rebuild your confidence and push back against manipulation.

Yet, individuals cannot bear this burden alone. Organizations must create cultures of transparency, accountability, and psychological safety to prevent such abuses from taking root. Leaders trained in respectful communication and clear policies on emotional abuse are essential to foster environments where supervisors can lead effectively without fear.

Above all, remember: your perceptions and experiences are valid. Trust yourself, seek support, and never underestimate your value as a leader. By standing firm against gaslighting, you not only protect your own well-being but also contribute to a healthier, more respectful workplace for everyone.

Chapter 11
Unpredictable Behavior and Mood Swings from Above

"When leadership's mood rules the day, stability disappears."

Unpredictable behavior from those above you creates an environment of anxiety and uncertainty. Mood swings can turn a supportive workplace into a minefield, where no one knows what to expect or how to respond.

This emotional rollercoaster undermines trust and hampers your ability to lead with confidence. Understanding the impact helps you develop strategies to maintain your footing amid the chaos.

Introduction

One of the more challenging and destabilizing experiences a supervisor can face is dealing with erratic and unpredictable behavior from upper management. When those in leadership fluctuate between extremes—ranging from overly approving one moment to harshly critical the next—it creates an unstable work environment. This emotional volatility not only undermines the supervisor's confidence and effectiveness but also impacts the broader team's morale and productivity.

This chapter explores what unpredictable mood swings from upper management look like, why they occur, the effects on supervisors and teams, and strategies for navigating and coping with this difficult dynamic.

What Does Unpredictable Mood Swings from Management Look Like?

Supervisors who face mood swings from their superiors often describe experiences such as:

- **Sudden shifts in tone:** A manager who praises one day but criticizes harshly without warning the next.
- **Inconsistent decision-making:** Rules or expectations change frequently and without a clear explanation.
- **Unpredictable reactions:** Seemingly minor issues trigger disproportionate anger or frustration.
- **Emotional withdrawal:** Periods of silence or disengagement followed by bursts of intense interaction.
- **Favoritism swings:** One day, a supervisor feels supported, the next feels singled out or blamed.

These swings leave supervisors guessing how to approach their superiors, unsure of what behavior will be met with approval or disapproval.

Why Do Managers Exhibit Mood Swings?

While every individual's emotional regulation varies, certain factors contribute to unpredictable moods in leadership:

- **Stress and Pressure:** High demands and stress can lead to irritability and emotional volatility.
- **Poor Emotional Intelligence:** Some managers lack the skills to manage emotions constructively.
- **Lack of Self-awareness:** Without reflection, leaders may not realize how their mood impacts others.
- **Personal Issues:** Problems outside work can spill over into professional behavior.
- **Power Dynamics:** Sometimes, mood swings are an unconscious tactic to control or intimidate.

Understanding these root causes can help supervisors contextualize the behavior, though it does not excuse the negative effects.

The Impact on Supervisors

Dealing with unpredictable moods from above causes several challenges:

- **Emotional Exhaustion:** Constantly trying to "read" moods is draining.
- **Reduced Confidence:** Mixed signals make it hard to know if work is meeting expectations.
- **Increased Anxiety:** Fear of sudden outbursts creates chronic stress.
- **Impaired Decision-Making:** Unclear guidance leads to second-guessing and mistakes.
- **Damaged Relationships:** Inconsistency damages trust between supervisor and manager.

For example, Sarah, a retail store supervisor, reported feeling "like walking on eggshells" around her director, who praised her in the morning but reprimanded her harshly in the afternoon without clear reasons. Over time, Sarah's stress affected her sleep and focus, impacting her ability to lead her team effectively.

Effects on the Team and Organization

Unpredictable leadership affects not only supervisors but their teams and the organization as a whole:

- **Lowered Morale:** Teams sense tension and uncertainty, reducing engagement.
- **Higher Turnover:** Stressful environments push employees to leave.
- **Reduced Productivity:** Distraction and fear hinder performance.
- **Communication Breakdowns:** Mixed messages cause confusion at all levels.

- **Toxic Culture:** Persistent volatility fosters mistrust and resentment.

Strategies for Supervisors to Navigate Mood Swings

While supervisors cannot control their managers' emotions, they can adopt strategies to minimize the impact:

1. **Maintain Professional Boundaries:** Keep interactions focused on work and avoid personal emotional involvement.
2. **Document Communications:** Keep records of meetings and instructions to clarify expectations amid inconsistent messages.
3. **Develop Emotional Resilience:** Practice stress management techniques such as mindfulness, exercise, and seeking social support.
4. **Use Clear, Calm Communication:** When addressing concerns, use neutral language and avoid reacting emotionally to outbursts.
5. **Seek Support:** Find mentors, peer groups, or HR allies who can provide advice and advocacy.
6. **Clarify Expectations Regularly:** Request clear, written guidance when possible to reduce ambiguity.
7. **Know When to Escalate:** If mood swings become abusive or impair job function, involve HR or higher leadership.

Organizational Responsibilities

Organizations must recognize the damage unpredictable leadership causes and foster healthier environments by:

- **Providing Emotional Intelligence Training:** Teaching leaders to manage emotions and lead with stability.
- **Encouraging Feedback:** Creating safe channels for supervisors to raise concerns.
- **Promoting Leadership Accountability:** Holding managers responsible for their impact on teams.
- **Offering Support Services:** Providing counseling and coaching for managers and supervisors.

Conclusion

Unpredictable mood swings from upper management create a ripple effect that destabilizes supervisors, teams, and entire organizations. While understanding the causes helps frame the problem, active strategies and organizational commitment to emotional intelligence and support are vital to restoring stability and respect.

Supervisors facing this challenge can protect their mental health and leadership effectiveness by setting boundaries, documenting interactions, seeking support, and advocating for more transparent communication. Ultimately, organizations thrive when leadership is steady, predictable, and respectful.

Real-Life Examples of Unpredictable Mood Swings from Management

Example 1: The Praise-Then-Punish Cycle

Emma, a warehouse supervisor, described her new manager as "a rollercoaster." One week, he would commend her team for hitting targets, showering praise during meetings, and even sending thank-you emails. The following week, without warning, he would criticize Emma harshly for minor errors, such as a delayed report, in front of her team. This sudden shift left Emma anxious, unsure when praise would turn into criticism. She found herself overworking to avoid mistakes, but the unpredictability only increased her stress.

Example 2: The Silent Treatment and Sudden Outburst

James managed a team at a tech company. His director often withdrew completely from communication for days—ignoring emails and calls. Then, without explanation, he would erupt over a small, missed deadline or perceived slight. The silence bred confusion and frustration, and the outbursts created a tense atmosphere where James struggled to keep his team motivated.

Example 3: Changing Expectations Without Notice

Linda, a healthcare supervisor, found that her manager would frequently change priorities and goals mid-project without informing her. One day, she was instructed to focus on patient satisfaction metrics; the next, she was reprimanded for not meeting staffing targets she hadn't been told to prioritize. This inconsistency made it difficult for Linda to lead confidently and keep her team aligned.

Emotional Support Strategies for Supervisors and Their Teams

1. Recognize and Normalize Emotional Responses

It's natural to feel anxious, frustrated, or confused when leadership is inconsistent. Supervisors should acknowledge these feelings without self-judgment and understand they are a typical response to unstable environments.

2. Foster Open Team Communication

Encourage regular, honest check-ins with team members to share concerns and support each other. Transparent conversations can alleviate the uncertainty caused by leadership unpredictability.

3. Build a Personal Support Network

Seek out mentors, trusted colleagues, or professional counselors who can offer advice, perspective, and emotional support outside the immediate work context.

4. Practice Mindfulness and Stress Reduction Techniques

Techniques such as deep breathing, meditation, or short breaks during the workday can help manage stress levels and maintain focus amid emotional turbulence.

5. Develop Emotional Boundaries

Supervisors should strive to separate their self-worth from their manager's fluctuating moods. Reminding themselves that unpredictable behavior is about the manager's issues, not their own competence, protects emotional health.

6. Encourage Self-Care and Team Well-being

Promote healthy work-life balance, exercise, and downtime for both supervisors and their teams to build resilience.

Closing Thought

Dealing with unpredictable mood swings from above is like steering a ship through stormy seas—the turbulence can shake confidence and disrupt calm waters. Yet, with awareness, support, and coping tools, supervisors can weather the storm and continue guiding their teams safely toward success.

How Organizations Can Prevent and Address Unpredictable Mood Swings in Management

Unpredictable mood swings in leadership often reflect deeper organizational issues such as stress, poor communication, or a lack of emotional intelligence training. To create a healthier workplace, organizations must take proactive, systemic steps that promote consistent, respectful leadership and support supervisor well-being.

1. Leadership Development Focused on Emotional Intelligence

Why it Matters:

Leaders who understand and manage their emotions effectively create stable environments. Emotional intelligence (EI) training equips managers with skills like self-awareness, empathy, and emotional regulation.

Practical Steps:

- Implement mandatory EI workshops as part of leadership training programs.
- Use 360-degree feedback tools so managers receive honest insights from peers and subordinates.
- Encourage ongoing coaching and mentoring focused on emotional regulation strategies.

Example:

A multinational tech company introduced EI training for all managers. Over one year, they reported a 30% decrease in employee complaints related to managerial behavior, showing that better emotional regulation benefits everyone.

2. Clear Communication Channels and Feedback Loops

Why it Matters:

Unpredictable moods often stem from misunderstandings or pressure build-up. Transparent communication channels allow concerns to be voiced early, reducing tension and surprises.

Practical Steps:

- Establish regular one-on-one meetings between managers and supervisors to discuss workload, challenges, and expectations.
- Create anonymous feedback systems so employees and supervisors can report erratic behavior safely.
- Promote an open-door policy where supervisors can approach higher management without fear of retaliation.

Example:

A hospital system implemented monthly feedback forums where supervisors and upper management could discuss issues openly. This reduced "outburst" incidents by allowing problems to be addressed before escalating.

3. Workload Management and Support Systems for Leaders

Why it Matters:

Stress and burnout in managers are major contributors to mood instability. Organizations must ensure leaders have realistic workloads and support to perform effectively.

Practical Steps:

- Conduct regular workload assessments to prevent manager burnout.
- Provide resources such as administrative assistants or technology tools to streamline managers' tasks.
- Encourage use of Employee Assistance Programs (EAPs) offering counseling and stress management resources.

Example:

A financial firm introduced a policy limiting the number of direct reports per manager and providing executive coaching. Managers reported feeling less overwhelmed, leading to more consistent leadership behavior.

4. Establishing a Culture of Accountability and Respect

Why it Matters:

Tolerating erratic leadership behavior undermines trust and morale. A culture that prioritizes accountability ensures managers understand the impact of their mood swings and face consequences if their behaviors continue unchecked.

Practical Steps:

- Include behavioral expectations in performance evaluations for managers, with clear consequences for harmful conduct.
- Train HR and senior leaders to intervene promptly when erratic behaviors are reported.
- Celebrate leaders who model calm, consistent, and empathetic behaviors.

Example:

An international retailer launched a "Respect in Leadership" initiative. Managers received scores on emotional stability as part of promotions. This shift reduced reports of unpredictable mood swings by 40% within 18 months.

5. Support Networks and Peer Groups for Managers

Why it Matters:

Leadership can be isolating, and having a support network reduces stress and improves emotional resilience.

Practical Steps:

- Create peer support groups or leadership forums where managers can share experiences and coping strategies.
- Encourage cross-department mentorship programs to build broader support networks.
- Promote wellness activities tailored to leaders, such as mindfulness retreats or resilience workshops.

Example:

A non-profit organization formed monthly "Leadership Circles" for managers to discuss challenges and share advice. Participants reported feeling less isolated and better equipped to manage stress-related mood swings.

Conclusion

Addressing unpredictable mood swings from management requires a comprehensive approach: building emotional intelligence, promoting transparent communication, managing workload stress, enforcing accountability, and fostering supportive networks. When organizations invest in these areas, they not only improve leadership behavior but also boost supervisor morale, team performance, and overall workplace well-being.

Real-World Examples: Companies Successfully Managing Unpredictable Mood Swings in Leadership

1. Google's Emotional Intelligence and Leadership Development

What they did:

Google didn't just focus on technical skills for managers — they recognized that handling emotions well is key to good leadership. So, they developed the "Search Inside Yourself" program, which teaches mindfulness (being fully present and aware) and emotional regulation. This helps leaders stay calm, even when things get stressful, and respond with empathy rather than frustration or anger. The training isn't a one-time thing — they embed it in their leadership curriculum worldwide and encourage managers to practice regularly with peer coaching groups.

Outcome:

As a result, Google's internal surveys found that managers were more emotionally steady and employees felt happier and less stressed. This reduced the kind of conflicts and unpredictable mood swings that often derail teams. Basically, by investing in emotional intelligence, Google made their leadership more consistent and supportive.

Why it matters:

It shows how teaching leaders to manage their emotions isn't just "nice to have" — it directly improves workplace atmosphere and productivity. When leaders stay calm and empathetic, teams feel safer and perform better.

2. Southwest Airlines' Culture of Transparency and Support

What they did:

Southwest Airlines made openness a cornerstone of their leadership style. Managers regularly check in with their teams and keep lines of communication wide open. They foster a "family" feeling by encouraging honest conversations and sharing how decisions are made. This transparency prevents misunderstandings that can cause stress or mood swings in managers and employees alike.

Outcome:

Because employees trust their leaders and understand what's going on, leadership feels predictable and fair. This trust shows in Southwest's high employee retention and excellent customer service — people want to stay and perform well because they feel respected and informed.

Why it matters:

Clear, frequent communication isn't just about information sharing — it builds trust and emotional stability. When people aren't left guessing, managers are less likely to react erratically, and the whole team feels more grounded.

3. Salesforce's Workload Management and Wellness Initiatives

What they did:

Salesforce realized that many mood swings and leadership challenges come from burnout. So, they took active steps to reduce managers' stress: they limited how many direct reports each manager had (making it more manageable), enforced mandatory breaks for wellness, and provided executive coaching focused on stress and emotional management.

Outcome:

Managers felt less overwhelmed and reported better control over their emotions. This led to improved productivity and a significant drop in turnover, with fewer supervisors quitting because of stress.

Why it matters:

Even the best leadership skills can crumble under too much pressure. Managing workload and providing mental health support isn't a luxury — leaders need to maintain steady, effective performance.

4. Zappos' Accountability and Respect Culture

What they did:

Zappos embedded expectations for emotional stability and respectful behavior into their leadership evaluations. They made sure HR had the power and responsibility to act quickly if any manager behaved erratically or disrupted the team. This accountability meant that no bad behavior went unnoticed or unchecked.

Outcome:

This approach helped Zappos build and maintain a positive reputation for its leadership style. Reports of mood-related conflicts remained low, and leaders stayed responsible for their actions, which kept teams healthy and functioning well.

Why it matters:

When leadership is held accountable for their behavior, it discourages emotional outbursts or manipulation. A culture of respect starts at the top and is enforced consistently, setting a strong example for everyone.

5. Patagonia's Peer Support Networks for Leaders

What they did:

Patagonia recognized that leadership can feel lonely and stressful, so they created "Leadership Huddles," where managers come together regularly to share challenges, swap coping strategies, and support each other. They also offer wellness programs specifically tailored for leaders, knowing their unique pressures.

Outcome:

Leaders who participate in these peer support groups report feeling more emotionally resilient and better able to maintain steady moods and manage their teams effectively.

Why it matters:

Sometimes, just knowing you're not alone and having a safe space to talk can make all the difference. Peer support networks give leaders the tools and emotional backing to handle stress without losing their cool.

Summary:

Each of these companies addresses the challenge of unpredictable mood swings in leadership in different, but complementary ways — by developing emotional intelligence, fostering open communication, managing workload, enforcing accountability, and building peer support. Together, these strategies create healthier, more stable leadership that benefits everyone.

Key Takeaways from These Examples

- **Invest in emotional intelligence and ongoing leadership development.**
- **Maintain open, transparent communication channels to avoid misunderstandings.**
- **Manage manager workloads to prevent burnout.**
- **Establish clear accountability for behavior and provide support when needed.**
- **Foster peer networks to reduce isolation and encourage shared learning.**

These real-world cases offer valuable blueprints for organizations seeking to reduce unpredictable mood swings and build more decisive, more stable leadership.

Chapter 12
Unfairly Blamed for Others' Failures

"Taking the fall for what you didn't break steals more than credit — it steals your peace."

Being blamed for mistakes you didn't make is demoralizing and unjust. When others deflect responsibility onto you, it undermines your credibility and strains your professional relationships.

This chapter explores how to recognize unfair blame and protect your integrity in the face of misplaced accusations.

Introduction

In any workplace, supervisors are on the frontline of managing teams and projects, often bearing the brunt of responsibility when things go wrong. However, there are times when failures or setbacks are caused by factors outside their control — such as poor decisions by upper management, resource shortages, or external circumstances — yet supervisors still find themselves unfairly blamed. This misplaced accountability is a common but damaging form of workplace injustice.

Why Supervisors Become the Fall Guys

Supervisors often find themselves stuck in the middle — trying to balance demands from upper management while managing frontline teams. When things go wrong, it's tempting for organizations to look for someone to blame quickly, and supervisors often end up in that spotlight. Here's why:

Causes of Misplaced Blame:

- **Lack of Transparency**
  - When senior leaders don't clearly communicate decisions, changes, or the reasoning behind them, supervisors are left in the dark.
  - Without the full picture, supervisors can't manage effectively, yet they're held accountable for outcomes that depend on information they never had.
  - This creates a gap where supervisors become easy targets because they appear to "drop the ball," even though the real issue was poor communication.
- **Pressure to Show Accountability**
  - Organizations demand accountability to improve results and manage risks, which is good in theory.
  - But when there's pressure to assign blame quickly, rather than investigate root causes, supervisors often become scapegoats.
  - It's simpler to say "the supervisor failed" than to face complex systemic issues that require deeper analysis or leadership changes.

119

- **Power Dynamics**
  - Blaming a supervisor shifts the spotlight away from upper management, who may be responsible for poor decisions or a lack of support.
  - This protects senior leaders from criticism or having to admit mistakes.
  - It also reinforces hierarchical control, reminding supervisors that they're accountable but have limited power — creating a dynamic where supervisors absorb the fallout.
- **Misaligned Expectations**
  - Often, goals and deadlines are set without realistic input from those on the ground.
  - Supervisors might be asked to deliver more with fewer resources, inadequate staffing, or outdated tools.
  - When these expectations are impossible to meet, supervisors face the consequences, even though the root cause is bad planning or resource shortages.
  - This mismatch sets them up for failure and unfair blame.

Real-World Example: The Warehouse Woes

Consider the case of James, a warehouse supervisor at a large distribution center. A sudden supply chain disruption caused delays in shipments, but management had not informed James in time to adjust schedules or communicate with his team. When customer complaints surged, upper management blamed James for poor planning and team performance.

Despite his efforts to explain the circumstances, James's reputation suffered. He felt demoralized and questioned his ability to lead — a direct consequence of being unfairly held accountable for external factors.

The Impact of Unfair Blame on Supervisors

Psychological Effects:

- **Eroded Confidence:** Constant blame undermines self-esteem and decision-making confidence.
- **Increased Stress:** Pressure to "fix" problems beyond control causes anxiety and burnout.
- **Reduced Engagement:** Feeling undervalued may lead supervisors to disengage or withdraw effort.

Effects on Team Dynamics:

- **Loss of Respect:** Teams may lose faith in a supervisor unfairly blamed, impacting morale.
- **Poor Communication:** Fear of blame can discourage honest dialogue or innovation.
- **Higher Turnover:** Demoralized supervisors and teams are more likely to seek other opportunities.

Strategies to Handle and Prevent Unfair Blame

1. Document Everything

Maintain detailed records of decisions, communications, and resource limitations. Documentation builds a factual basis to demonstrate what was and wasn't within your control.

2. Clarify Expectations

Seek written confirmation of goals, resources, and deadlines. Proactively discuss potential obstacles with your manager to set realistic expectations.

3. Communicate Upward Transparently

Regularly update higher management on progress, risks, and challenges. Early warnings reduce surprises and help shift blame when issues arise.

4. Build Alliances

Develop strong relationships with peers and mentors who can provide support and advocacy when unfair blame occurs.

5. Use Formal Feedback Channels

If blame becomes unjust and repeated, use HR or other formal processes to raise concerns professionally.

Conclusion

Being blamed for failures outside your control is a painful but unfortunately common experience for many supervisors. Recognizing the systemic nature of these challenges, documenting your efforts, and fostering open communication can help mitigate the damage. Ultimately, organizations must strive to hold all levels accountable fairly to build trust and sustain effective leadership.

Real-Life Case Study: Sarah's Marketing Campaign

Sarah, a marketing supervisor at a mid-sized tech firm, was tasked with launching a new product campaign. However, key decisions on budget cuts and staffing changes were made at the executive level without her involvement. When the campaign failed to meet targets, Sarah was held responsible.

She documented all communications and the last-minute changes made by leadership. Sarah then presented her evidence during a review meeting, showing how the setbacks were due to factors beyond her control. Though initially defensive, management acknowledged the oversights and worked to clarify roles and improve communication channels moving forward.

Sarah's experience highlights the importance of clear documentation and transparent dialogue in pushing back against unfair blame.

Expert Perspectives

Dr. Emily Carter, Organizational Psychologist, explains:

"When organizations fail to distribute accountability clearly, supervisors lack the systems and support needed to succeed. Relying on transparent communication and thorough documentation helps shield them from unfair blame."

Gallup research supports this, finding that teams with highly engaged managers are up to **59% less likely to leave** the organization compared to teams with disengaged leadership. Poor managerial support is a major driver of turnover and disengagement.

A 2022 study in the *Journal of Occupational and Organizational Psychology* found that employees who perceive their supervisors as scapegoats or unsupported are significantly more likely to experience stress, distrust leadership, and consider leaving their roles. The study emphasizes the importance of fair treatment and psychological safety in leadership structures.

Chapter 13
Forced into Ethical Conflicts or Compromises

"When 'just follow orders' means betraying your values."

Sometimes, the demands aren't just unfair — they ask you to choose between your job and your integrity. Whether it's cutting corners, hiding truths, or sacrificing others, these forced compromises are a corrosive form of pressure. They erode trust in leadership and leave lasting wounds on your conscience.

Introduction

Supervisors are often the moral compass of their teams, entrusted to balance company goals with integrity and fairness. But sometimes, they face scenarios where upper management pressures them into decisions that conflict with their values or professional ethics. Being forced into such ethical dilemmas creates profound stress, damages credibility, and can leave lasting moral scars.

This chapter explores how supervisors are placed in these difficult situations, the impacts on their mental health and leadership, real-world examples, and strategies to navigate and push back against such unethical pressures.

What Are Ethical Dilemmas in a Supervisory Context?

Ethical dilemmas occur when supervisors are torn between doing what's "expected" by higher-ups and doing what they believe is right. These moments aren't always dramatic, but they're emotionally and professionally taxing — especially when the stakes involve people's well-being, safety, fairness, or legal compliance.

These dilemmas often take shape in subtle (or not-so-subtle) ways:

• **Being asked to misrepresent data or inflate performance metrics**

- Example: A supervisor is told to report that a team met its targets, even though a portion of the project is incomplete.
- **The conflict**: Lying may protect them short-term, but risks their credibility, the company's integrity, and even legal consequences.

• **Pressured to favor certain employees unfairly or overlook harassment**

- Example: A senior manager tells the supervisor to "let it slide" when a high performer behaves inappropriately.
- **The conflict**: Protecting one employee at the expense of others violates ethical standards and damages team trust.

• **Directed to prioritize short-term profit over safety, fairness, or compliance**

- Example: Management demands pushing forward with production despite unresolved safety concerns.
- **The conflict**: Meeting performance goals might earn praise — but it could lead to accidents, lawsuits, or moral injury.

• **Required to conceal errors or risks from stakeholders**

- Example: A supervisor discovers a quality issue in a product but is told not to inform the client.
- **The conflict**: Staying quiet protects the company in the moment, but can break long-term trust and possibly violate regulations.

Why Do Supervisors End Up in These Dilemmas?

These situations rarely happen in a vacuum. They usually stem from deeper organizational issues that push supervisors into impossible choices:

1. Culture of "Do Whatever It Takes"

- In some companies, hitting targets or beating deadlines is glorified — no matter how it's achieved.
- **Result**: Ethical shortcuts become normalized. Supervisors may feel that "success" means bending the rules, or worse, turning a blind eye.

2. Lack of Ethical Frameworks

- When a company doesn't have clear ethical guidelines or doesn't model ethical behavior from the top, supervisors are left to "figure it out."
- **Result**: Supervisors may feel unsure about what's right or allowed — leading to inconsistent or unsafe decisions.

3. Fear of Reprisal

- Speaking up can feel dangerous. Supervisors may fear retaliation, poor evaluations, exclusion from leadership circles, or even losing their jobs.
- **Result**: Many stay silent or go along with unethical directives, not because they agree, but because they feel trapped.

4. Ambiguous Roles or Responsibilities

- Sometimes, supervisors are held accountable for things beyond their control or aren't given enough clarity about their role.
- **Result**: They might not know who owns a decision or what the "right" path is — making ethical boundaries fuzzy.

Human Insight

Ethical dilemmas can lead to deep stress, guilt, and isolation. Supervisors in these positions often carry the emotional burden alone — caught between loyalty to their employer and their own moral compass.

But acknowledging these dilemmas is the first step toward addressing them constructively — through clearer ethics policies, stronger support systems, and open conversations about integrity in leadership.

Ethical Dilemmas in Detergent Manufacturing

In the fast-paced world of detergent manufacturing, supervisors are constantly balancing production demands, safety protocols, and quality standards. Yet, when the expectations of senior leadership conflict with what's realistically achievable on the factory floor, supervisors often find themselves stuck in ethical gray zones. These moments require difficult choices — between doing what's right and protecting their position or performance metrics.

1. Misreporting Data to Meet Targets

Scenario: A production supervisor is asked to confirm that all scheduled safety inspections were completed on time, even though two inspections were delayed due to equipment issues.

The Dilemma: Do they report the truth and risk criticism from leadership, or fudge the numbers to avoid disruption?

"I was pressured to simply 'check the box' and say all the safety inspections were done on time, even though some had been delayed because of equipment issues. They told me we'd catch up later, but deep down, I knew that if something went wrong, that falsified report would come back to haunt me. It's a terrible feeling, being caught between meeting deadlines and doing what's right."

— *Production Supervisor, Manufacturing Facility in Delhi*

2. Overlooking Harassment to Maintain Output

Scenario: A top-performing machine operator is known for using harsh, aggressive language with team members. Complaints have reached HR, but management urges the supervisor to avoid stirring the pot during peak production.

The Dilemma: Do they speak up and risk being seen as a troublemaker, or stay silent to keep production on track?

"It really felt like I was stuck between a rock and a hard place. I wanted to step in and address the aggressive behavior, but every time I tried, I was told, 'We need him to meet production targets right now, so just let it slide.' It was frustrating because I knew it was hurting the team, but the pressure to keep things running smoothly was overwhelming."

— *Line Supervisor, Manufacturing Facility in Ontario*

3. Prioritizing Speed Over Safety or Quality

Scenario: A detergent batch ends up with a slightly elevated concentration of one ingredient. The plant manager tells the supervisor to ship it anyway — it's "close enough," and reworking would cause delays.

The Dilemma: Do they halt the process and risk falling behind schedule, or go along with instructions and risk customer dissatisfaction or regulatory issues?

"My instincts told me to stop the production line because the batch didn't meet the exact standards we usually follow. But then the plant manager stepped in and said, 'It's within tolerance, just let it go,' which made me second-guess myself. It's tough when you feel responsible for quality but are told to prioritize speed and deadlines over safety or precision."

— *Shift Supervisor, Manufacturing Plant, Ontario*

4. Concealing Operational Failures

Scenario: A malfunctioning valve causes minor cross-contamination between two product lines. The quality assurance team recommends documenting and investigating it, but upper management insists on quietly flushing the line and moving on.

The Dilemma: Do they log the issue and risk backlash for delays, or stay silent and keep production running?

"The contamination wasn't huge, and management insisted we just clean it up quietly without making a big deal. But even if it seemed minor, it didn't sit right with me. Ignoring issues like that can snowball into bigger problems down the line, and I felt caught between following orders and doing what's right for the product and the customers."

— *Quality Assurance Supervisor, Manufacturing Facility, New Jersey*

Why These Dilemmas Are Common in Manufacturing

1. A "Push Through No Matter What" Culture

- Meeting production deadlines is critical — sometimes at the cost of ethics.
- Supervisors are pressured to prioritize speed over accuracy or safety.

2. Lack of Clear Ethical Guidelines

- Many mid-sized factories don't have formal ethical frameworks in place.
- Without guidance, supervisors are left to navigate tough calls on their own.

3. Fear of Retaliation

- Pushing back against questionable directives can be career-limiting.
- Supervisors often worry about getting labeled "difficult" or being passed over for promotion.

4. Ambiguous Responsibility

- Supervisors are expected to take ownership of results without having full decision-making power.
- This imbalance often leaves them shouldering blame for issues beyond their control.

Broader Industry Examples of Ethical Dilemmas

Example 1: Inflating Performance Metrics

In a large retail chain, a regional supervisor is asked to underreport return rates to make the brand's quarterly performance look stronger. Returns have actually increased due to a product defect, but this truth could spook investors.

- **Impact:** Critical quality issues are hidden. The team feels uneasy, and the supervisor bears the ethical and legal risk of misrepresentation.

Example 2: Ignoring Safety for Speed

A warehouse supervisor is told to bypass standard safety inspections to keep pace with a holiday shipping rush. An accident happens a week later, and it's revealed that the inspections were skipped.

- **Impact:** Trust in leadership erodes. The supervisor faces guilt, liability, and possible disciplinary action. The company also incurs regulatory penalties.

Example 3: Avoiding Harassment Investigations

A supervisor receives multiple complaints about inappropriate behavior from a high-performing team member. Leadership insists it's "not the right time" to take action due to the employee's value to the company.

- **Impact:** The team loses trust in leadership. The supervisor feels complicit in silencing valid concerns. The company risks long-term damage to morale and reputation.

The Impact of Forced Ethical Dilemmas

1. **Emotional Toll**
   - **Moral distress:** Feeling forced to act against one's conscience.
   - **Guilt and shame:** When unethical actions harm others.
   - **Chronic stress:** Frequent ethical conflict leads to anxiety and burnout.
2. **Professional Consequences**
   - Damaged credibility within the organization and industry.
   - Fear of taking future initiative or responsibility.
   - Risk of losing license, certification, or encountering legal penalties.
3. **Team and Cultural Damage**
   - Loss of team respect and loyalty.
   - Higher turnover as employees refuse to become part of unethical practices.
   - Normalization of unethical behavior in workplace culture.

Strategies for Addressing Ethical Dilemmas

1. Know Your Moral and Professional Boundaries

- Reflect on your core values and professional rules before crises emerge.
- Use this understanding as an internal compass when facing pressure.

2. Document Directives

- Keep a discreet written record of unethical requests, noting date, time, and content.
- This documentation can be vital if issues escalate to HR, compliance departments, or external authorities.

3. Seek Advice from Trusted Mentors or Ethics Committees

- Confidentially consult with experienced professionals or ethics officers.
- Shine light on the dilemma without raising alarms to start exploring safe solutions.

4. Frame Your Refusal Constructively

- *"I'm concerned that this directive could put us at legal risk. Can we explore an alternative that achieves our goal transparently?"*
- This preserves respect while asserting ethical boundaries.

5. Use Formal Reporting Channels

- Every organization should have a whistleblower or ethics hotline.
- If necessary, escalate confidentially via HR or compliance.

6. Prioritize Self-Care and Support

- Ethical dilemmas impact mental health deeply.

- Seek counselling, peer support, or professional resources through EAPs or external advisors.

7. Plan for Possible Consequences

- Have contingency plans; stiff resistance may lead to retaliation.
- Ensure financial stability and network connections are in place if a job becomes untenable.

Organizational Responsibility

For organizations to truly support supervisors and employees in making ethical decisions, they must create a strong foundation rooted in integrity. This means going beyond just words and putting practical systems and culture in place that encourage and protect ethical behavior.

- **Establish a Clear Ethics Code and Provide Regular Training**
- Organizations need to develop straightforward guidelines that explain what ethical behavior looks like in everyday situations. These shouldn't be vague rules but clear, practical principles that everyone understands. Regular training sessions help reinforce these standards, keeping ethics top of mind, and equip employees to handle difficult situations confidently.
- **Maintain Multiple and Confidential Reporting Channels**
- It's crucial for employees to have safe ways to speak up when they encounter unethical behavior. Offering several options — like anonymous hotlines, confidential email addresses, or third-party reporting services — ensures people can choose the method they feel most comfortable with. Knowing their concerns will be heard without retaliation encourages honesty and accountability.
- **Enforce Zero-Tolerance Policies for Retaliating Against Ethical Behavior**
- Employees should never fear backlash for raising concerns or standing up for what's right. Organizations must strictly enforce rules that protect whistleblowers or those who report misconduct. Clear consequences for retaliation create a safer environment where ethical behavior is respected and protected.
- **Provide Ethics Support, Such as Committees or Third-Party Helplines**
- Sometimes, ethical dilemmas are complex and require advice or mediation. Having dedicated ethics committees or access to independent third-party counselors gives supervisors a trustworthy resource to discuss challenges confidentially and find guidance. This support helps prevent mistakes and encourages thoughtful decision-making.
- **Promote Leaders Who Model Ethical Behavior, Reinforcing Value-Based Culture**
- Leadership sets the tone for the entire organization. When managers and executives consistently demonstrate integrity and fairness, it reinforces that ethical behavior isn't optional—it's expected. Celebrating and promoting these leaders sends a powerful message throughout the company, inspiring others to follow their example.

Conclusion

Supervisors often find themselves caught in the middle—facing tough ethical dilemmas where they must balance the demands of upper management with their own values and the well-being of their teams. These situations can feel like no-win battles, requiring not only personal courage but also clear thinking and strategic action. However, the burden should never fall solely on individuals.

Organizations play a crucial role in creating environments where ethical behavior is expected, supported, and protected. This means fostering a culture of transparency and accountability, providing clear ethical guidelines, and ensuring that supervisors have safe channels to speak up without fear of retaliation. When companies prioritize integrity and back it up with real systems and leadership commitment, they not only protect their people but also build stronger, more resilient workplaces where trust and respect thrive.

In the end, navigating ethical challenges is a shared responsibility—one that demands both personal strength from supervisors and a firm, ongoing commitment from organizations to do what's right.

Chapter 14
Threats of Demotion or Termination

"Fear is a leash disguised as leadership."

Threats don't motivate — they intimidate. When your future is dangled like a carrot or a sword, it's not a negotiation. It's coercion. Constant threats to your position create a toxic atmosphere where fear trumps respect, and survival replaces engagement.

Introduction

One of the most stress-inducing tactics supervisors face is the looming shadow of punishment—frequent threats of demotion, pay cuts, or job loss from upper management. These threats, whether overt or covert, keep supervisors feeling constantly on edge, choking creativity, and undermining trust. This chapter dives into how such threats manifest, their profound impact on individuals and teams, real-world examples, and strategies for navigating these threats constructively—all in a grounded, human voice.

What Constant Threats Look Like

Threats in the workplace rarely come in the form of blunt commands or obvious ultimatums. Instead, they often appear as subtle messages or hints that create an underlying tension and insecurity for supervisors. Here's how these threats can show up:

1. **Subtle Warnings in Performance Reviews**
2. You might hear phrases like, "We can't afford underperformance," or "We expect improvements immediately." While they sound like typical feedback, these comments carry an unspoken warning: fall short, and your job could be on the line. It's a way to keep you on edge without explicitly saying so.

    Example: During your yearly review, your manager says, "We really need everyone to hit their goals this quarter." It sounds like encouragement, but you leave the meeting wondering if your job's safe if you don't deliver. That pressure stays with you every day.

3. **Frequent References to Roles Being "At Risk"**
4. Managers might casually mention that your position "isn't guaranteed" or "could be affected by upcoming changes." These offhand remarks linger in your mind, making you second-guess your job security every day—even if no formal action is happening.

    Example: Your boss drops comments like, "With the budget cuts, no one's position is completely secure right now." You don't know if it's just talk, but it's enough to make you watch every step, afraid to make even minor mistakes.

5. **Demotion as a Tool to Reassert Control**
6. Sometimes, supervisors are threatened with being moved to a less senior or less influential role if they don't meet certain targets. Hearing something like, "If results don't improve, we'll need to move you back to a coordinator role," is a direct pressure tactic designed to remind you who holds the power.

   Example: After missing a project deadline, you're told, "If we don't see improvement soon, we might have to shift you back to a less demanding role." The threat hangs over your head, making you question your future every morning.

7. **Threatening Language in Emails or Instant Messages**
8. Short, sharp messages such as "Mistakes like this can cost jobs" can feel like a punch to the gut. Unlike face-to-face conversations, these written notes linger and can amplify anxiety, creating a toxic atmosphere where fear of making errors dominates.

   Example: You get a short email from your supervisor: "Mistakes like this aren't acceptable and can cost jobs." No room for explanation or discussion — just fear and stress flooding your inbox.

9. **Public Suggestions That the Team Needs "New Leadership"**
10. Even vague comments made in meetings about "needing fresh leadership" chip away at your authority. They undermine your confidence and your team's trust in you, making it harder to lead effectively.

    Example: In a team meeting, a senior exec casually mentions, "Maybe it's time for some fresh leadership around here." Everyone hears it, and suddenly your team looks uncertain, doubting your ability to lead.

Why Leadership Uses Threats

Understanding why some leaders resort to threats helps make sense of this damaging behavior— and opens the door to addressing it:

1. **Control Through Fear**
2. For some managers, threatening job security or status is an easy shortcut to get compliance. It's a quick fix to push people into action. But while fear may work in the short term, it destroys motivation, creativity, and trust in the long run.

   Example: A manager uses threats to push a deadline, warning, "If this project isn't done on time, there will be consequences." It might get the job done, but team members start feeling like they're walking on eggshells instead of being motivated.

3. **Avoiding Accountability**
4. When upper management isn't willing to take responsibility for problems, they can use threats as a way to shift blame downward. Instead of fixing systemic issues or their own mistakes, they pressure supervisors to carry the weight—and the risk—of failure.

Example: When a big mistake happens, senior leaders point fingers at frontline supervisors instead of looking at their own poor planning. By blaming you, they protect themselves but leave you carrying the fallout.

5. **Performance Culture Run Amok**
6. In workplaces obsessed with hitting numbers or results at all costs, threats become normalized. When success is the only metric that matters, leaders may believe fear is necessary to keep performance up, ignoring the human cost behind the scenes.

Example: In a company obsessed with hitting quarterly sales goals, threats about "losing your job" for missing targets become common. The pressure to perform is so intense that no one talks about balance or well-being.

7. **Insecurity and Inexperience**
8. Some leaders lack the confidence or skills to lead effectively, especially under pressure. Threats then become a defense mechanism—a way to cover up their own vulnerabilities by intimidating others rather than inspiring them.

Example: A newly promoted manager feels overwhelmed and unsure, so they use threats to assert authority. It's less about real consequences and more about covering their own uncertainty with fear tactics.

The Psychological Impact on Supervisors

- **Chronic Stress & Anxiety**
- The brain stays on high alert—heart pounds, sleep is disrupted, and decision-making muddies.
- **Decreased Confidence**
- Even capable managers begin second-guessing all their choices.
- **Fearful Leadership**
- Supervisors stop inspiring their teams, resorting to micro-controlling to avoid mistakes.
- **Impaired Mental Health**
- Anxiety can spiral into burnout, depression, or physical symptoms like headaches and insomnia.

The Impact of Job Threats on Employee Well-Being:

Threats of job loss and ongoing job insecurity are more than just stressful words — they can have serious effects on employees' mental health and workplace performance. While exact numbers vary, research consistently shows that employees facing these pressures experience increased anxiety, decreased engagement, and higher turnover intentions.

For example, studies in Canada highlight that many workers report worsening mental health when job security feels uncertain. According to Statistics Canada, mental well-being among employed Canadians declined notably during times of economic uncertainty, with increased reports of stress and anxiety linked to workplace conditions. Similarly, surveys reveal that financial and job-related pressures significantly contribute to symptoms of anxiety and depression.

Real-World Examples Carlos's Retail Challenge:

During a tough sales quarter, Carlos's district manager hinted that leadership roles might be reviewed. Despite factors beyond his control affecting performance, Carlos became anxious and overly fixated on short-term numbers, which made it hard to focus on long-term goals.

Aisha's Tech Team Struggles: After her VP expressed doubts about her role due to product delays, Aisha imposed strict new controls on her team. This eroded trust and lowered productivity, compounding stress for everyone involved.

These examples illustrate how even indirect threats or ambiguous messages from leadership can unsettle supervisors and teams, ultimately impacting morale and results.

Strategies for Supervisors to Respond

1. **Ask for Specific Feedback**
2. "Can you help me understand exactly what's being measured, and how I can improve?" Shifts the threat into a developmental conversation.
3. **Request Formal Goals & Clarity**
4. Ask for written, measurable goals and timelines. Without clarity, threats remain nebulous and intimidating.
5. **Seek Allies & Mentors**
6. Get insight from HR, peers, or trusted mentors. They offer perspective and guidance when threats seem overwhelming.
7. **Maintain Detailed Records**
8. Document conversations that feel threatening. Logs will matter if discussions escalate.
9. **Practice Emotional Regulation**
10. Use deep breathing, short walks, or mini mindfulness practices when anxiety peaks.
11. **Know When to Escalate or Exit**
12. If threats become veiled bullying or harassment, involve HR or consider alternative roles or employers.

Organizational Responsibilities

1. **Encourage Transparent Performance Reviews**
2. Goals should be clear, measurable, and realistic—not based on fear or vague "at risk" language.
3. **Develop Performance-Focused Support Policies**
4. Use goals—and support like training or mentorship—instead of threats and fear.
5. **Train Managers in Feedback Delivery**
6. Supervisors should learn to provide corrective feedback without fear tactics.
7. **Implement Safe Escalation Paths**
8. HR must be trusted to handle situations involving frequent threats of job loss.

9. **Measure Psychological Safety**
10. Survey employees regularly to identify if fear-based tactics are widespread and harmful.

Chapter Summary

Threatening supervisors with demotion or job termination is a deeply damaging tactic—one that harms individuals, teams, and organizational culture. While leaders may assume it drives performance, it often produces the opposite results: anxiety, disengagement, and diminishing returns.

Supervisors can defend themselves through documentation, clear communication, support-building, and emotional resilience—but real change requires organizational accountability. Transparent goals, manager training, and psychological safety initiatives are key to replacing fear-based tactics with sustainable, trust-driven leadership.

Scripts for Responding to Job Threats

1. When the Threat Is Vague or Implied

"Your role may not be necessary if things continue like this."

Response:

"I hear your concern, and I want to ensure I'm meeting expectations. Can we review the specific areas where I need to improve and clarify the performance standards being used? That way, I can take focused action to align with team and organizational goals."

Why it works: It redirects the conversation from vague fear to measurable improvement while showing accountability.

2. When You're Blindsided in a Meeting or Review

"You know we can always find someone else."

Response:

"I'd appreciate it if we could keep this conversation centered on my performance and contributions. I want to understand what's not working and how we can move forward constructively. I'm committed to this role and the team."

Why it works: This affirms professionalism and encourages a shift away from intimidation toward collaboration.

3. When Threats Are Repeated Over Time

"I've mentioned before—your position is under review."

Response:

"I've noticed that this concern has come up more than once, and I take it seriously. I'd like to request a written performance development plan or schedule a formal review with HR. I want to make sure expectations and support are clearly documented."

Why it works: This moves the interaction into a formalized space, which protects the supervisor from arbitrary actions or verbal threats.

4. When a Manager Uses Fear Instead of Feedback

"If we see another mistake like this, there will be consequences."

Response:

"I understand the importance of avoiding errors, and I take responsibility. I'd like to talk about how we can reduce risk in this area—whether that's with clearer protocols, support, or additional training. My goal is to improve the process, not just avoid punishment."

Why it works: It acknowledges accountability without accepting a culture of blame, and offers to problem-solve.

5. When You Feel Retaliated Against

You report a problem, and your job is suddenly "under review."

Response (to HR or a neutral party):

"After raising concerns about [issue], I received feedback that my position is being reconsidered. I'm documenting this because I want to ensure there's no misunderstanding or retaliation. I'd like support in clarifying performance expectations and discussing the next steps openly."

Why it works: This starts a paper trail and puts the issue in a professional context without sounding defensive.

A Note on Tone

When delivering these responses:

- Stay calm and composed—even if the threat feels personal.
- Speak slowly and deliberately. Don't rush.

- Use "I" language to stay grounded: *"I'd like clarity…"*, *"I take this seriously…"*, *"I want to collaborate…"*.
- Avoid blame but be firm about boundaries and fairness.

Chapter 15
Retaliation for Reporting Concerns or Misconduct

"Speaking up shouldn't punish you — but often, it does."

When you raise concerns about harassment, discrimination, or mismanagement, you expect to be heard — not targeted. Retaliation comes in many forms: exclusion, extra scrutiny, stalled projects, or outright demotion. This backlash silences others and protects the very abuse you tried to expose.

Introduction

When supervisors step up to report unethical behavior—harassment, safety violations, financial mismanagement—they are performing a vital leadership duty. Yet, instead of being praised, many face retaliation: frozen promotions, hostility, budget cuts, exclusion, or even job loss. Retaliation not only punishes moral courage; it tells everyone else to stay silent.

In this chapter, we explore how retaliation shows up, its psychological and professional toll, real-world examples, and proactive strategies to protect both one's team and conscience.

What Retaliation Looks Like

Retaliation doesn't always arrive in obvious or dramatic ways. Often, it's subtle, strategic, and deniable — which makes it even harder for supervisors to address or report. Here are some of the most common signs, explained through the lens of real workplace dynamics:

1. Undermined Authority After Filing Complaints

After raising a concern — whether it's about harassment, safety, ethics, or management conduct — you might notice your decisions are suddenly being second-guessed.

- **Example:** You approve a schedule or process that previously went unchallenged, but now a senior leader steps in to reverse or override your decision in front of your team.
- **Impact:** It sends a message to others that your authority is weakening, making it harder for you to lead confidently or maintain your team's trust.

2. Exclusion from Projects or Resources

Where you were once looped in, now you're left out. Project assignments, budget approvals, or team meetings start happening without your involvement.

- **Example:** You find out a key strategic meeting occurred — one you would normally be part of — and you weren't invited, with no explanation.
- **Impact:** This chips away at your influence and leaves you sidelined, both professionally and emotionally. It can feel like you're being "phased out" without anyone saying it out loud.

3. Negative Performance Reviews Without Cause

Suddenly, your performance is "not meeting expectations" — even though your results haven't changed or have even improved. No clear explanation is given, and feedback is vague or inconsistent.

- **Example:** You're told your "leadership tone" is a concern, though no prior complaints or evidence support this.
- **Impact:** These reviews can damage your credibility, affect promotion or bonus opportunities, and create a paper trail that justifies future disciplinary action or dismissal — all while being difficult to dispute.

4. Isolation from Leadership

You once had an open line of communication with senior management — now, responses are delayed or missing. Invitations to informal check-ins or leadership briefings stop coming.

- **Example:** You used to be consulted on major decisions. Now, you're hearing about them second-hand or through email chains you were never copied on.
- **Impact:** This isolation breeds insecurity and signals to others that your standing with leadership has diminished. It's a form of quiet punishment that chips away at your sense of belonging.

5. Overt Threats or Intimidation

Sometimes, retaliation isn't subtle. It comes in the form of backhanded comments or verbal pressure.

- **Example:** You're told in private, "You might want to rethink how far you're pushing this," or "People who stir the pot don't last long here."
- **Impact:** These statements may not be recorded or formal, but they are deeply chilling. They create a hostile environment that discourages transparency and deters others from speaking up.

Why It Matters

Retaliation is not just unfair — it's corrosive. It punishes integrity and discourages ethical behavior. For supervisors caught in the middle, it sends the message: "Protecting what's right will cost you." And that cost often comes quietly — through lost trust, missed opportunities, and increasing professional isolation.

By learning to recognize these patterns early, supervisors can better protect themselves and seek support when necessary. Organizations, in turn, must take these signs seriously and address them swiftly to build a culture of respect, not fear.

Case Study: Retaliation via Weaponized Compliance from a Direct Report

Weaponized Compliance from Direct Reports: A Supervisor's Retaliation Nightmare

In one organization, a highly qualified and policy-driven supervisor consistently enforced company rules, regularly holding meetings with his direct reports to reinforce expectations around safety, quality, and productivity.

Despite his proactive leadership, one employee deliberately avoided his responsibilities and instead captured footage of a coworker violating a safety policy. The intent wasn't to report the issue through proper channels—but to **hold it as leverage**.

Later, when this employee was disciplined and ultimately terminated for poor performance, he retaliated by showing the footage to upper management. Instead of investigating the motive or circumstances behind the incident—or acknowledging that the supervisor was unaware of the violation—leadership held the supervisor accountable for "failing to prevent" the event.

He was fired.

This was not a case of negligence or mismanagement. It was a clear act of retaliation, enabled by a system where **supervisors carry all the responsibility but receive little to no protection**, even when acting in good faith.

The incident served as a stark warning to others: supervisors can be sacrificed not because they failed in their duty, but because no one in leadership is willing to stand behind them when it's inconvenient.

💬 **Reflection:**

"When direct reports can weaponize misconduct and leadership refuses to investigate, the supervisor becomes the scapegoat—not the leader."

Psychological & Professional Toll

Speaking up about wrongdoing is often portrayed as the right thing to do — and it is. But for many supervisors, reporting misconduct feels less like a triumph of integrity and more like stepping into a storm with no umbrella. The emotional and career-related fallout can be far more damaging than expected, especially when retaliation is subtle but relentless.

• Guilt and Regret

After filing a complaint or reporting unethical behavior, many supervisors carry a heavy emotional weight. Not because they believe they did the wrong thing, but because of the unintended consequences that follow.

You may begin to wonder: *Did I just put a target on my team? Did my report create tension for everyone around me?*

Some feel responsible for the ripple effects — like strained workplace dynamics or lost promotions — even though the real problem was the misconduct they tried to correct.

"I thought I was protecting the team. But after I spoke up, budgets got tighter and a few people got reassigned. It was hard not to feel like it was my fault — even though I knew what I did was right."

• Self-Doubt

Retaliation doesn't always come with sirens. It sneaks in through meetings you're not invited to anymore, tasks quietly reassigned, or leadership suddenly questioning your competence. Over time, this can chip away at your confidence.

You might even begin to wonder: *Was I overreacting? Did I misunderstand what happened? Should I have just let it go?*

When your concerns are dismissed or minimized, it becomes easy to second-guess your own judgment — even if your observations were accurate and your actions justified.

• Stress and Anxiety

The uncertainty of "what happens next" is one of the hardest parts. You don't know if today will bring a disciplinary notice, a passive-aggressive comment from your boss, or a new assignment designed to set you up for failure.

This chronic stress can affect your sleep, your energy levels, and even your relationships outside of work. You may feel constantly on edge, unable to fully relax, even on weekends.

Some supervisors describe it as *"waiting for the other shoe to drop,"* day after day.

• Damaged Credibility

When you report a problem and leadership does nothing — or worse, quietly punishes you for it — your professional credibility can take a hit.

Team members may stop bringing issues to you, assuming that raising concerns leads nowhere. Your authority may weaken, not because of anything you did wrong, but because others see you as "out of favor" or no longer protected.

This damage can be especially painful for supervisors who've worked hard to build trust, only to watch it unravel after doing the right thing.

Studies across various sectors show that many whistleblowers experience lateral transfers, stalled advancement, exclusion from new projects, or other forms of career impact within a year of reporting unethical behavior.

This toll is real. And while it shouldn't discourage ethical action, it highlights a hard truth: organizations must do far more to protect those who speak up — not just with policies, but with culture, leadership accountability, and long-term support.

Real-World Examples

Example 1: The Financial Misreporting

A finance supervisor noticed that revenues were being overstated to meet quarterly targets. When he reported it to internal audit, leadership froze his budget, removed him from high-profile projects, and refused him developmental training. His team, fearing budget cuts, stopped consulting him on decisions.

Example 2: The Safety Cover-Up

At a manufacturing plant, a supervisor reported repetitive safety incident reports being silenced. Overnight, she was excluded from planning meetings, and a "performance improvement" plan appeared—though all metrics were being met before. Colleagues stopped including her in casual hallway conversations.

These examples reflect how retaliation transforms principled action into a personal cost.

What the Law Says

Under Canadian federal law and most provincial human rights codes, **retaliation against whistleblowers is illegal**. Protected activities include reporting safety concerns, harassment, discrimination, or financial wrongdoing. Retaliation includes termination, demotion, harassment, or refusal to provide opportunities. Legal remedies can consist of:

- Reinstatement
- Compensation for lost wages
- Damage to reputation

How Supervisors Can Protect Themselves

1. Know Your Rights and Company Policy

Read annual ethics, whistleblower policies, or staff handbooks. If unclear, consult HR or a legal advisor before reporting.

2. Document Everything

Keep time-stamped records of:

- Incidents and conversations
- Your report and to whom it was directed
- Symptoms of retaliation—budget cuts, exclusion, performance feedback

This provides a valuable record in escalation or legal processes.

3. Use Established Channels

Report through official avenues—HR complaint forms, safety hotlines, audit requests—not hallway conversations. This creates a formal acknowledgement of your action.

4. Seek Support

- Connect with a union representative, employee advocate, or mentor
- Engage with external counsel or the provincial Workplace Safety and Insurance Board
- Confide in trusted peers to maintain emotional balance

5. Request Formal Follow-Up

After reporting, ask for confirmation and updates:

"Could you confirm receipt of my concern and outline next steps?"

This notice signals that you're monitoring the process—and documentation helps protect you later.

6. Prioritize Well-Being

Facing retaliation is isolating and emotionally draining. Lean into:

- Professional counseling or EAP services
- Physical self-care: sleep, exercise, mindfulness
- A trusted personal support network

7. Escalate When Necessary

If retaliation continues or worsens:

- File an internal grievance
- Contact provincial agencies (e.g., Ontario's Whistleblower Protection Office)
- Consult a labor lawyer.
- Document each communication and escalate within your comfort and risk tolerance.

What Organizations Must Do

Creating a genuinely ethical and supportive workplace isn't just about drafting policies—it's about embedding integrity into everything the organization does. Let's dive deeper into each critical area:

1. Clear, Confidential Whistleblower Policies

Employees need to *understand* how to report concerns and *feel safe* doing so. A transparent, straightforward policy reassures people that speaking up won't backfire.

- **Example: Siemens**
- After its major corruption scandal in the 2000s, Siemens overhauled its compliance systems. By 2019, an impressive **80% of employees said they felt secure reporting wrongdoing**, thanks to a revamped whistleblower program FNLondon+4Psicosmart+4Vorecol Blogs+4.

Case Study: Siemens – Rebuilding Trust After Crisis

In the early 2000s, Siemens faced one of the largest corporate corruption scandals in history. The fallout was massive, shaking the company's global reputation and forcing a complete overhaul of its internal systems. But rather than patch things up superficially, Siemens took a long-term, culture-driven approach to reform.

The company implemented a comprehensive compliance program that included:

- A confidential and anonymous whistleblower hotline, available worldwide.
- Robust training programs to educate employees on ethical reporting.
- A stronger internal audit and compliance team with direct access to senior leadership.
- Clear consequences for unethical behavior—regardless of role or rank.

By 2019, Siemens had made measurable progress. According to data shared by Transparency International, approximately **80% of Siemens employees** said they felt **safe reporting unethical behavior** without fear of retaliation. This level of confidence is rare in the corporate world and reflects years of consistent effort, leadership buy-in, and cultural change.

Why It Matters:

Siemens shows what's possible when organizations go beyond surface-level ethics policies. They built a structure and culture where speaking up was not only allowed, but respected and protected.

2. Whistleblower Protection Training for All Staff

It's not enough to write a policy—people need to feel its protection. Regular training ensures all levels of staff know what to do, how to do it, and what happens afterward.

- Training changes culture. When employees see managers and colleagues backing whistleblowers, it reduces stigma and fear—and makes ethical choices easier.

3. Zero Tolerance for Retaliation (With Real Consequences)

It's not enough for companies to say they don't tolerate retaliation — they have to prove it with action. When employees come forward to report wrongdoing, they're taking a big risk. If organizations let retaliation slide, it sends a loud message: "Speaking up will cost you." This fear can silence voices that are crucial for fixing problems and protecting the workplace.

What Zero Tolerance Looks Like:

- Clearly defining what retaliation means, from demotions and pay cuts to subtle exclusions or bullying.
- Promptly investigating any complaints of retaliation with transparency and fairness.
- Enforcing real consequences when retaliation is confirmed, no matter who's responsible.
- Publicly reinforcing the message that retaliation won't be ignored or accepted.

Example: Starbucks — Strengthening Protections Against Retaliation

In response to widely publicized incidents highlighting racial bias, Starbucks took steps to improve its workplace culture and reinforce its commitment to equality. The company introduced enhanced whistleblower programs and made public commitments to address misconduct more effectively. Following these efforts, reports of misconduct reportedly declined, and employee confidence in reporting concerns increased, according to statements made by the company and third-party observers.

This example shows how organizations can take meaningful action to foster a safer, more inclusive environment where employees feel supported in speaking up.

4. Regular Auditing of Cases to Ensure Integrity

Handling whistleblower reports properly requires ongoing review—not just one-off investigations. Regular audits check whether cases are resolved fairly and identify recurring risks.

- Audits can show: Are claims being prioritized? Are patterns emerging in certain departments? This data helps prevent future issues.

5. Anonymous, Multi-Channel Reporting Systems

Not everyone feels comfortable raising concerns in the same way. Some employees prefer speaking directly to a trusted person, while others need the security of complete anonymity to feel safe. Providing multiple reporting options ensures that everyone can find a way to speak up that suits them.

Why this matters:

Offering different channels—like anonymous hotlines, confidential online forms, or direct conversations with ethics officers—makes reporting accessible and builds trust. When people know they won't be forced into a single method, they're more likely to share concerns early, preventing small issues from becoming major problems.

Example: Deloitte

Deloitte, a global professional services firm, recognized the need for diverse, confidential reporting options. They introduced an anonymous hotline alongside clear, structured follow-up procedures to ensure every report was taken seriously and acted upon. Over two years, this approach contributed to a significant reduction—about 40%—in compliance incidents reported within the company.

Employees appreciated having choices for how to raise issues, and the company's commitment to follow-up helped build confidence that speaking up would lead to real change—not just empty promises.

Bottom line:

When organizations offer multiple, trustworthy ways to report concerns—and back them up with genuine action—they create safer workplaces where employees feel heard and protected, no matter how they choose to come forward.

Chapter Summary

Reporting wrongdoing takes real courage, but many supervisors who do the right thing face retaliation. This backlash can harm careers, damage team morale, and erode trust within organizations. However, supervisors equipped with clear documentation, supportive allies, and a solid understanding of their rights can stand firm. At the same time, organizations must foster safe, transparent cultures where speaking up is recognized as a strength—not a risk.

Legal Frameworks – Protecting Supervisors Who Speak Up

Introduction

Supervisors who report wrongdoing—whether safety violations, fraud, harassment, or ethical breaches—often face retaliation. Strong legal protections can make a vital difference, offering a safeguard against unfair treatment. This chapter outlines key whistleblower protection laws in Canada, with comparisons to the United States and United Kingdom, and offers practical advice for supervisors seeking to leverage these protections.

Canada

1. Public Servants Disclosure Protection Act (PSDPA)

- **Scope:** Applies to federal public sector employees.
- **Protections:** Shields employees from reprisals such as discipline, demotion, or termination for disclosing wrongdoing or cooperating with investigations. Maintains confidentiality of whistleblower identity.
- **Process:** Employees must file reprisal complaints within 60 days of the incident. Cases are reviewed by the Integrity Commissioner and may proceed to the Public Servants Disclosure Protection Tribunal.
- **Enforcement:** The Tribunal can order reinstatement, financial compensation, or reversal of disciplinary actions.

2. Provincial & Sector-Specific Laws

- Various provinces (Ontario, Alberta, British Columbia, Quebec) have laws protecting whistleblowers under workplace safety and employment standards statutes.
- Sector-specific protections exist for environmental, privacy (PIPEDA), competition, and securities breaches.

3. Criminal Code Protections

- Section 425.1 prohibits employers from threatening reprisals against employees who report suspected criminal wrongdoing.

United States

1. Whistleblower Protection Act (WPA)

- Protects federal employees disclosing government misconduct, waste, or abuse.
- Covers reprisals such as demotion, threats, or pay cuts. Enforcement handled by the Merit Systems Protection Board.

2. Sarbanes-Oxley Act (SOX) & Dodd-Frank Act

- SOX (2002) protects employees of publicly traded companies from reporting fraud, with civil penalties for violators.
- Dodd-Frank (2010) expands whistleblower rewards and anti-retaliation protections.

United Kingdom & European Union

1. Public Interest Disclosure Act 1998

- Protects workers who disclose wrongdoing in the public interest.
- Shields employees from dismissal, demotion, or other penalties, with claims heard in employment tribunals.

2. EU Whistleblower Directive

- Requires member states to establish safe reporting channels and protect whistleblowers across sectors.

Key Themes Across Jurisdictions

Feature	Canada	U.S.	U.K./EU
Protected Reporting	Wrongdoing, including safety, legal, and criminal breaches	Federal misconduct, financial fraud	Public interest disclosures
Protection	Reinstatement, compensation, restored reputation	Reinstatement, monetary damages, SEC enforcement	Compensation, job reinstatement
Reporting Channels	Public Sector Integrity Commissioner	DOL, SEC, EPA, DoJ, internal hotlines	Internal, prescribed persons, tribunals

Real-World Case Examples

- **CIA Case:** A whistleblower reporting sexual misconduct was terminated despite legal protections, with national security concerns complicating enforcement.
- **UK Kabul Evacuation Case:** Civil servant Josie Stewart won an unfair dismissal claim after whistleblowing on evacuation mismanagement.

What Supervisors Should Do

1. **Know Your Protections:** Understand the laws relevant to your country and sector.
2. **Follow Official Channels:** Use designated systems like the PSDPA, hotlines, or internal audits.
3. **Document Everything:** Keep detailed, dated records of wrongdoing, reporting efforts, and any adverse reactions.
4. **Seek Guidance:** Consult HR, legal counsel, or external bodies such as labor ministries.
5. **Escalate if Needed:** If retaliation occurs, file formal claims within legal timeframes (e.g., 60 days for PSDPA).
6. **Protect Confidentiality:** Request anonymity when possible to reduce retaliation risk.

Final Thought

Legal frameworks aim to protect supervisors who stand against unethical or illegal behavior. While protections vary in scope and enforcement, being informed and prepared empowers supervisors to safeguard their careers and conscience. Moreover, it helps build workplaces that are safer, fairer, and more ethical for everyone.

Chapter 16
Deliberate Isolation from Team and Leadership

"Exile at work isn't accidental — it's engineered to break you."

You notice fewer invitations. Meetings happen without you. Casual conversations turn into inside jokes you don't hear. This isn't just social awkwardness — it's a calculated exclusion. Isolation is a weapon designed to silence, demoralize, and make you invisible where it matters most.

Introduction

Feeling isolated—cut off from both your team and leadership—is one of the most painful forms of workplace marginalization. Supervisors depend on connectedness to lead effectively: to receive guidance, provide direction, and foster unity. When communication is withheld, invitations stop, and trust erodes; supervisors feel ineffective, undervalued, and unsupported. This chapter explores what workplace isolation looks like, its profound impacts, and actionable strategies to restore connection and influence.

What Isolation Looks Like

Isolation is often subtle and gradual, but its impact is immediate and deep:

- **Being Left Out of Meetings:** Meetings relevant to your role occur without your inclusion—often emailed as summaries after the fact.
- **Communication Gaps:** Email threads, Slack channels, or informal chats exclude key information or decisions.
- **Physical and Social Exclusion:** Your office door remains closed, invitations disappear, and casual morning chats stop.
- **Decision-Making Exclusion:** Leadership makes team or operational decisions without input or notice.
- **Lack of Recognition or Mentions:** Your name is omitted when credits or accomplishments are shared.

Why Isolation Happens

These precede and perpetuate isolation:

- **Power Plays:** Excluding supervisors can be a way to reduce their influence and centralize control.
- **Neglect by Default:** When communication systems are informal or ad hoc, anyone can easily slip through the cracks.
- **Personal or Cultural Bias:** Supervisors can be sidelined for who they are or for unconscious biases about their capabilities or background.

- **Punitive Measures:** Isolation is sometimes used as punishment for speaking up or making mistakes.
- **Organizational Silos:** Structural issues can degrade collaboration and unintentionally leave supervisors out.

Real-World Examples

Story 1: Sarah, the Healthcare Supervisor

Sarah noticed she was no longer invited to weekly policy meetings. Suddenly, she'd learn of decisions via hallway whispers. Her attempts to gather updates only led to frustrating apologies and vague reasons. Eventually, morale among her nursing team dipped—they felt directionless and undervalued.

Story 2: Raj, the IT Supervisor

Raj found Slack and Teams channels confusingly excluding him. Important project deadlines were shared elsewhere. When he asked about it, leaders replied, "Oh, I thought it wasn't relevant." His team took longer to deliver projects and felt unsupported. Raj questioned whether his contributions mattered.

Impact on Supervisors, Teams, and Organizations

For Supervisors:

- **Decreased Authority:** Teams lose respect when supervisors lack current information.
- **Imposter Syndrome:** Frequent exclusion leads to self-doubt.
- **Burnout and Stress:** Constantly chasing updates is exhausting.
- **Loss of Career Momentum:** Continued exclusion erodes visibility and potential.

For Teams:

- **Confusion:** Without your direction, team members lack clarity.
- **Low Engagement:** Feeling excluded leads to disengagement and turnover.
- **Reduced Performance:** Lack of guidance affects efficiency.

For Organizations:

- **Operational Risk:** Decisions made without frontline input can miss key insights.
- **Cultural Decline:** Isolation leads to toxic "us vs. them" dynamics.
- **Leadership Gaps:** Hidden dysfunction affects overall performance and innovation.

Strategies to Overcome Isolation

1. Seek Formal Inclusion

Request to be explicitly included in relevant meetings, channels, and discussions—ideally documented via email or shared calendar invites.

"I'd appreciate being included in policy meetings and communication threads related to X and Y—this helps me align my team more effectively."

2. Maintain Your Own Communication Channels

Proactively create weekly team newsletters or status updates that flag critical issues and share them with leadership and peers.

3. Build Informal Relationships

Seek casual meetups or regular check-ins with peers and leaders. Be big-hearted, genuinely curious, and open.

4. Clarify Role Expectations

Ask leaders: "When I was assigned this project, I assumed I'd be included in all relevant decisions—how can we ensure that moving forward?"

5. Document Missed Opportunities

When exclusion leads to project delays, document the lessons learned. Share constructively: "We experienced a delay after missing the planning call—can we schedule the next one with all supervisors?"

6. Escalate When Necessary

If repeated exclusion is harming team outcomes—and your requests are ignored—make a case to HR or senior leadership. Provide examples and emphasize the mutual benefits of inclusion.

Organizational Responsibilities: Making Inclusion Intentional

In any workplace, especially those with layered reporting lines, it's easy for communication gaps and unintentional exclusion to creep in. When supervisors aren't looped into decisions, updates, or planning conversations, it undermines their ability to lead effectively. These five strategies help organizations build inclusive systems where all voices—especially frontline leaders—are heard and respected.

1. Implement Inclusive Meeting Protocols

What it means: Make it standard practice to include all relevant stakeholders—especially supervisors—in meeting invites and agenda planning.

Why it matters: Supervisors are often the bridge between strategic direction and operational execution. Excluding them from early conversations leads to disconnects, confusion, and frustration.

What it looks like: Before scheduling a meeting, consider who will be affected by the topic or outcome. Invite them proactively and give them the chance to shape the agenda.

"We used to loop in supervisors after decisions were made—then wondered why implementation was rocky. Now they're at the table from the start."

— HR Manager, Manufacturing Sector

2. Monitor Communication Equity

What it means: Leadership should periodically review how information is shared—and who is consistently kept in the loop.

Why it matters: Sometimes, leaders unintentionally favor certain communication lines, like going straight to department heads or skipping middle management. Over time, this creates silos and exclusion.

What it looks like: Conduct short quarterly audits or surveys: Are supervisors getting timely updates? Do they feel informed and involved in decision-making?

"We didn't realize our email distribution lists left out most site-level supervisors. Once fixed, we saw a huge improvement in engagement."

— Internal Communications Lead

3. Train on Collaborative Leadership

What it means: Offer training that helps managers and senior leaders recognize unconscious biases and learn how to lead inclusively.

Why it matters: Exclusion isn't always malicious—it can stem from habit, assumption, or comfort. Training helps leaders identify these blind spots and create intentional inclusion practices.

What it looks like: Host workshops on inclusive decision-making, cross-level collaboration, and the risks of top-down communication. Use real case studies to drive the message home.

"Some of our team leads didn't even realize they were gatekeeping info. Training helped shift the culture from control to collaboration."

— Inclusion & Equity Officer

4. Use Collaboration Tools Properly

What it means: Don't just install software—use it to actively share information, track updates, and allow supervisors access to what they need.

Why it matters: Tools like Slack, Microsoft Teams, or shared project dashboards only help if everyone's included and knows how to use them. If supervisors are left out of channels, they're left out of decisions.

What it looks like: Create shared folders, group chats, and meeting notes that automatically include supervisory staff. Document expectations for how these tools are used.

"We had all the tech, but the setup excluded the very people driving the day-to-day. Just changing access permissions made a big difference."

— Operations Manager

5. Review Role Clarity Regularly

What it means: Hold structured check-ins—at least quarterly—to align on roles, expectations, and how inclusion is being practiced in communication flows.

Why it matters: As organizations evolve, people assume responsibilities shift. Without regular reviews, gaps in communication and authority become normalized.

What it looks like: During team reviews or one-on-ones, ask: Does each supervisor feel heard? Are they getting updates early enough to plan effectively? Are decisions being made without their input?

"One quarter, our supervisors flagged feeling out of the loop. We adjusted our org chart comms protocols, and accountability went up immediately."

— Director of Field Operations

Closing Reflection

Inclusion, transparency, and connection are more than nice-to-haves—they're essential to thriving leadership. When supervisors are empowered with information, respected for their input, and trusted to act, everyone benefits: teams stay aligned, trust flourishes, and organizational performance strengthens.

As you move through this book, ask yourself:

- **What's one change I can make today**—in a meeting, an email, or a check-in—that helps a supervisor feel seen and included?
- **Where in your organization** might unseen silos be holding back talent and collaboration?

Small, intentional steps toward inclusion can reshape workplace culture—one conversation, document, or invitation at a time.

Reflection & Application

Use the following prompts for personal insight or team discussion:

✦ For Supervisors (Self-Reflection)

- When have you felt excluded from key conversations or decisions at work? How did it affect your leadership?
- What strategies have helped you re-establish connection or visibility?
- Is there a recent situation where you wish you had spoken up about being left out?

✦ For Leadership Teams

- How do we currently decide who gets "looped in" for meetings or updates? Is that process equitable?
- Have we unintentionally isolated any team members or roles from the information they need?
- What one change could improve communication and inclusion across levels?

Try This: "Inclusion in Action" Micro-Exercise

Think of a recent decision or meeting:

1. Who was included?
2. Who wasn't—but probably should have been?
3. What was the impact of their absence?

Discuss or journal your thoughts. If relevant, share insights with your team or manager.

Want to Go Deeper?

Explore these resources:

- **"Dare to Lead" by Brené Brown** – Courageous leadership with a focus on vulnerability and inclusion.
- **Harvard Business Review:** *"Why Managers Need to Involve the Front Line in Decision-Making."*
- **Catalyst.org** – Practical guides for inclusive leadership and workplace equity.

Part III: Recognition, Reward, and Advancement Denied

When growth, credit, and fairness are systematically denied.

Chapter 17
Biased and Inaccurate Performance Reviews

"When the scorecard is rigged, the game isn't fair."

You work hard, hit targets, and innovate — but your review tells a different story. Critiques are vague, unfair, or based on hearsay. Biased evaluations aren't honest assessments; they're tools to hold you back or push you out. When reviews lose integrity, so does your career.

Introduction

Performance evaluations are meant to provide honest feedback, recognize achievements, and identify areas for growth. They are critical in shaping a supervisor's career trajectory, affecting promotions, compensation, and professional reputation. Unfortunately, many supervisors face biased and unfair reviews that undermine their contributions and limit their opportunities. These unfair assessments often stem from subtle prejudices, miscommunication, or intentional manipulation by upper management. The consequences can be devastating—not only for the individual but also for the broader team and organization.

This chapter delves into the nature of biased performance reviews, how they manifest, their impact, and strategies for supervisors to navigate and challenge these unfair practices.

Understanding Biased Performance Reviews

Bias in performance evaluations can be conscious or unconscious and take many forms, including:

- **Halo and Horn Effect:** Where a manager's overall impression (positive or negative) colors the entire review, regardless of specific achievements or failures.
- **Similarity Bias:** Favoring supervisors who share the same background, personality traits, or interests.
- **Gender, Race, and Age Bias:** Studies consistently show that women, minorities, and older workers often receive lower performance ratings or less favorable feedback.
- **Recency Effect:** Overemphasis on recent events rather than the whole review period.
- **Confirmation Bias:** Managers interpret information in a way that confirms their preconceived opinions.

For example, a female supervisor who has delivered strong results might be labeled as "too aggressive" or "not a team player," while a male counterpart exhibiting similar behaviors may be praised for leadership. Similarly, supervisors from minority groups may be unfairly scrutinized or receive vague feedback that lacks actionable steps for improvement.

Real-World Examples

Example 1: Sarah's Stalled Career

Sarah, a mid-level supervisor in a tech company, consistently exceeded her targets and received positive feedback from her team. However, her performance reviews rarely reflected these successes. Instead, her manager focused on minor communication style critiques and occasionally questioned her "fit" with company culture. Despite her efforts, Sarah was passed over for promotion twice. Later, an internal diversity audit revealed that female supervisors in her department were systematically rated lower than their male peers, pointing to deep-seated gender bias.

Example 2: Carlos' Compensation Freeze

Carlos, a supervisor in a manufacturing plant, received glowing verbal praise but was told his official performance review "did not warrant" a raise. His manager cited vague concerns about "attitude," which Carlos believed was linked to cultural misunderstandings and his direct communication style. Over time, Carlos noticed that his peers were promoted and compensated more generously, despite their lower output. His frustration led him to seek external mentorship and eventually HR intervention.

The Impact of Unfair Reviews

Unfair performance reviews aren't just a paperwork issue — they strike at the heart of professional identity. For supervisors who work hard to support their teams and meet expectations, receiving a review that feels biased, inaccurate, or incomplete can be disheartening and damaging.

Let's break down what that impact really looks like:

1. Decreased Motivation and Engagement

When supervisors invest time, energy, and care in their roles, only to receive vague or unbalanced reviews, it can sap their enthusiasm. Over time, this discouragement turns into disengagement.

"After I got a 'meets expectations' rating on a year where I clearly went above and beyond, I stopped volunteering for stretch projects. What was the point?"

— Operations Manager, logistics sector

Without acknowledgment or constructive feedback, even high performers begin to dial back their efforts.

2. Erosion of Trust

Performance reviews are often viewed as a reflection of how leadership sees you. When the process feels subjective, inconsistent, or politically driven, it chips away at trust — not just in the manager delivering the feedback, but in the system as a whole.

"It felt like the rating had been decided before the conversation even started."

— Team Lead, tech industry

This mistrust can make supervisors hesitant to give feedback themselves, perpetuating a cycle of unclear expectations and uneven standards.

3. Stunted Career Growth

Supervisors rely on fair evaluations for promotions, bonuses, and access to leadership programs. A single unfair review — especially if uncorrected — can stall upward movement for years.

"They said my leadership skills needed work, but gave no examples. A month later, someone with less experience got the promotion."

— Line Supervisor, manufacturing

When reviews don't reflect actual performance or growth, career paths become blocked — not due to lack of skill, but due to systemic inequity.

4. Higher Turnover

No one wants to stay in a workplace where they feel invisible or undervalued. Over time, unfair appraisals cause burnout, disengagement, and eventually, resignation.

"I loved my team, but the constant under-rating from leadership made me feel invisible. Leaving was the only way forward."

— Supervisor, healthcare

Organizations that fail to recognize and reward talent often lose it to competitors who value fairness and transparency.

5. Negative Team Climate

Supervisors shape the tone for their teams. When unjust reviews dishearten them, it often trickles down. Team members may sense tension, morale may drop, and retention can suffer.

"After my review, I struggled to stay positive. My team picked up on that — and it started affecting them, too."

— Frontline Manager, retail

Fair treatment of supervisors isn't just about their well-being — it's about sustaining the health of the whole team.

Final Thought

Unfair reviews aren't just about a missed bonus or promotion — they're a breach of trust. For supervisors on the front lines, performance evaluations should be tools for growth, recognition, and honest reflection. When done poorly, they do real harm. When done well, they unlock potential and drive teams forward.

Research consistently shows that when employees perceive their performance reviews as fair—especially regarding the process and feedback—they report more substantial commitment to the organization and a greater intention to stay. At the same time, supervisors who experience unfair appraisals are more likely to report higher stress and burnout, which can negatively affect team productivity.

Why Do Biased Reviews Happen?

Unfair performance reviews usually don't come out of nowhere. Several common factors — both personal and systemic — contribute to why some supervisors end up with biased or unjust evaluations:

• Managerial Inexperience

Many managers have never been adequately trained on how to give fair, objective feedback. Without the right skills, it's easy for personal feelings or assumptions to cloud judgment.

"My boss just repeated vague criticisms without examples — I don't think she knew how to evaluate me properly."

• Organizational Culture

If the workplace tolerates favoritism, cliques, or discrimination — whether based on race, gender, or politics — those biases seep into performance reviews, often unnoticed or unchallenged.

"The same few people always get great reviews, no matter what."

• Lack of Clear Criteria

When expectations and performance standards are fuzzy or applied unevenly, managers have too much room for interpretation, which can lead to unfair ratings.

"I wasn't sure what goals I was being judged on — no one ever told me."

• Fear or Insecurity

Some managers may feel threatened by supervisors who raise concerns or challenge policies. Rather than addressing the issue, they might retaliate through harsh reviews to maintain control or silence dissent.

"After I reported safety violations, my next review criticized my leadership style — completely out of the blue."

• **Poor Feedback Practices**

Feedback that's rare, vague, or only given during formal reviews makes it hard to correct misunderstandings or biases early. Without ongoing dialogue, minor issues can snowball into unfair assessments.

"I got blindsided by my rating because I hadn't heard any concerns all year."

• **Retaliation for Raising Concerns**

Supervisors who speak up about unethical or harmful practices risk being targeted. Negative reviews can be a subtle form of punishment, discouraging others from speaking out.

"I tried to push back against a policy I felt was wrong, and suddenly my review was full of 'areas for improvement' that never came up before."

• **Resistance to Change**

Managers uncomfortable with new ideas or challenges to the status quo might unfairly rate supervisors who advocate for improvements or transparency.

"I suggested a better reporting process, and my manager seemed annoyed. My next review reflected that frustration."

Final Thought

Biased reviews are rarely accidental — they reflect deeper issues within leadership, culture, and communication. Understanding these causes is the first step to building fairer, more transparent appraisal systems that encourage honesty, growth, and trust instead of fear or silence.

Strategies for Supervisors Facing Biased Reviews

1. Document Your Achievements

Keep a detailed record of accomplishments, metrics, and positive feedback throughout the review period. Use objective data to support your case during evaluations.

2. Seek Regular Feedback

Request ongoing feedback rather than waiting for annual reviews. This helps correct misunderstandings early and demonstrates commitment to growth.

3. Prepare Thoughtful Responses

If you believe a review is unfair, calmly request a meeting to discuss specific points. Use evidence to clarify discrepancies and express your perspective professionally.

4. Build Allies and Mentors

Develop relationships with other leaders or HR professionals who can advocate for you or provide guidance.

5. Know Your Rights

Understand your organization's policies on performance management and anti-discrimination. If bias persists, consider formal complaint channels.

Real Experience: When Fair Reviews Turn Unfair

In 2023, a shift supervisor received an *exceeds expectations* rating, reflecting strong performance and leadership. His team thrived under his guidance, and his results were consistently solid.

However, in 2024, despite maintaining or even improving his work, his review was downgraded to *meets expectations*. The surprising change was attributed not to his actual performance but to perceived resentment from senior management. This stemmed from his raising a genuine concern about a longstanding policy issue—a concern that had been voiced before but remained unresolved.

Rather than being recognized for his courage in speaking up, the supervisor felt that his willingness to address this issue created friction with upper management, which was then reflected unfairly in his evaluation.

This example illustrates how standing up against problematic policies can sometimes lead to biased performance reviews, which in turn damage motivation, trust, and career growth. Organizations must ensure appraisal systems are transparent and fair, protecting supervisors who advocate for positive change instead of penalizing them.

When Ratings Are Changed Without Input: A Hidden Bias in Performance Reviews

Another concern that often goes unnoticed—but is deeply unfair—is how performance reviews are sometimes handled in certain organizations (though not all). In some companies, shift supervisors are responsible for evaluating their direct reports based on firsthand experience. They know their team members' strengths, challenges, and day-to-day contributions better than anyone.

However, after these evaluations are submitted, the management team may review and finalize ratings behind closed doors—sometimes changing them entirely without involving the supervisor or seeking their input. This means a supervisor's detailed and informed assessment can be overridden by people who may have had little to no direct interaction with the employees being reviewed.

What's more troubling is that employees who didn't meet the criteria for higher ratings are still given *exceeds expectations*, while others who truly earned it are downgraded. This kind of process not only disrespects the supervisor's judgment but also undermines the integrity of the review system and damages trust across the team.

In the long run, practices like these don't just impact individual morale—they weaken leadership, accountability, and the fairness that high-performing workplaces depend on.

What Organizations Should Do

To promote fairness, organizations can:

- Implement structured and standardized evaluation processes.
- Provide bias-awareness training for managers.
- Use 360-degree feedback to gather diverse perspectives.
- Encourage transparency and open dialogue about performance criteria.
- Regularly audit evaluations for patterns of bias or disparities.

Conclusion

Biased and unfair performance reviews are a pervasive form of disrespect and discrimination that hinders supervisors' careers and damages workplace culture. Recognizing the signs and understanding the mechanisms behind these biases empowers supervisors to advocate for themselves. At the same time, organizations bear the responsibility to design and enforce equitable evaluation systems that uphold dignity, trust, and fairness.

Inspirational Quote to Close the Chapter

"Fairness is not an attitude. It's a professional skill that must be developed and exercised."

— Brit Hume

Chapter 18
Blocked from Promotions Without Cause

"When the ladder is pulled up, merit means nothing."

You meet every goal, train others, and show leadership potential — yet the promotion always goes elsewhere. The explanation is vague, the criteria unclear. Sometimes, career stalls aren't about readiness — they're about gatekeepers protecting their own power. Being blocked isn't a failure; it's a barrier designed to keep you down.

Introduction

One of the most demoralizing forms of workplace injustice is when supervisors are passed over for promotions or advancement—despite consistent performance and credentials. This form of bias not only stalls individual careers but also corrodes trust in leadership and organizational fairness. In this chapter, we'll examine how unexplained advancement barriers arise, their impact, real-world examples, and strategies for navigating and resolving them.

Understanding Promotion Bias

Even when supervisors exceed expectations, unseen factors can prevent their advancement:

- **Opaque Decision-Making** – Promotion criteria are vague or inconsistently applied.
- **Favoritism and Nepotism** – Friends or family of decision-makers get preferred treatment.
- **Unconscious Bias** – Decisions influenced by gender, race, age, or personality.
- **Gatekeeping** – Higher-ups exclude deserving individuals from networking or visibility.
- **Lack of Advocacy** – Supervisors without influential mentors or sponsors often fail to get promoted.

Unexplained blocks signal that performance alone doesn't determine advancement—and this disconnection can erode motivation and faith in the system.

Real-World Examples

Case 1: Jamie's Marketing Leadership Stalemate

Jamie, a marketing supervisor, consistently led successful campaigns, including a 20% increase in brand engagement. Despite accolades from peers and clients, he was passed over for the director role. Instead, a less experienced colleague—who had closer ties to senior leadership—was promoted. When Jamie asked for feedback, he received vague statements like "we felt Jane had a better cultural fit." Unable to identify performance gaps, Jamie felt blocked for reasons beyond his control.

Case 2: Priya's Engineering Oversight Exclusion

Priya led her engineering team through a major software transition on time and under budget. Her manager praised her in performance meetings but didn't support her candidacy for a vacant higher-level manager position. Instead, the role was filled by someone from another department. No reason was given, and Priya's requests for clarification were met with polite but non-specific responses. Without explanation, she felt overlooked and undervalued.

The Impact of Being Unjustly Passed Over

Being passed over for a promotion, especially when you've earned it, isn't just a career setback—it's a deeply personal blow. Here's how it affects supervisors and their teams:

• Emotional Toll

Supervisors may feel frustrated, resentful, or even question their own worth. After investing significant time and effort, being overlooked can trigger self-doubt and a sense of injustice.

"I'd put my heart into the role, but getting passed over made me feel invisible—and that hurt more than any deadline missed."

• Career Stagnation

Without promotion, opportunities for growth—both in responsibility and compensation—dwindle. The result is a career standing still while peers move forward. That plateau can be discouraging, especially when goals feel out of reach.

• Reduced Engagement

Once advancement is perceived as unfair, motivation takes a hit. If good work isn't rewarded, even high-performing supervisors may see little reason to go the extra mile.

• Team Ripple Effects

Supervisors set the tone. When they're overlooked, their teams notice. It sends a message: "If they won't reward merit here, why should I?" Over time, disengagement spreads—and performance suffers.

• Organizational Consequences

Repeatedly overlooking strong performers damages credibility. Organizations risk losing their best talent and reputational standing. Attracting driven employees becomes harder when news spreads that merit isn't valued.

What the Research Shows

Multiple studies in organizational behavior indicate that perceived fairness in promotion processes correlates strongly with employee engagement, retention, and performance. Supervisors who feel overlooked—especially without clear feedback—are far more likely to disengage or even leave.

Real-World Reflection: When Recognition Gets Missed

A shift supervisor at a mid-sized manufacturing firm had consistently exceeded performance targets, improved team morale, and trained two junior team leads—yet when a promotion opportunity opened up, the role was given to someone with less experience but closer ties to upper management.

No feedback was offered. When the supervisor asked for clarity, the response was vague: "It was a strategic decision."

Over the following months, the supervisor remained professional but stopped volunteering for extra duties. Eventually, they began exploring opportunities elsewhere—and left quietly six months later. The team felt the loss deeply.

This isn't an isolated story. It's a reminder that promotion decisions shape not just one person's path, but the culture and cohesion of a workplace.

Final Thought

Ensuring that advancement opportunities are transparent and based on objective criteria is crucial—not just for individual morale, but for the vitality of entire teams and organizations. Recognizing and rewarding merit restores trust and fuels sustained success.

How to Navigate and Resolve Blocked Promotions

Facing unfair promotion decisions can be really frustrating and disheartening. But even in challenging situations, there are practical steps supervisors can take to advocate for themselves and create positive momentum. The following strategies can help you get clear about what's expected, build a supportive network, and take charge of your career growth.

1. **Request Clear Feedback and Criteria**
2. Don't hesitate to ask for specific guidance. You might say something like:
3. *"Could you help me understand what I need to do to be competitive for the director role in six months? I want to map out a clear plan to get there."*
4. Knowing precisely what's required reduces guesswork and shows you're serious about growing.
5. **Build Your Advocate Network**
6. Find mentors and sponsors who can champion your work, offer advice, and gently remind decision-makers about your contributions when promotion discussions happen.
7. **Document Your Achievements**
8. Keep track of your wins—whether it's project results, positive feedback, or leadership moments. Having a solid record makes it harder for your efforts to be overlooked.

9. **Ask for Visibility Opportunities**
10. Look for chances to work on high-profile projects or cross-department initiatives. These experiences help you get noticed by senior leaders and expand your influence.
11. **Raise Concerns Professionally**
12. If you suspect unfairness, approach the topic calmly and constructively. For example:
13. *"I've observed several leadership roles filled without a clear process. Could we work toward ensuring promotions are handled transparently and fairly?"*
14. This keeps the door open for dialogue without sounding confrontational.
15. **Set a Timeline**
16. It's okay to ask for a follow-up:
17. *"If a promotion doesn't happen this time, can we revisit it in six months? I'd like to focus on the right areas to prepare."*
18. Having a timeline helps hold everyone accountable and keeps your growth on track.
19. **Know When to Move On**
20. If barriers persist and the leadership isn't responsive, it might be time to consider other opportunities—while making sure to leave on good terms and with professionalism intact.

What Organizations Must Do

For organizations to truly be fair and keep their best supervisors engaged, it takes more than good intentions. Clear systems, open communication, and ongoing support are essential. Here's what companies can do to make promotions more transparent and equitable:

1. **Clarify Promotion Criteria and Make Them Public**
2. Everyone must know exactly what it takes to move up. Companies should clearly outline the skills, experience, and results expected for each level—and share these openly. When promotion goals aren't a secret, supervisors can aim confidently and avoid confusion or guesswork.
3. **Use Structured Promotion Reviews**
4. Rather than leaving decisions up to one person, promotions should be reviewed by a group of stakeholders—like HR, managers, and senior leaders—who follow a consistent set of written criteria. This reduces bias and ensures decisions are fair, balanced, and based on evidence.
5. **Offer Mentorship and Sponsorship Programs**
6. Promising supervisors need champions in leadership to help them grow. Mentors provide advice and encouragement, while sponsors actively promote their protégés for opportunities. These programs help talented supervisors get noticed and supported as they prepare for bigger roles.
7. **Audit Demotion or Pass-over Data**
8. Companies should regularly examine who's being promoted and who's passed over, categorizing this by factors such as gender, race, or department. This helps identify patterns that may indicate unconscious bias or unfair practices, allowing them to address problems before they worsen.
9. **Embed Feedback Loops**
10. For supervisors who don't get promoted, organizations must offer clear, actionable feedback and a path forward. This could include coaching, training, or a formal

reapplication process. Knowing how to improve helps maintain high motivation and demonstrates the company's care for its employees' growth.

Summary

Being blocked from promotion without a clear reason is a form of workplace disrespect that undercuts morale, retention, and performance. Supervisors can protect their careers by requesting transparency, building advocacy, and securing visibility. Organizations must respond by clarifying, structuring, auditing, and mentoring to ensure promotions reflect merit—not confusion or bias.

Inspirational Quote

"Don't sit down and wait for the opportunities to come. Get up and make them."

— **Madam C.J. Walker**, America's first self-made female millionaire

Chapter 19
Unequal Pay or Compensation

"Fair pay isn't a favor — it's a right."

When colleagues doing similar work earn more, it's not a coincidence. Unequal pay breeds resentment and highlights systemic biases. Being underpaid for your work diminishes your value, motivation, and future prospects. It's a silent injustice that too often goes unchallenged.

Introduction

Fair compensation is a fundamental aspect of professional respect and motivation. For supervisors, receiving equitable pay is not just a matter of personal income—it signals recognition of their work, leadership, and dedication. Yet many find themselves repeatedly denied raises or discover their pay lags behind peers despite similar roles and responsibilities. This pitting of effort against inequity breeds frustration, distrust, and diminished effectiveness.

This chapter examines how pay disparities emerge, the real-world consequences, and practical strategies supervisors can use to advocate for fair compensation.

Understanding Pay Inequity: Why It Happens

Unequal pay often results from a mix of systemic biases and organizational shortcomings:

- **Lack of Pay Transparency:** When salary ranges are secret, starting offers and raises become subjective.
- **Negotiation Disparities:** Those who are more comfortable negotiating may receive higher raises, while others are passed over.
- **Bias—Conscious or Unconscious:** Gender, race, age, or background can affect managers' perceptions of worth.
- **Role Creep Without Compensation:** Supervisors take on expanded duties without pay adjustments.
- **Inequitable Performance Reviews:** Lower performance ratings—sometimes unfairly applied—can block salary increases.

These factors combine to create slow, invisible, and often undetected wage disparities.

Real-World Examples

1. Maria's Untransparent Raise Process

Maria, a production supervisor, led a record-breaking quarter and took on extra shifts. However, when annual reviews came, her raise was minimal. After privately comparing notes with a peer in another department, she learned he received 15%—far more than her 2%. No explanation was provided, and higher-ups said, "Budgets are always tight."

2. Daniel's Role Expansion Without Pay

Daniel, an IT supervisor, had overseen a small team for three years. When budget cuts left other departments understaffed, he absorbed extra responsibilities. Still, his salary remained stagnant. Eventually, he realized that others with similar expanded roles received pay adjustments, while he was overlooked, and no feedback was ever given.

The Impact

Pay isn't just a number—it's a signal of respect, fairness, and organizational values. When supervisors feel underpaid or overlooked, the effects ripple far beyond personal income. Here's what typically happens:

• Declining Motivation

When supervisors see their hard work go unrewarded, engagement inevitably fades. A surprising 59% of employees report they'd stay for less pay if they felt fairly valued, showing that perceived fairness can be more influential than just higher wages.

• Team Morale Drops

Teams look to their leaders for signals about how the organization values them. When a supervisor is underpaid or passed over, it sends a message that effort doesn't pay off. This kind of disconnect saps energy across the board.

• Erosion of Trust

Trust in leadership depends on fairness. One study found that organizations prioritizing transparent salary practices experienced a 20% decrease in turnover and a 31% boost in productivity PsicoSmart+1Psico-Smart Blog+1. When pay seems equitably handled, trust follows.

• Higher Turnover Risk

Underpaid supervisors are more likely to explore other opportunities. A 2022 MIT Sloan School of Management report found that companies investing in pay equity initiatives saw a 15% improvement in retention, and often saved on costly turnover PsicoSmart.

• **Systemic Inequality**

Persistent pay gaps along gender or racial lines hurt not just individual supervisors but the organization's diversity and innovation. For instance, addressing pay imbalances has been linked to a 20% reduction in employee turnover and higher engagement across teams en.wikipedia.org+15PsicoSmart+15psicosmart.net+15.

Why Pay Equity Matters

Pay equity isn't just fair—it's foundational to a healthy, purposeful workplace. According to equity theory (Adams, 1965), people naturally compare their input-to-output ratio to others. When they perceive imbalance—especially at managerial levels—motivation collapses, and relationships deteriorate en.wikipedia.org+1PsicoSmart+1.

Final Thought

Fair and transparent compensation is a cornerstone of trust, engagement, and team cohesion. By aligning pay with performance—and making it clear how and why decisions are made—organizations don't just reward effort—they reinforce the very values that drive success.

Strategies for Supervisors

1. Know Market Benchmarks

Use salary surveys, industry reports, and online tools (e.g., PayScale, Glassdoor) to understand where your pay stands relative to similar roles.

2. Document Your Contributions

Keep detailed records of achievements, expanded duties, team results, and accolades. Use data to build your case for compensation reviews.

3. Request Transparent Dialogue

Open a discussion with your manager:

"I'd like to review my compensation in light of additional responsibilities and recent performance. Can we look at market benchmarks together?"

This shows professionalism and invites accountability.

4. Practice Salary Negotiation

Even inside an organization, negotiation is key. Frame your request around team impact and outcomes—not just personal need.

5. Seek Mentors or HR Advice

Confide in trusted internal mentors or HR to explore whether others in your role are paid similarly. They can guide you through the process.

6. Consider Formal Compensation Review

Refer to your company's HR or compensation committee if informal discussions fail. A documented career progression and contribution record strengthen your case.

7. Prepare Your Exit Strategy

If inequity persists and internal interventions fail, explore opportunities elsewhere. Often, moving roles is the most effective way to align pay with performance.

What Organizations Should Do

To foster truly fair and motivating compensation practices, organizations must go beyond policies—they need to lead with intention, transparency, and accountability. These five steps build a culture where people feel respected, rewarded, and empowered.

1. Implement Clear Salary Bands

Why it matters: When employees (and their managers) don't know what fair pay looks like for a role, assumptions and confusion creep in. This is where resentment and inequity can start.

What it looks like: Share role-based salary ranges with all employees. For example, a "Shift Supervisor Level 2" role might have a clear published range, such as $60,000–$72,000.

The impact: When people know where they stand—and where they can go—they trust the system more and are more likely to stay and grow with the company.

2. Conduct Equity Audits

Why it matters: Pay gaps aren't always intentional, but they can become invisible until someone actively checks.

What it looks like: HR or external consultants regularly analyze salary data across factors like gender, race, geography, and tenure. They flag and correct any patterns that don't reflect fair practice.

The impact: Equity audits send a clear message: this company doesn't just *say* it values fairness— it's willing to prove it and make changes.

3. Train Managers on Fair Pay Practices

Why it matters: Many managers want to be fair but often lack the tools or awareness to do so objectively.

What it looks like: Regular workshops or e-learning that cover unconscious bias, how to assess performance fairly, and how to use compensation data correctly.

The impact: Empowered managers make more consistent, inclusive, and justifiable pay decisions—benefiting both individuals and the company's reputation.

4. Ensure Transparency

Why it matters: Silence around pay can lead to suspicion, gossip, or even lawsuits. People want to understand how and why compensation decisions are made.

What it looks like: Leaders clearly explain how raises, bonuses, and promotions are determined. Compensation frameworks should be accessible, and open-door policies should be encouraged for pay-related questions.

The impact: Transparency builds trust—and prevents good employees from leaving because they assume unfairness where there may be none.

5. Recognize Role Growth with Mid-Year Reviews

Why it matters: Roles evolve—especially for high-performing supervisors. If pay doesn't evolve with it, people feel taken for granted.

What it looks like: When a supervisor starts leading additional shifts, mentoring new team leads, or overseeing special projects, they don't have to wait until the annual review. A mid-year salary discussion can acknowledge that extra effort.

The impact: This responsiveness shows employees that leadership is paying attention and that going the extra mile is actually valued and rewarded.

Final Thought

Fair compensation is more than just a budget item—it's a signal of trust, recognition, and belonging. When organizations are intentional about how they set, audit, and communicate pay, they don't just reduce turnover—they build a workplace people are proud to grow in.

Summary

Demoralizing and damaging, denied raises and unequal pay undermine supervisors, teams, and the organization as a whole. By grounding requests in data, documentation, and open conversation—and by encouraging transparency and equity processes—supervisors and companies alike can ensure pay fairness and strengthen workplace trust.

Chapter 20
Manipulated Metrics to Undermine Performance

"Numbers can lie — especially when they're chosen to hurt."

You've done your best, but the metrics tell another story. Goals change without notice. Benchmarks move. Data is cherry-picked. Manipulating performance indicators is a subtle sabotage tactic, turning honest efforts into apparent failures. When the numbers aren't fair, neither is the judgment.

Introduction

Numbers should tell the truth, but in some workplaces, they're twisted to serve hidden agendas. One of the most insidious forms of manipulation is when supervisors' performance metrics are deliberately altered or misapplied to make them appear incompetent. Whether through unfair quotas, inconsistent data definitions, or selective reporting, this tactic erodes trust, morale, and the supervisor's standing within the organization.

How Metrics Can Be Manipulated

1. Changing Targets Midstream

Targets are reset without warning, making goals impossible to reach.

- *Example:* A sales supervisor's monthly target is raised mid-month due to "new priorities." Despite meeting the original target, performance is marked as poor.

2. Selective Data Tracking

Only negative or out-of-context data is used to assess performance.

- *Example:* A production supervisor's defect rate is tracked during the toughest shift, ignoring earlier successful shifts or quality improvements made earlier in the period.

3. Redefining Key Performance Indicators (KPIs)

KPIs are redefined so the supervisor appears to underperform.

- *Example:* Customer satisfaction used to be based on comprehensive post-sale surveys; now it's based solely on same-day returns—even though this reflects operational changes unrelated to the supervisor.

4. Cryptic or Irrelevant Metrics

Performance is evaluated on data that is irrelevant to the actual job or outdated.

- *Example:* A call center supervisor is evaluated on average call time without regard for demonstrated improvements in first-contact resolution and customer feedback.

Why Management Manipulates Metrics

1. **To Shift Blame:** When projects fail, management may adjust numbers to scapegoat a supervisor.
2. **To Control Behavior:** People chase goals; changing metrics manipulates priorities.
3. **To Mask Leadership Failures:** Dirty metrics obscure broader systemic issues.
4. **To Impose Power Dynamics:** Manipulated metrics reinforce hierarchy and control.

Real-World Examples

1. The Retail Turnover Trap

A retail supervisor improved store sales by 12%. Mid-review, the district manager changed the formula to subtract online transactions, making the supervisor appear to underperform. The altered metric was never shared.

2. The Hospital Readmissions Rate

A hospital ward supervisor oversaw a team that reduced readmissions. Suddenly, readmissions were counted within seven days of discharge—even though the supervisor had no control over post-discharge care—resulting in a worsened performance report.

Impact on Supervisors and Teams

- **Damaged Reputation:** When metrics are arbitrarily manipulated, the supervisor looks ineffective.
- **Loss of Motivation:** Fighting a phantom against impossible targets drains energy.
- **Eroded Trust:** Teams lose confidence in leadership when performance reporting seems arbitrary.
- **Stress and Demoralization:** Unwinnable or shifting targets generate sustained anxiety.

Strategies for Setting the Record Straight

1. Maintain Your Own Records

Keep copies of original reports, email confirmations, and historical metrics. Documentation provides context for comparison.

2. Ask for Clear Definitions

During goal-setting, clarify how metrics are calculated and documented. Request written KPIs before targets are assigned.

3. Review Metrics Regularly

Set monthly or weekly check-ins to monitor numbers. Call out any sudden changes immediately—and ask for written notification.

4. Question Inconsistencies Immediately

If you notice odd changes, ask:

"I noticed our sales goal dropped from 'Total Units Sold' to 'Units Sold In-Store'. Can you help me understand why?"

This shows proactivity—and prevents being blindsided.

5. Get Data from Multiple Sources

Validate reported numbers with independent data—shared systems, exported spreadsheets, or peer comparisons.

6. Escalate If Necessary

If you're repeatedly penalized by unexplained metric changes, bring the issue to HR or auditing. Provide the documentation of original goals and performance levels.

What Organizations Must Do

To ensure metrics are fair and transparent:

- **Publish KPI Definitions:** Make calculation methods visible to all stakeholders.
- **Freeze Targets Mid-Cycle:** Any changes must be documented and agreed upon by affected parties.
- **Include Data Audits in Reviews:** HR should review the data basis behind performance reports.
- **Provide Dispute Channels:** Allow formal challenges to metric-based feedback.

- Deming, W. E. (1986). *Out of the Crisis*. MIT Press. (On the dangers of poorly designed performance metrics.)

Summary

Manipulated metrics mask reality and sabotage honest supervisors. By demanding clarity, documenting performance, checking numbers, and challenging dubious changes, supervisors can protect their credibility. Organizations must build transparent systems that measure what matters—not what can be twisted.

Chapter 21
Favoritism Toward Select Employees

"When fairness is replaced by favoritism, trust crumbles."

You see it clearly: some get praised for the same work you do, others get perks or second chances. Favoritism isn't just unfair — it fractures team morale and sows resentment. When leaders pick favorites, they create a workplace divided by loyalty, not merit.

Introduction

Favoritism occurs when certain employees—by friendship, personal traits, or other connections—receive advantages in projects, recognition, or advancement. While occasional flexibility isn't always unfair, consistent preference erodes trust, damages morale, and marginalizes supervisors who are equally or more qualified. In this chapter, we explore how favoritism presents itself, its harmful consequences, and how supervisors and organizations can confront it constructively.

What Favoritism Looks Like

Favoritism manifests in subtle and overt ways, such as:

- **Unequal Access to Opportunities:** A favored supervisor is given high-visibility projects, while capable peers are passed over.
- **Skipping the Approval Process:** Favorites bypass standard protocols in hiring, resourcing, or budget approvals.
- **Public Praise Disparity:** Announcements and promotions highlight favorites, not those who earned it.
- **Social Privileges:** Favorites are included in leadership retreats, informal gatherings, or off-site meetings.
- **Lenient Treatment:** Favorites are forgiven for poor performance or mistakes others wouldn't get away with.

Why Favoritism Happens

While not always malicious, favoritism can arise from:

- **Personal Biases:** Connections based on hobbies, background, or personality influence decisions unconsciously.
- **Desire for Ease:** Leaders often "go with someone they trust," even if another is more competent.
- **Inadequate Oversight:** Lack of checks and transparent processes allows personal preferences to slip in.

- **Fear of Conflict:** Leaders avoid confrontations by favoring those they find agreeable.

Real-World Examples

Example 1: The LA Tech Division

In one technology firm, two supervisors were competing to lead a new AI pilot. One, a former colleague of the division director, received the project without meeting the stated criteria. The other, who had delivered similar pilots before, was told to "wait for the next round." Staff noted a drop in team spirit, feeling that decisions were arbitrary.

Example 2: Hospital Scheduling Bias

A nursing supervisor noticed that her favored colleague would always get holiday slips first and day-shift preferences. Meanwhile, she consistently filled less desirable time slots. When she raised the issue, leadership dismissed it as "just standard rotation," despite clear favoritism.

The Effects of Favoritism

1. **Supervisor Disillusionment:** Seeing others rewarded for connections, not performance, damages motivation.
2. **Team Fracturing:** Teams divide into "favored" and "unfavored," reducing trust and collaboration.
3. **Culture of Resentment:** When rules apply unevenly, morale erodes, and turnover increases.
4. **Lost Opportunity:** Talent is wasted when merit isn't rewarded; innovation suffers.

A McKinsey report (2021) found that organizations with perceived favoritism were twice as likely to have disengaged employees and reported 30% lower team performance.

Strategies for Supervisors Facing Favoritism

1. Collect Objective Evidence

Track instances when opportunities are assigned without transparent criteria. Collect documentation or witness support when favoritism is clear.

2. Seek Clarification Professionally

"I noticed Sarah was selected for the project—what criteria were used? I'd like to understand the process for similar future opportunities."

This demonstrates interest in clarity, not accusation.

3. Highlight Your Achievements

Present your contributions regularly—during team meetings, status updates, or one-on-ones. Document successful outcomes to build your case.

4. Network Broadly

Build relationships across leadership levels and departments to create your own sources of advocacy and visibility.

5. Form Peer Coalitions

If favoritism is systemic, quietly align with others who've been affected. A shared voice can encourage HR or leaders to reassess decisions.

6. Escalate When Necessary

If favoritism leads to clear inequity in promotion, resources, or respect, bring it up confidentially with HR or a trusted senior leader. Focus on fairness and business impact—not personal grievance.

What Organizations Can Do

Favoritism in the workplace isn't always intentional—but its effects are deeply felt. When leaders consistently favor certain individuals, it erodes trust, morale, and equity. The good news? Organizations can actively build cultures that prevent favoritism and promote fairness—without micromanaging or creating rigidity.

Here's how:

1. Create Transparent Opportunity Processes

Why it matters: When special assignments, promotions, or leadership roles are handed out behind closed doors, it often feels like favoritism—even if it's not.

What it looks like:

- Use open application processes for internal opportunities.
- Post criteria publicly: Who's eligible? What's required?
- Rotate high-visibility projects among capable staff—not just the "usual" people.

The impact: Everyone feels they have a shot, not just those closest to senior leaders. Transparency shows fairness is a standard, not a secret.

2. Implement Decision Audits

Why it matters: Without tracking how decisions are made, it's hard to spot patterns of bias—or fix them.

What it looks like:

- HR or leadership regularly reviews decisions about who's promoted, selected for development programs, or put on key projects.
- Look for trends: Are the same types of people always advancing? Are certain departments or backgrounds underrepresented?

The impact: These audits surface invisible barriers and help organizations adjust processes before they become unfair habits.

3. Train Leaders on Unconscious Bias

Why it matters: Even well-meaning managers can fall into bias traps—favoring those who look like them, agree with them, or are part of their informal social circles.

What it looks like:

- Offer interactive workshops on how unconscious bias shows up in evaluations, hiring, and mentoring.
- Include scenarios and reflection exercises that challenge assumptions.
- Make this part of ongoing leadership development—not a one-time checkbox.

The impact: Leaders make more thoughtful, inclusive decisions—and become more self-aware in the process.

4. Gather Regular Feedback from Employees

Why it matters: If favoritism is happening, employees often feel it long before HR or leadership notices.

What it looks like:

- Conduct anonymous pulse surveys to gauge employee perceptions of fairness, recognition, and opportunity.
- Include open-text questions like: "Do you feel advancement decisions are based on merit?"
- Use feedback to shape manager training and organizational strategy.

The impact: Employees feel heard, and leadership gets early insight into potential blind spots or culture cracks.

5. Hold Leaders Accountable for Equity

Why it matters: If inclusive behavior doesn't influence a manager's own growth, it won't be a priority.

What it looks like:

- Include metrics on fairness, team inclusion, and talent development in performance reviews.
- Reward leaders who grow diverse talent—not just those who meet financial targets.
- Make equity part of promotion criteria for managers and executives.

The impact: Fairness becomes part of leadership excellence—not an afterthought. When equity is tied to outcomes, it stops being optional.

Final Reflection

Favoritism thrives in ambiguity and silence. But organizations that prioritize transparency, feedback, and accountability can turn that tide. The result? A workplace where people are chosen for what they bring—not who they know. And that's where real leadership culture begins.

Summary: Why Fairness Matters More Than Ever

Favoritism in the workplace isn't just an uncomfortable dynamic—it's a serious obstacle to trust, performance, and morale. When certain individuals are consistently favored over others, it creates ripple effects: hardworking supervisors begin to question their worth, team members lose motivation, and resentment quietly grows beneath the surface.

For supervisors, being overlooked or sidelined despite strong performance can feel deeply personal. It's not just about recognition—it's about fairness, dignity, and the belief that effort should lead to opportunity. That's why it's essential to speak up respectfully, document inconsistencies, and, when necessary, raise concerns through the right channels. Doing so isn't just about self-advocacy—it's about helping to build a culture where all voices matter.

Organizations, in turn, have a responsibility to take favoritism seriously. This means designing transparent processes, providing equal access to growth opportunities, and holding leaders accountable for equitable treatment. When fairness becomes part of the system—not just a talking point—people feel safe to contribute, innovate, and grow.

At its core, fairness is not a "nice to have." It's foundational to a healthy workplace where everyone, regardless of personality or proximity to power, has a chance to thrive.

Chapter 22
Excluded from Networking and Visibility Opportunities

"Out of sight means out of mind — and out of the running."

The right connections open doors. But when you're left out of key meetings, social events, or mentorship, those doors stay closed. Exclusion from networking is a quiet career killer. Without visibility, your talents remain hidden, your potential overlooked.

Introduction

Networking is the invisible thread that weaves together career advancement, visibility, and opportunity. For supervisors, being kept out of networking events—both formal and informal—is more than a minor inconvenience; it limits access to mentors, critical information, and relationships essential for success. Feeling excluded sends a message: you are not trusted enough to shape the future. In this chapter, we'll explore how this exclusion occurs, its true impact, and strategies supervisors and organizations can use to build inclusive cultures.

How Networking Exclusion Happens

Exclusion from networking can arise in both overt and subtle ways:

1. **Invitation Bias**
2. Network events—executive luncheons, off-sites, or social gatherings—often exclude certain supervisors without transparent selection criteria.
3. **Selective Visibility**
4. Leadership shares info and opportunities only with their favorites, bypassing others.
5. **Unshared Knowledge**
6. Key informal channels, such as hallway conversations or internal groups, often exclude supervisors, despite the vital lessons shared there.
7. **Event Scheduling Decisions**
8. Workshops or after-hour meetups are scheduled when some supervisors can't attend (due to family or personal reasons), and are treated as essential career-building steps.

Why Networking Access Matters

- **Visibility and Sponsorship**
- Informal interactions often lead to sponsor relationships, which are essential for promotions and strategic projects.
- **Access to Information**

- News travels informally—through lunch chats or corridor conversations. Missing this means missing critical context.
- **Career Development**
- Networking helps supervisors learn best practices, hear about new roles, and build confidence by seeing peers recognized.
- **Connection is Confidence**
- When deprived of peer networks, supervisors feel isolated, undervalued, and disconnected from organizational culture.

Real-World Examples

Case 1: The Hidden Leadership Meeting

At a non-profit organization, a "strategy lunch" was organized for upcoming campaign directors. A high-performing supervisor was skipped, despite being directly involved in campaign strategy. She only learned about the lunch after it took place—along with insider connections she didn't know existed.

Case 2: The After-Hours Omission

A tech firm hosted monthly "mentor mixers" in the office lounge after 6:00 p.m. Supervisors with young children were unable to attend. Hi-liners assumed that mixing wasn't critical for career paths—leading to unspoken bias in promotions.

Impacts of Exclusion

Exclusion in the workplace—especially when it affects supervisors—doesn't just bruise egos. It can quietly dismantle morale, distort opportunities, and create invisible walls across teams. Here's how the effects show up across individuals, teams, and entire organizations:

On Supervisors

- **Lowered Morale and Lack of Belonging**
- When supervisors are left out of meetings, updates, or decisions that affect their teams, it sends a clear message: *You're not essential.* Over time, this erodes confidence and chips away at a sense of purpose. Even high-performing leaders may begin to feel invisible, undervalued, or disconnected from the larger mission.
- **Reduced Ability to Influence Decisions**
- Supervisors serve as critical bridges between frontline teams and leadership. Exclusion limits their ability to raise concerns, provide insights from the field, or shape decisions that impact operations. This weakens both their influence and the quality of the decisions being made.
- **Hindered Access to Unspoken Organizational Knowledge**
- So much of what drives success in an organization isn't in a handbook—it's in hallway conversations, informal networks, and "who you know." Excluded supervisors miss this

unspoken context, making it harder for them to navigate culture, anticipate changes, or align their teams effectively.

- **Missed Promotion or Project Opportunities**
- Supervisors who are out of the loop often miss the chance to raise their hands for high-visibility projects or development pathways. When leadership doesn't see or hear from them regularly, they're less likely to be considered for advancement—even if their results are strong.

On Teams

- **Managerial Isolation Filters Down**
- When a supervisor feels excluded or sidelined, that disconnect often trickles down to the team. Employees may feel less informed, more uncertain, or sense that their manager lacks the authority to act decisively. Over time, this breeds frustration and confusion at the frontline.
- **Reduced Ability to Advocate for Their Teams**
- Supervisors play a vital advocacy role. They secure resources, resolve cross-functional issues, and push for recognition. But they can't do that if they're not in the room. Exclusion weakens their ability to fight for their teams and stalls problem-solving across departments.

On Organizations

- **Cultures Fracture into Insular Groups**
- When some leaders are looped in and others are left out, silos form. These informal power circles often reinforce inequality, create turf wars, and make collaboration harder. Instead of one unified culture, you end up with inner rings and outer rings.
- **Leaders Are Promoted Based on Who They Know, Not What They Know**
- Favoritism often hides behind exclusion. When promotions depend on visibility and relationships instead of results, the organization rewards familiarity over merit. That undermines credibility and leaves top talent disillusioned—or walking out the door.
- **Innovation Suffers When Information Is Unevenly Shared**
- Innovation thrives when ideas and insights move freely across levels. But when only a select few hold key information, creativity stalls. Valuable ideas from frontline teams and their supervisors never surface, simply because the communication channels aren't open or inclusive.

Exclusion may start subtly—skipped meetings, missing context—but its long-term effects are profound. A healthy organization depends on transparency, access, and the belief that everyone's voice matters—especially those tasked with leading others.

What Supervisors Can Do

Exclusion often isn't intentional—but the effects are still real. For supervisors, especially those not part of upper leadership circles, it can feel like essential conversations and connections are happening without them. Here's how you can take initiative—without seeming pushy—to become more visible and involved.

1. Raise Awareness—Tactfully

Sometimes, people don't even realize they're excluding others. A gentle, respectful nudge can go a long way.

Try saying:

"I heard about the strategy lunch—sounds like a great conversation. I'd love to join next time. How can we make those spaces more inclusive for all supervisors?"

This signals interest without blame and subtly highlights the need for broader access.

2. Schedule Your Own Network Events

You don't need to wait for leadership to create a connection. Host a 30-minute roundtable, coffee session, or virtual meetup just for fellow supervisors.

This builds a sense of community, strengthens horizontal relationships, and gives you a chance to support each other—even across departments or shifts.

3. Use Mentorship Requests to Signal Engagement

If you're seeking growth, don't be afraid to ask a senior leader to mentor or guide you.

When you initiate these relationships, it shows that you're proactive—and helps put you on the radar for future opportunities.

You might say:

"I admire how you lead strategic initiatives. I'd appreciate 30 minutes of your time sometime to learn from your experience."

4. Build Peer Networks

Create informal spaces where you and your fellow supervisors can regularly check in.

Coffee chats, walking meetings, or even short "Monday catch-ups" can keep you connected, reduce isolation, and help you navigate challenges together.

These small moments build immense trust over time.

5. Make Your Involvement Visible

If you're invited to a high-level meeting, training, or event—share what you learned with others.

This reinforces your presence, strengthens peer ties, and shows that you're part of a larger leadership conversation.

Being seen *sharing* knowledge is just as important as being seen in the room.

What Organizations Can Do

Creating equitable access to informal and formal networking opportunities is not just a "nice to have"—it's essential for developing and retaining diverse, capable leaders. Here's how organizations can do better:

1. Set Objective Invitation Policies

Be intentional about how people are selected for events, lunches, off-sites, or stretch assignments.

Instead of inviting "favorites," create clear guidelines:

- All supervisors after one year of service
- One rep per department, rotating each quarter
- Or open sign-up based on interest

Transparency prevents cliques and builds trust.

2. Schedule Inclusively

Plan events at varied times of day and with flexible formats. Not everyone can attend a 7:30 a.m. breakfast or a 6 p.m. happy hour.

Consider:

- Rotating time zones
- Offering virtual or hybrid options
- Avoiding exclusion of caregivers or remote staff

Being flexible shows respect for diverse lives.

3. Create Open Social Spaces

Don't make networking a special occasion—make it part of the routine.

Examples:

- 15-minute "connection corners" before meetings

- Monthly supervisor lunch tables
- Open calendar slots where anyone can join a leader for a coffee chat

Everyday moments can foster lasting relationships.

4. Promote Peer-to-Peer Networking

Support supervisor-only forums or project-based cohorts where peers can connect and collaborate. This allows supervisors to learn from one another, swap strategies, and grow together—without relying solely on senior leadership to drive engagement.

5. Track Participation and Feedback

You can't improve what you don't measure.

- Regularly analyze who's attending visibility events, getting stretch roles, or joining mentorship programs. Then ask:

- Are all departments and demographics represented?
- Do people *feel* included?

Annual inclusion surveys or focus groups can surface blind spots early.

Final Thought

Inclusion in networking isn't just about events—it's about access, visibility, and shared belonging. When supervisors feel seen, connected, and supported, they lead with more confidence—and that energy flows to every team they manage.

Chapter Summary: Reclaiming Connection Through Fair Access

Being excluded from networking opportunities isn't just about missing a lunch or a chat by the coffee machine—it's about missing crucial moments where relationships form, decisions get made, and careers quietly move forward. For supervisors, these missed moments can have lasting impacts: promotions delayed, voices unheard, and confidence quietly chipped away.

This kind of exclusion often isn't deliberate—but the effects are real. When certain people are consistently left out, others are unintentionally elevated, creating a two-tier system where access, visibility, and advancement rely more on who you know than what you contribute. That erodes trust and stifles innovation, as the same voices continue to dominate the same discussions.

But there is a better way.

Supervisors can take small, meaningful steps to build their own visibility—by speaking up, creating peer networks, and advocating for inclusion. These aren't just professional strategies—they're acts of self-respect and leadership.

At the same time, organizations must stop leaving connections to chance. Fair networking systems don't rely on favoritism, popularity, or informal power dynamics. They are intentional, transparent, and equitable—designed to bring in a wide range of perspectives and ensure every supervisor has not just a seat at the table, but an authentic voice in the conversation.

Because when networking is inclusive, it doesn't just benefit individuals—it uplifts teams, strengthens leadership, and builds a culture where everyone has room to grow.

Chapter 23
Achievements Ignored or Unrecognized

"Silence in place of praise speaks volumes about what they value."

You nailed a tough project, saved the team from disaster, or exceeded every goal. Yet, no one says a word. Ignoring achievements isn't oversight — it's a strategy to minimize your worth. Recognition is more than a pat on the back; it's proof that you belong and matter.

Introduction

Recognition is more than a pat on the back—it's confirmation that your work matters and signals respect, trust, and motivation. Yet many supervisors face the frustrating reality of achievements being overlooked or taken for granted. When success is ignored, it chips away at confidence, undermines morale, and discourages continued excellence. This chapter explores how the absence of recognition manifests, why it's damaging, and how supervisors and organizations can restore a culture of appreciation.

How Lack of Recognition Happens

Even high-performing supervisors can go unnoticed—not because they aren't doing great work, but because recognition isn't baked into the culture. Here's how it often shows up:

1. Silent Celebrations

A major deadline is met. A tough project wraps up. Metrics improve. But no one pauses to say, "Well done." No email, no shout-out, no moment of shared pride. When wins aren't acknowledged, they start to feel invisible—even to the person who achieved them.

"It's like shouting into the wind—did anyone even notice?"

2. Credit to Others

Sometimes, supervisors do the heavy lifting—but someone else, often higher up or more vocal, gets the praise. Whether intentional or not, the impact stings. It quietly tells the contributor: your voice, your presence, didn't carry weight in the room.

"That was my idea... but I watched someone else get the handshake."

3. Belittling Acknowledgment

A simple "thanks" can lift someone's spirits—but a dismissive comment like, *"Well, that's your job,"* or *"I expected no less,"* can flatten enthusiasm. When effort is met with minimization, it sends the message that going above and beyond isn't really valued.

"It felt like nothing I did would ever be good enough to notice."

4. Selective Applause

Certain teams or projects always seem to be in the spotlight—often those closer to senior leadership. Meanwhile, quietly critical work gets overlooked. When recognition feels political or popularity-driven, trust erodes.

"They always recognize the flashy stuff, never the foundational work."

5. One-Time Praise, No Follow-Up

You might get a "great job" on launch day—but then nothing. No follow-up, no mention in reviews, no added opportunities. Praise that doesn't translate into growth, visibility, or rewards can feel hollow.

"It was a pat on the back—then back to business, like it never happened."

Why Recognition Matters

Recognition isn't just about feeling good—it's about being seen, respected, and given the energy to keep leading well. Here's why it makes a difference:

• Motivation & Engagement

Supervisors are often driving performance from behind the scenes. When their work is acknowledged, it fuels them. Positive reinforcement is a well-documented psychological driver—people repeat the behaviors they feel are valued.

"That one thank-you note kept me going all month."

• Credibility & Influence

When a supervisor's successes are visible to others, it enhances their reputation and influence across the organization. Recognition isn't just appreciation—it's social proof. It builds trust with teams and earns respect from peers and leaders.

"When leaders see your name tied to results, they start listening differently."

• **Retention**

People don't just leave bad jobs—they leave when they feel invisible. A Gallup study found employees who feel recognized are nearly **3x more likely** to stay. For supervisors, especially, consistent recognition helps prevent quiet burnout.

"I didn't need a trophy—I just needed to know it mattered to someone."

• **Team Inspiration**

Recognition is contagious. When a supervisor is appreciated, it sets a tone of gratitude and momentum. Teams feel proud, more connected, and more likely to go the extra mile when they see their leader valued.

"When they celebrated my work, my whole team felt lifted."

Real-World Examples

1. The Launch No One Noticed

Dan, senior operations supervisor, led a three-month process improvement that reduced cycle time by 25%. Despite clear savings and praise from the client, upper management made no mention in company-wide communications. Dan's initiative lacked visibility, slowing future support for his team.

2. Parachute Recognition

Maria, coding supervisor, submitted a new feature update that earned industry acclaim. Yet she discovered a manager took the credit in a press release without naming her or her team. The omission created frustration across her department.

Why Recognition Doesn't Happen

Even when people do excellent work, it doesn't always get seen—or appreciated. Recognition is often assumed to be automatic, but in reality, many small (and big) factors get in the way. Here's why it slips through the cracks:

• **Leadership Oversight**

Sometimes it's not intentional—it's just that leaders are overwhelmed. With calendars packed, goals stacking up, and urgent issues constantly demanding attention, even well-meaning leaders forget to pause and say, "Thank you" or "Great work."

"It's not that they didn't care—they just never said it. I was quietly hoping they'd notice, but the moment passed."

Without systems that prompt leaders to reflect on and reward contributions, recognition becomes sporadic—and some people are left wondering if what they did really mattered.

• Visibility Gaps

Not all great work happens in the spotlight. Roles like logistics, compliance, tech support, or shift supervision often run behind the scenes—and when things go smoothly, that effort becomes invisible. The irony is: the better you do your job, the less people notice.

"The project didn't stall, the process didn't break—and that's because of me. But all they saw was silence, not success."

If leaders only recognize the "loud wins" (like flashy sales numbers or high-profile launches), they unintentionally ignore the backbone work that keeps the organization functioning.

• Culture Doesn't Encourage It

Some workplaces operate with a "no news is good news" mindset. The culture leans heavily toward fixing problems instead of celebrating progress. Recognition is seen as optional, fluffy, or even "unprofessional."

"You only heard something if you messed up. But when you pulled off something tough? Just silence."

Over time, this kind of environment drains morale and makes people feel replaceable, not respected. It signals that excellence is expected—but not celebrated.

• Managerial Bias

In some teams, praise isn't based on performance—it's based on preference. Managers might repeatedly acknowledge the same few people they feel closest to, while others are sidelined, regardless of their work quality.

"I trained the new hire, fixed the process, and hit my goals—but the person who goes out to lunch with the boss got all the credit."

When recognition is tied to relationships instead of results, it breeds resentment and erodes trust—especially for supervisors trying to lead by example.

The Takeaway

Lack of recognition doesn't mean the work wasn't valuable—it often means the system (or the people in it) didn't have the time, tools, or awareness to reflect it back. That's why both individual advocacy and organizational change matter: to ensure great work isn't just done—it's seen, appreciated, and built upon.

What Supervisors Can Do

1. **Track Wins Methodically**
2. Sometimes, great work gets forgotten—not because it didn't matter, but because no one wrote it down. Keep a simple log of your team's achievements: completed projects, resolved issues, and positive feedback from peers or clients. Even small wins, when documented consistently, tell a powerful story over time. Mention these casually in check-ins or end-of-week summaries. It's not about bragging—it's about making sure hard work is visible.
3. **Celebrate Internally**
4. You don't need a trophy to make someone feel seen. A quick thank-you in a team meeting or a message in a group chat can go a long way. When you regularly acknowledge your team's contributions, you create a ripple effect—others feel appreciated, morale improves, and it becomes easier for everyone to recognize good work. It also models the kind of behavior you want to see in your organization.
5. **Create Upward Visibility**
6. Leaders are often juggling too much to notice everything. Make it easier for them. Use quick updates like, "Just wanted to share—we hit our onboarding targets a week early" or "Our team just completed the Q3 report with 10% fewer errors than last quarter." These short highlights don't just inform—they remind your manager that you and your team are making a difference.
7. **Share Success Stories**
8. Don't let accomplishments live in isolation. Write a quick summary after a major project—what went well, what was learned, and who contributed. These can be shared in internal newsletters, dashboards, or even just a hallway conversation. Framing your work as a story helps others see its value more clearly.
9. **Ask for Feedback and Spread the Credit**
10. After a big effort, ask your team and leaders: "What do you think went well? Who deserves a shout-out?" This gives others a voice in the recognition process and helps you highlight contributions you might've missed. It also reinforces a culture where appreciation is shared—not hoarded.

What Organizations Can Do

1. **Establish Recognition Rituals**
2. If praise only happens during annual reviews, it's not enough. Build rituals that make appreciation part of the rhythm of work—weekly wins emails, monthly "shout-out" boards, team huddles that begin with a highlight. Rituals make recognition predictable, visible, and culturally expected.
3. **Train Leaders on Celebratory Leadership**
4. Some managers simply weren't taught how to recognize others effectively. Provide training that focuses on how to give authentic, timely praise. Help them understand that recognition isn't just a "nice to have"—it's a core leadership skill that motivates people, builds loyalty, and strengthens team performance.
5. **Tie Recognition to Performance Reviews**

6. Want to make it matter? Make it measurable. When reviewing supervisors, assess not just what they achieved, but how they elevated others. Did they celebrate team wins? Did they foster a culture of gratitude? Linking recognition to formal evaluation signals that it's valued by the organization.

7. **Make Visibility Part of the Job**

8. Some roles, like compliance or quality control, operate behind the scenes—so their wins are less visible. Help departments connect their work to broader outcomes. For example, "Because of your early QA process, the product shipped with zero defects." Everyone should be able to see how their work contributes to success.

9. **Measure Recognition Culture**

10. Data helps. Simple pulse surveys asking, "Have you felt appreciated at work this month?" or "Do your efforts get acknowledged by your manager?" can surface blind spots and patterns. Recognition should feel like a shared experience—not a random perk that only a few receive.

These practices, when combined, create a workplace where people don't just work hard—they **feel valued for it**. And that changes everything—from morale, to retention, to performance.

Chapter Summary: Why Recognition Matters More Than You Think

Sometimes, **the absence of recognition** can feel heavier than direct criticism. When no one acknowledges your effort, it chips away at your motivation and confidence. It sends a quiet, but powerful message: "What you did doesn't matter." Over time, that message erodes joy, stifles momentum, and leaves even high-performing supervisors wondering if they should bother going the extra mile again.

For supervisors, this isn't just a personal issue—it affects how they lead. When recognition is missing, it's harder to keep morale high, model appreciation for others, or feel connected to the bigger mission. That's why one of the most empowering things supervisors can do is **track wins**, celebrate progress (even the small stuff), and make sure successes are visible—not just to their teams, but to leadership as well.

But supervisors can't carry the entire burden alone. **Organizations have a responsibility** to build a culture where appreciation isn't left to chance. That means creating real systems—**consistent rituals, intentional habits, and shared expectations**—that ensure people are seen when they do meaningful work. Whether it's through structured recognition programs or informal shoutouts during meetings, every gesture counts.

Ultimately, celebrating contributions isn't just about being "nice." It's about **strategy, retention, and human connection**. When people feel valued, they stay longer, perform better, and bring their best selves to the table. A workplace that shines a light on its wins doesn't just feel better—it works better.

Chapter 24
Training and Development Withheld

"Growth requires opportunity — and sometimes, those are denied."

The world changes fast. Without training or development, skills stagnate, and so do careers. When opportunities to learn are withheld, it's not just about missing out on growth — it's a way to keep you stuck, dependent, and easily replaced.

Introduction

Training and professional development are essential to both career advancement and the ability to perform effectively in a leadership role. Yet, many supervisors find themselves locked out of these opportunities—passed over for leadership courses, conference attendance, or specialized training. When development is blocked, it's not merely frustrating: it stunts potential, diminishes skillsets, and signals that the organization does not truly value the individual's growth. This chapter explores why this happens, how it impacts supervisors and teams, and what can be done about it.

How Development Blockades Occur

Development can be blocked in various forms:

1. **Overlooking Eligibility**
   - Supervisors are not considered for leadership programs despite long service or high performance.
   - Example: Kelly, who has led her team for two years, was not invited to a mentoring circle open to others at her level.
2. **Resource Constraints as an Excuse**
   - Budget cuts are used to justify excluding certain supervisors from training, without transparency.
   - Example: In a hospitality chain, managers claimed they lacked funds for workshops—but later booked executives to attend.
3. **Informal Gatekeeping**
   - Access is granted only to favorites or those with personal ties to decision-makers.
   - Example: Only supervisors from one department were asked to attend conference sessions, without any formal criteria.
4. **Last-Minute Withholding**
   - Invitations are rescinded or postponed, citing workload or timing issues.
   - Example: Just before a training week, John was told he "might be needed" on the warehouse floor, so he was taken off the attendee list.

These occurrences may appear isolated—but together they form a pattern of blocked development.

Why It's Important

Development isn't a luxury—it's a necessity. When supervisors are denied opportunities to grow, the effects ripple far beyond one individual. Here's why supporting their learning and advancement truly matters:

• **Performance Limitations**

When supervisors aren't given access to training, coaching, or skill-building opportunities, it becomes harder for them to do their jobs well—especially in fast-changing environments. Whether it's new technology, leadership methods, or compliance expectations, today's workplaces demand continuous learning. Without it, supervisors can feel overwhelmed or out of step, unable to lead change or offer solid mentorship to their teams confidently. It's like asking someone to run a marathon without training them first.

• **Career Frustration**

Imagine watching peers move forward—taking on new challenges, gaining visibility, and receiving promotions—while you're stuck in place, not because you lack potential, but because development wasn't offered to you. That kind of stagnation breeds disappointment, disengagement, and even resentment. Talented supervisors may start to question their value or future at the organization, and that emotional toll builds quietly until they decide to leave.

• **Team Impact**

When a supervisor isn't supported in their own growth, their team feels it too. Supervisors who aren't current with new practices or leadership strategies may struggle to help others develop or adapt. This can result in missed opportunities for innovation, slower adoption of new initiatives, and teams that fall behind—not because of lack of effort, but because of lack of updated guidance.

• **Cultural Message**

When an organization deprioritizes supervisor development—or treats it as something earned only by a select few—it sends an implicit message: *"You're not worth investing in."* That message doesn't just affect individuals; it undermines trust, inclusion, and equity across the board. Development should be seen as a right tied to the role—not a reward for being favored or perfectly polished.

Bottom line:

When development is blocked, people stop raising their hands. They stop dreaming bigger, taking risks, or speaking up. That means potential gets silenced—not because it doesn't exist, but because it wasn't nurtured. For organizations committed to long-term success, investing in supervisor growth isn't optional—it's strategic and deeply human.

Real-World Examples

Example 1: International Conference Snub

Sarah, head of quality, had consistently improved departmental standards but was not included in a cross-region conference attended by other leaders. She only discovered the event when photos appeared in internal newsletters.

Example 2: Virtual Training Bumped

During a remote learning week, Raj was enrolled in a digital leadership program but was removed due to "urgent project needs." Meanwhile, his peers remained enrolled, and the program proceeded.

Example 3: Selective Budgeting

In a manufacturing company that is tightening training budgets, Maria's request to attend a workshop on new compliance standards was rejected due to "limited seats." Yet, two seats went unused in her supervisor's peer group.

Impact on Individuals and Teams

When professional development isn't prioritized or equitably offered, the impact doesn't stay confined to a single supervisor. It affects morale, performance, and the future of entire teams. Here's how:

• Skill Obsolescence

Leadership today isn't what it was even five years ago. New technologies, cultural shifts, remote team dynamics, and evolving compliance standards all require updated tools and approaches. When supervisors aren't offered training, they can feel left behind—like they're using yesterday's map for today's terrain. Over time, this gap in knowledge creates real challenges: they may hesitate to take initiative, feel uncertain in meetings, or struggle to guide their teams effectively. Not because they lack talent—but because no one gave them the updated tools.

• Burnout

When you're trying to lead without the skills or resources to do it confidently, everything takes more effort. Supervisors in this position often feel like they're in a constant state of catch-up—putting in long hours just to stay afloat. The stress of feeling underprepared, unsupported, and constantly behind wears people down. Over time, this leads to emotional exhaustion, reduced motivation, and that familiar, heavy question: *"Am I even cut out for this anymore?"* In reality, they're not failing—the system is.

• Inequality and Demoralization

When some supervisors are regularly selected for leadership programs, certifications, or visibility-building projects—and others aren't—it sends a silent but powerful message about who is valued. Over time, this creates divisions between departments or individuals: those who are "in the loop" and those who feel left out. Teams begin to question fairness, leading to mistrust, resentment, and disengagement. The damage isn't always loud—but it runs deep.

• Retention Risk

People don't leave jobs just because of workload—they often leave because they stop seeing a future. When supervisors are denied growth opportunities year after year, they begin to look elsewhere. It's not always about chasing a promotion—it's about wanting to learn, contribute meaningfully, and feel like their work is part of something bigger. When that hunger is ignored, organizations risk losing some of their most loyal and capable leaders.

Bottom line:

Growth is fuel—for individuals and for the teams they lead. When development is blocked or distributed unfairly, it doesn't just slow people down—it dims their spark. And when that happens across a team or organization, momentum stalls, trust erodes, and progress suffers.

Strategies for Supervisors

When access to development feels out of reach, it's easy to assume that it's personal—or permanent. But it doesn't have to be. With the right approach, supervisors can advocate for fair learning opportunities in ways that are both respectful and effective.

1. Track and Request Systematically

Sometimes being left out of training is accidental. Other times, it's a pattern. The best way to address either is with facts, not frustration.

Start a personal **development log**: note the dates of trainings you've attended (or missed), what topics you'd like to explore, and how they connect to your current role. Then schedule time with your manager and say something like:

"I noticed I wasn't included in the last leadership cohort. I'd really like to be part of the next one. Could we talk about how to get on that track?"

It shows professionalism, not complaint, and helps you get on their radar.

2. Propose Alternatives

Not every company has a big training budget or bandwidth for in-person seminars. That doesn't mean development has to stop.

Supervisors can suggest **cost-effective or flexible formats**, like:

- Webinars or recorded sessions
- Peer-to-peer learning circles
- Lunch-and-learns hosted internally
- Online certifications

By offering solutions instead of just pointing out the problem, you position yourself as resourceful and ready to grow—without placing extra burden on leadership.

3. Leverage Internal Networks

Just because you missed a session doesn't mean you have to miss the learning. Reach out to peers who *were* included:

"Hey, I heard you attended the conflict resolution workshop—any chance you'd want to grab coffee and share a few takeaways?"

This not only helps you stay sharp but also builds trust and camaraderie across teams. Knowledge-sharing is a leadership trait in itself.

4. Advocate for Role-Based Learning

If leadership training feels like a "nice-to-have" to others, reframe it as a **business advantage**.

For example:

"If I attend this customer service metrics training, I can bring back a system to track response time across our team. It could help reduce ticket backlog."

Link your learning request to cost savings, efficiency, improved morale, or better service. When you show how training benefits more than just you, it's easier for others to say yes.

5. Escalate Tactfully if Needed

If you've repeatedly raised your hand for growth and keep being overlooked without explanation, it may be time to escalate—but with professionalism and poise.

You might say:

"I want to raise a concern respectfully. I've expressed interest in development multiple times, and I haven't had a clear pathway forward. I'm committed to this role and want to contribute more—could we discuss how to ensure access to learning is fairly distributed?"

This centers your intention (growth, contribution) and avoids blame. Escalation isn't about creating conflict—it's about creating clarity.

Final Thought:

You don't need to wait for someone else to hand you a development path. With a bit of strategy and courage, you can help create one—and open the door for others, too.

What Organizations Should Do

Supervisors are the backbone of day-to-day operations—but many feel forgotten when it comes to development opportunities. If organizations want to retain capable, motivated leaders, they must build growth into the system. That means not just offering training—but ensuring it's fair, visible, and meaningful.

1. Establish Clear Development Paths

Professional growth shouldn't feel like a guessing game. When expectations are unclear, it leaves room for confusion and favoritism. Organizations need to **make development part of the job**, not just a bonus for those who ask.

- Define the leadership skills and competencies required at each level.
- Clarify what training or milestones are needed for advancement.
- Make it clear how a supervisor moves from "good at the job" to "ready for the next step."

When development is structured, everyone knows the goal—and how to get there.

2. Ensure Equitable Access

All supervisors deserve a shot at learning—not just the most visible, vocal, or connected ones.

- Set **transparent criteria** for selecting participants for leadership programs.
- Rotate opportunities so supervisors across departments, shifts, and locations get equal chances.
- Create application processes that allow interested employees to self-nominate or express interest.

Access shouldn't depend on who's in the room when decisions are made. Equity means **opportunity is intentional and inclusive**.

3. Prioritize Budget Allocation

Training is often the first thing to go when budgets are tight—but that short-term thinking leads to long-term leadership gaps.

- Protect a portion of the training budget specifically for frontline and mid-level leaders.
- If external training isn't feasible, invest in internal facilitators or digital resources.
- View development not as a luxury—but as an essential part of business continuity.

Even small investments in growth send a powerful message: *We believe in your future here.*

4. Formalize Peer Learning

Not all development requires formal courses. Some of the most potent growth happens through connection.

- Launch **peer mentoring** between new and experienced supervisors.
- Host informal "lunch and learn" sessions where staff share lessons from recent challenges.
- Rotate who leads sessions so a variety of voices are heard—not just the usual ones.

When knowledge-sharing is built into the culture, learning becomes a daily practice—not an annual event.

5. Monitor and Report

Tracking who gets development—and who doesn't—helps prevent unconscious bias from shaping opportunity.

- Collect data on training attendance by team, role, gender, shift, or other relevant demographics.
- Review who is promoted, how long it takes, and whether training access played a role.
- Share results transparently and use them to improve programs and close gaps.

If one group is consistently underrepresented, it's a sign to dig deeper—not look away. Accountability leads to equity.

In Short:

Organizations can't leave supervisor development to chance. By building **intentional, transparent, and inclusive systems**, they grow stronger leaders—and send a clear message: *You matter here, and your growth matters too.*

Chapter Summary: When Growth Is Denied

Being excluded from training and development opportunities doesn't just slow someone down—it sends a message, loud and clear: *You don't matter as much here.* For a frontline or mid-level supervisor who's putting in the work, solving daily challenges, and guiding a team, this can be disheartening and deeply personal.

The impact goes beyond skills—it touches confidence, engagement, and future potential. When others around you are growing, gaining certifications, or being mentored while you're standing still, it's hard not to wonder: *What did I do wrong? Or am I just invisible?*

For organizations, the cost of this invisibility is steep. Denying growth doesn't just hurt the individual—it weakens the entire system. Innovation slows. Morale dips. Promising leaders leave.

And equity takes a hit when some groups—especially women, shift workers, or underrepresented staff—are repeatedly overlooked.

But change is possible. Supervisors can take a proactive role by tracking their needs, asking for support, and finding creative ways to keep learning—such as peer groups, webinars, and internal mentorship. And organizations? They have the power to reimagine what development looks like. By creating **clear pathways, fair selection processes, and intentional support structures**, companies can show that leadership potential exists everywhere—not just in the loudest or most visible corners.

Growth shouldn't be a privilege—it should be a promise.

When learning becomes accessible, visible, and equitable, everyone benefits: the individual, the team, and the culture as a whole. It's not just about training supervisors—it's about building the future of leadership, one opportunity at a time.

Part IV: Personal Invasions and Boundaries Crossed

When your private life and dignity are no longer respected.

Chapter 25
Harassment Involving Family or Personal Life

"Attacking who you love is the cruelest form of workplace abuse."

Harassment that crosses into your personal life cuts deeper than anything professional. Threats or insults aimed at your family or private relationships invade your sense of safety and dignity. It's a calculated attempt to destabilize and control beyond the office walls.

Introduction

Our personal and family life should be a sanctuary. But for some supervisors, it becomes a battleground where upper management or colleagues intrude—questioning parental choices, mocking family circumstances, or imposing unrealistic schedules that ignore caregiving needs. This form of harassment breaches personal boundaries, affects mental and emotional well-being, and undermines professional performance. In this chapter, we'll explore how such harassment appears, its real impact, and ways for supervisors and organizations to confront it with dignity and resolve.

What This Harassment Looks Like

When workplace conversations cross the line, they don't just sting—they reveal a kind of judgment that sends a message: "your personal life doesn't belong here." Here's how that shows up:

1. Inappropriate Comments

• "You've got kids; you couldn't possibly manage this project."

• "Single moms don't have time to lead."

These types of remarks reduce complex lives to unfair assumptions. When someone's work is evaluated not by skill or impact, but by their family structure, it stings on both professional and personal levels. It jolts your identity and communicates that your worth at work is conditional—based on who you are at home.

2. Unrealistic Scheduling Expectations

• Assigning important tasks after traditional work hours—or scheduling 6 AM meetings—without consideration of caregiving responsibilities.

It's not just the timing—it's the expectation. When managers schedule non-urgent meetings without flexibility, they're implying that everyone can—and should—drop everything for work. It forces people to choose between doing well at home and doing well at work, and that's a choice no one should have to make.

3. Mocking Caregiving Choices

• Ridicule over "leaving early for daycare," taking elder-care leave, or working part-time.

These remarks trivialize valid life choices. When someone's caregiving decisions become a punchline, it sends the message that their personal responsibilities are somehow a barrier—and not a normal, acceptable part of working life.

4. Unwarranted Inquiries

• Repeated, probing questions—about divorce, illness, childcare—that have nothing to do with job performance.

Inquiring about personal circumstances—when not directly relevant—can feel invasive. It can transform a supervisor's private life into open territory for judgment, gossip, or office snark. It sends a clear signal that you're under surveillance, not supported.

5. Punitive Measures

• Denying remote work requests, imposing rigid hours, or denying training because "you're always away" for family reasons.

These behaviors punish responsibility rather than support it. When caregiving is treated as a liability, the organization effectively discourages honesty. It pressures people to hide parts of their lives—or risk losing professional growth and opportunity.

Why It Matters

Taken together, these actions do more than disrupt work—they chip away at dignity, trust, and inclusion:

- **They signal** that who you are outside the office doesn't count.
- **They build pressure**, making you question whether your personal life or your career should come first.
- **They fracture trust** between managers, teams, and the organization.

Many well-meaning companies overlook these behaviors—or dismiss them as "tough work culture." However, the emotional cost is high: burnout, turnover, and the lost contributions of people who feel forced to choose between their families and their careers.

What You Should Do

- Note the pattern—track comments and decisions that feel discriminatory.

- Speak to a trusted mentor, HR representative, or peer to explore what boundaries feel reasonable.
- If possible, have a direct, respectful conversation with the person involved: "I want you to know that my caregiving schedule is important—I'd appreciate planning meetings that respect that."
- If the behavior doesn't change, escalate with documentation, asking for cadenced accommodations or anti-harassment training to address the culture.

Setting boundaries matters. So does building a workplace where "family-friendly" isn't a nice-to-have—but a fundamental value.

Why It Matters

- **Erodes Trust:** It sends a message that "who you are" is secondary to "what you are at work."
- **Drains Mental Well-being: Supervisors internalize guilt, shame, or exhaustion,** leading to stress and burnout.
- **Discourages Diversity:** When careers suffer due to family commitments, organizations lose diverse perspectives and talent.
- **Damages Reputation:** Harassment over personal life breeds disengagement and accelerates turnover—especially of caregivers and marginalized groups.

Studies from the *Canadian Mental Health Association* show that discriminatory remarks related to family responsibilities contribute significantly to work-related stress and depression.

Real-World Examples

Example 1: Afternoon Meeting Penalty

A retail supervisor casually mentioned her kids in a team update. The response? The next month's schedule landed her on **mandatory late shifts every Friday**. When she asked for some flexibility, leadership implied her priorities were out of line.

The result: Her team's morale dropped. Retention suffered. They felt punished for caring, creating distrust and burnout.

Example 2: Jokes About Choosing Kids Over Career

In a staff meeting, a supervisor recently back from parental leave tried to contribute. A colleague smirked: "Do you still have time for work now that you're a parent?" The room laughed—she froze.

Inside: She felt humiliated and began questioning whether her leadership potential was still taken seriously.

Impact on Supervisors and Teams

- **Personal Well-Being Eroded**
- Facing jokes, guilt-trips, or schedule penalties related to family life causes anxiety, distraction, and defensive guilt. It steals focus from work—and peace of mind from home.
- **Work Performance Effects**
- Supervisors under this pressure skip breaks, rush tasks, and avoid professional development—worried that time-based commitments will "prove" their priorities lie elsewhere.
- **Team Disillusionment**
- Team members watch their respected leader get "punished" for asking for reasonable accommodation. It breeds cynicism: "If that can happen to them, what about me?"
- **Cultural Decay**
- When intrusive scheduling or mockery is tolerated, it becomes "just how we do things." The values of respect, trust, and diversity quietly erode from the inside.

Strategies for Supervisors

1. **Set Clear Boundaries—Calmly**
2. Example response:

   > "I understand the meeting was important. Going forward, let's keep family topics out of the conversation and focus on my work contributions."

   These redirects focus on performance—not personal life.

3. **Share Context Without Apologizing**
4. Example:

   > "I have to leave by 3 PM today. I'll be fully present before then and will meet all deadlines."

   Affirm your capabilities without hiding your needs.

5. **Seek Ally Support**
6. Find coworkers who get it. When they witness insensitive remarks or scheduling issues, they can help reinforce your boundaries:

   > "Let's respect their schedule"—it's harder to ignore a small chorus than a single voice.

7. **Document Incidents**
8. Track jokes, unfair schedules, and the emotional or practical impact each has. Not for confrontation—but to build clarity and gather facts if escalation becomes necessary.
9. **Use Formal Channels When Needed**

10. If behaviors continue despite boundary setting, escalate the issue confidentially through HR or internal harassment protocols. Protecting your rights at work is never "too much."
11. **Lean on Legal & Policy Rights**
12. In Canada, provincial laws protect caregivers, including parental leave, flexible schedules, and accommodation rights. Don't hesitate to refer to these standards if needed:

> "According to [province] standards, employees in my situation are eligible for flexible scheduling, which I'm formally requesting."

Bottom Line

Work-life boundary violations—whether disguised as jokes or scheduling demands—aren't harmless. They erode trust, performance, and culture. Being a supervisor doesn't mean sacrificing empathy or equity—especially when caring responsibilities are involved.

You don't have to stay silent: **calm boundaries, documented patterns, and trusted allies help shift the culture toward respect and inclusion**—for you, your team, and everyone who follows.

What Organizations Should Do

Creating a workplace where supervisors don't feel penalized for their family responsibilities requires more than just policies—it takes a cultural change. Here's how organizations can move from silent tolerance to active inclusion:

1. Train Leaders on Family-Friendly Respect

Many managers don't intend harm—but they may carry outdated ideas about what "dedication" looks like. That's where training makes a difference.

- **What it means:** Add caregiving awareness to inclusive leadership training. Help managers recognize how bias can creep in, even unintentionally, through assumptions like "parents are too distracted" or "single caregivers can't take on big roles."
- **Why it matters:** When leaders are educated, they become more empathetic—and far less likely to judge or sideline someone because of their life outside work.

2. Ensure Scheduling Flexibility

Flexibility isn't a favor—it's a fair expectation.

- **What it means:** If a supervisor requests to avoid early morning calls or late evening shifts due to caregiving needs, they shouldn't be silently penalized or overlooked for advancement.
- **Why it matters:** Scheduling should support—not punish—real life. Accommodating personal needs helps retain talented, motivated supervisors who simply need room to manage both work and life with dignity.

3. Tackle Microaggressions Proactively

Snide jokes and throwaway comments can hurt more than outright bias.

- **What it means:** Leaders must be trained and expected to address and shut down inappropriate comments in real-time. Whether it's "Guess you're back on the 'mommy track,'" or "Must be nice to leave at 3 every day," silence isn't neutral—it signals approval.
- **Why it matters:** When one person speaks up, it gives others permission to feel safe. Setting the tone at the top helps build a culture of respect.

4. Normalize Care Choices

There's power in modeling.

- **What it means:** Encourage senior leaders to share when they've taken parental leave, adjusted their schedule for family, or chosen remote work during a life transition.
- **Why it matters:** It shows that balancing life and work isn't a career killer—it's a normal part of professional success. That simple visibility helps normalize and de-stigmatize caregiving at every level.

5. Audit Culture Dynamics

You can't fix what you can't see.

- **What it means:** Use regular, anonymous pulse surveys to ask whether employees feel respected in balancing personal and professional demands. Look for patterns—who's being left out? Who's staying silent?
- **Why it matters:** This data becomes your accountability tool. It helps organizations intervene early, close inclusion gaps, and track whether efforts to improve are actually working.

Final Thought

Respecting family boundaries isn't just about compassion—it's about creating a resilient, loyal workforce. When supervisors feel trusted to balance their lives without judgment or sacrifice, they bring their best to the workplace—and they stay.

Chapter Summary: When Work Crosses the Line into Home

Harassment that targets a person's family life or caregiving responsibilities isn't just a minor annoyance—it's deeply personal, and it cuts to the core of who someone is. Whether it's judgmental comments, unfair scheduling, or subtle mockery, these behaviors send a damaging message: that your role as a parent, caregiver, or simply someone with a life outside work makes you less capable, less committed, or less deserving.

For supervisors—many of whom already balance enormous pressure—this type of treatment can erode confidence, mental well-being, and trust in leadership. It creates environments where people second-guess their own worth and feel compelled to hide important aspects of their lives to stay competitive.

But supervisors aren't powerless. They can take meaningful steps: setting clear boundaries, asking for what they need without apology, documenting patterns, and seeking allies or formal support when necessary. These actions aren't just defensive—they're powerful declarations that one's full identity deserves respect.

Organizations, on the other hand, must take a hard look at the invisible rules and outdated assumptions that allow this kind of harassment to persist. True inclusion means recognizing that people are not machines—they have families, health needs, and lives beyond their job titles. A genuinely supportive workplace doesn't treat these realities as inconveniences. It embraces them as part of what makes each employee whole.

Because when people feel safe bringing their full selves to work, they don't just survive—they thrive. And so does the organization.

Chapter 26
Invasion of Privacy and Excessive Monitoring

"Surveillance at work is mistrust made permanent."

When every keystroke, message, and movement is tracked, the office stops feeling like a workplace — and starts feeling like a cage. Excessive monitoring breeds anxiety, stifles creativity, and erodes trust. It tells you loud and clear: you're not trusted, and you're always under watch.

Introduction

Supervisors thrive on trust—trust from their teams and trust in their leadership. But when upper management engages in excessive monitoring or invades personal privacy, that trust is shattered. From being tracked on location during off-hours to constant email surveillance, these practices feel more like micromanagement than oversight. This chapter examines how privacy-invasive behaviors occur, their impact, and how both individuals and organizations can address them respectfully and effectively.

How Privacy Invasion & Excessive Monitoring Appear

1. Location Tracking During Off-Hours

- **What happens:** A field supervisor carries a company-issued mobile device that uses GPS. Even during personal time at home, the manager receives location alerts.
- **Example:** One supervisor found that every evening her phone triggered a "home zone" alert on her boss's dashboard. Soon after, she began receiving spontaneous calls asking why she was "not working." The assumption shifted from a legitimate concern to unnecessary surveillance, making her feel watched even when she was off duty.

2. Email and Instant Messaging Surveillance

- **What happens:** Management reads through private workplace messages—not just for compliance, but to monitor tone, response times, and interpersonal communication.
- **Example:** A supervisor was questioned after sending a reply that included "Thanks, will get back soon." It was flagged as "unprofessional" and later used as a reason for a warning. The situation made the supervisor self-conscious, second-guessing every casual word— even in routine correspondence.

3. Detailed Activity Logging on Work Devices

- **What happens:** Software installed on work computers tracks every click, link visited, and screen viewed—without any notification, consent, or clear policy defining its scope.

- **Example:** A supervisor preparing materials for a team presentation was logged for copying internal documents and opening external websites. Hybrid work made no difference—since lunchtime browsing of the company intranet was also recorded, she felt that even benign activity was being scrutinized, impeding her sense of autonomy.

4. Camera or Screen Monitoring

- **What happens:** Monitoring tools periodically take screenshots or even activate webcams, capturing what users are viewing—whether or not they are actively working.
- **Example:** A remote supervisor logged into a training webinar and noticed random "snapshot" notifications in their taskbar. While muted and off-camera, he still received a cautionary note reminding him to remain "engaged" during what he expected to be a confidential session. The trust was utterly broken.

5. Unwarranted Personal Data Collection

What happens:

Employers may use personal wellness or fitness apps to monitor employees' health metrics—such as steps walked or sleep patterns—by linking this data to company systems. The issue arises when this data is collected without a clear or justifiable reason, and often without the employee's awareness or consent. This can result in employers having access to highly personal information, including biometric and location data, which may not be necessary for the employee's role or the company's needs.

Example:

In the provided example, a company's wellness program automatically shared data about employees' physical activity and sleep cycles through an internal health dashboard. One supervisor, who was undergoing medical treatment, saw that her personal health information—including fluctuations in her health due to her treatment—was visible to HR staff, including those who didn't need access to that data. This breach of privacy caused significant stress and discomfort, as the supervisor realized her personal health issues were being monitored and shared without her direct involvement or consent.

Why This Matters:

- **Crossing into personal time:** When monitoring extends to employees' private time (off-hours or during moments of personal space), it violates boundaries and can create undue stress.
- **Lack of transparency:** When companies lack a clear policy regarding what data is being collected, why it's being collected, and who has access to it, employees feel uncertain and vulnerable. This makes them less trusting of the system and the employer.
- **Misuse of data:** If data collected for well-being purposes is used to assess productivity, character, or even as a basis for evaluating job performance, it becomes problematic. The

purpose of such data should be to support the employee, not to scrutinize them. It can also lead to biased decisions or unfair evaluations based on health metrics.

- **Punitive or judgmental behaviors:** Instead of using health and wellness data to foster improvement, companies might use it to penalize or criticize employees, even though such data was never meant to judge work performance. This undermines trust and damages the employee's mental health, creating an environment of stress rather than support.

What Should Be Done:

- **Define precise purpose and limits:** Companies should be explicit about why they are collecting certain data and how it's relevant to the employee's work. If data is necessary for job functions, it should be collected with clear goals in mind, not as a blanket surveillance measure.
- **Ensure monitoring stops after hours:** Data collection should only happen during working hours. If monitoring extends beyond that, employees should be explicitly informed and given consent. This ensures that employees feel their personal time is respected and that their privacy is protected.
- **Use aggregated metrics, not granular data:** Employers should focus on overall trends and data that gives a broad picture of wellness (such as weekly averages) rather than minute-by-minute details. Granular data can create unnecessary pressure and invade privacy, whereas aggregated data provides a broader view that is more suitable for workplace wellness purposes.
- **Communicate openly:** Clear communication about what data is being monitored, the reason for it, and who has access to it is essential. Transparency helps build trust and allows employees to make informed decisions about their participation.
- **Make it adjustable:** Employees should have the ability to control or pause the monitoring system, especially during personal time or when they are not at work. Allowing employees to opt in or out of certain data collection activities ensures that their boundaries are respected and their autonomy is preserved.

Why These Practices Are Important:

The key idea behind all these recommendations is that employees' personal data, especially health-related information, should only be used to support their well-being and productivity—not to invade their privacy or intrude into their personal lives. When companies implement these practices thoughtfully, they help create an environment where employees feel trusted, respected, and supported, which can improve their overall well-being and job satisfaction.

In summary, clear guidelines, transparency, and respect for personal boundaries are essential when using personal wellness data in the workplace. Without these, companies risk damaging their relationships with employees and creating an atmosphere of mistrust and stress.

Why It Happens

- **Fear of Employee Absence or Loss of Control**
- Managers may feel anxious about accountability and overcompensate by using excessive tech surveillance.
- **Pressure from Above**
- Sponsors or owners demand full visibility into daily activity, leading to intrusive oversight tactics.
- **Lack of Policy Awareness**
- Some companies haven't considered privacy risks or legal boundaries when deploying monitoring tools.
- **Assumed Consent**
- The presence of company-owned devices gives managers the false belief that unlimited access is acceptable.

Impact on Supervisors and Teams

- **Violation of Trust**
- People feel treated like children—or suspects—even when their intentions are professional.
- **Heightened Stress and Anxiety**
- Knowing every move is tracked leads to constant worry about how it could be interpreted.
- **Mental Health Erosion**
- Research from the *Canadian Journal of Occupational Therapy* shows micro-monitoring contributes to burnout and depression.
- **Stifled Autonomy**
- Supervisors reduce independent decision-making when every action is scrutinized.
- **Damaged Rapport**
- Teams mirror the distrust from leadership, harming collaboration and cohesion.

Real-World Examples

Example 1: Logging Every Pause

A call-centre supervisor discovered that all team breaks were timestamped and reviewed by managers. She became anxious about taking a needed moment without thought, which increased tension.

Example 2: Photo Check-ins

A delivery supervisor had to submit timestamped selfies at the start and end of each shift. Once, under stress, she forgot—receiving a warning the next day. She felt infantilized.

How to Respond When You Feel Monitored Unfairly

Modern digital tools make it easy for companies to track employee activity—but without transparency and balance, that oversight can cross into surveillance. If you're a supervisor experiencing invasive monitoring, it's not only appropriate but essential to advocate for reasonable boundaries. Here's how to approach it thoughtfully and professionally:

1. Clarify the Purpose of Monitoring

Before jumping to conclusions, the first step is to ask for clarity—without defensiveness.

Sample phrasing:

"Can you help me understand why location tracking continues after hours? I want to make sure I'm aligned with expectations and compliance, especially around privacy boundaries."

This neutral question achieves three things:

- It signals your willingness to cooperate.
- It redirects the conversation toward mutual understanding rather than confrontation.
- It makes the manager or IT team reflect on whether the practice has a legitimate purpose or simply persists out of habit or convenience.

Example: Transportation supervisor Alex noticed that his GPS tracker had pinged dispatch long after his shift ended. When he asked respectfully for clarification, it was revealed that dispatch had no formal reason—only "just in case" thinking. This prompted a review and change in the system default settings.

2. Set Clear Boundaries

Once the issue is acknowledged, the next step is to draw firm—but fair—lines. Focus on *when*, *how*, and *why* monitoring is acceptable.

Here are examples of reasonable boundaries:

- **Work hours only:** Monitoring of location, emails, or screen activity should be restricted to the standard work schedule (e.g., 8:00 AM to 5:00 PM), unless otherwise agreed upon.
- **On-call exceptions:** If you're officially on-call or in an emergency role, acknowledge this exception—but reinforce that this should be pre-approved.
- **Personal time is off-limits:** Unless there's a contractual or legal reason (such as vehicle tracking for theft prevention), no data should be reviewed when you're off the clock.

Example: Maria, a hospital supervisor, set a boundary that wellness app data from her fitness tracker wasn't to be shared with HR after she realized her participation stats were being included in team health reports. Her polite objection helped her department establish an "opt-in only" rule.

3. Document Instances of Invasion

It's critical to keep a calm, factual record if you suspect overreach.

Record:

- **The date and time of the incident.**
- **What kind of data was accessed (e.g., email timestamp, GPS ping, camera check-in)?**
- **How it was used or referenced (e.g., mentioned in a meeting, flagged in an email).**
- **What impact did it have on your work or well-being?**

Example log entry:

March 12, 2025 – I received a call from my director at 9:20 PM asking about my location after my company phone triggered a home zone alert. I was not on call. This made me feel monitored during personal time and impacted my sleep due to stress.

Having a log shows patterns, not just isolated complaints, and strengthens your case if you need to escalate it.

4. Propose Balanced Alternatives

A supervisor's role already involves oversight and reporting. Instead of opposing monitoring entirely, offer better ways to achieve accountability:

- **Weekly summary reports** instead of daily live-tracking.
- **Project-based check-ins** rather than keystroke logs.
- **End-of-day summaries** in place of real-time screenshots.

Example: David, a remote team leader, negotiated a Friday "brief summary" format that replaced the need for webcam screenshots during meetings. His manager found it more useful—and less invasive.

5. Consult Privacy Policies and Laws

In Canada, there are established legal standards that protect employee data. Depending on your province or sector, different laws may apply:

- **PIPEDA (Personal Information Protection and Electronic Documents Act):** Federal law that protects employee personal data in private-sector organizations.
- **Alberta, B.C., and Quebec** have their own privacy legislation that covers how employers can collect, use, and disclose personal information.

Review your company's internal privacy policy or employee handbook. Look for:

- What data is your employer allowed to collect?
- How long it's retained?
- Who has access to it?
- The stated purpose for monitoring.

If you find contradictions—or the policy is vague—it's reasonable to raise this with HR.

Reference: Office of the Privacy Commissioner of Canada. *(www.priv.gc.ca)*

6. Seek Support or Escalate When Necessary

If efforts to clarify and resolve the issue internally are unsuccessful, it's appropriate to seek outside support.

Options include:

- **HR or Labor Relations:** Start with a formal conversation, referencing your documented incidents and the impact on your performance or well-being.
- **Union Representatives:** If unionized, you have the right to representation in disputes about workplace monitoring or privacy.
- **Provincial Privacy Commissioners:** You can file a complaint or request informal mediation.

Tip: Your goal is not confrontation but **restoring trust and fairness**. Privacy isn't a privilege—it's a protected right.

Final Thought

Surveillance at work should never come at the cost of psychological safety. Supervisors are professionals who deserve clarity, dignity, and autonomy. When that line is crossed—especially subtly—your job becomes not just harder but emotionally draining.

By taking action calmly, respectfully, and with evidence, you're not just protecting yourself—you're setting the tone for fairness and trust across the organization.

What Organizations Should Do to Respect Privacy

1. Create Transparent Privacy Policies

Why it matters: Without clarity, employees feel like they're working under unseen rules. This damages morale and erodes trust.

How to do it:

- **Clearly list what is monitored**—for example, GPS location, email content, or device usage.
- **Explain why the data is needed.** Is it for safety (e.g., lone-worker alerts), legal compliance, or performance analytics?
- **Specify who can access the data.** Only relevant parties, such as supervisors, HR, or IT, should have permission.

- **Set retention guidelines.** Define how long data is stored—say, 90 days for usage logs—and when it will be automatically deleted.

Example:

"We collect email metadata to ensure urgent messages are not overlooked. Only your direct supervisor and IT have access, and the metadata is purged after 60 days."

2. Monitor Only What's Essential

Why it matters: A flood of data creates analysis paralysis and leads to misuse. Too much surveillance overwhelms both employees and managers.

How to do it:

- **Identify critical metrics.** For instance, monitor GPS during driving shifts only, not weekends.
- **Avoid overreach.** Skip tracking idle-time details, such as individual keystrokes or screen clicks, unless legally required.
- **Review tool settings once a year.** Disable features that are no longer justified by business needs.

Example:

A delivery company decides GPS tracking is needed for route safety during work hours—but turns it off outside shift time.

3. Ensure Informed Consent

Why it matters: Consent builds respect and legal compliance. Employees need to understand what they're agreeing to.

How to do it:

- **Obtain written acknowledgment.** When introducing new tracking tools, ask employees to sign a simple consent form outlining details.
- **Hold an informative session.** Demonstrate how the tool is used, what it records, and who is responsible for monitoring it.
- **Allow questions.** Make space for employees to voice concerns openly and get clear answers.

Example:

Before deploying webcam screenshot software, the company schedules a briefing: "Here's how the software works, here's who can view captures, and here's how it benefits the team's security."

4. Offer Opt-out or Alternative Options

Why it matters: Not everyone is comfortable being tracked. Providing options shows respect for personal comfort and needs.

How to do it:

- **Allow personal device use.** Allow employees to handle non-sensitive tasks on their personal phones or laptops when appropriate.
- **Rotate monitoring roles.** If supervisors are each responsible for oversight tasks, create a fair rotation so that no one is always being watched or doing the watching.
- **Offer hybrid tools.** Provide a choice between live tracking and summary reporting—a weekly snapshot might replace daily check-ins.

Example:

An organization offers two options: a monthly productivity report via spreadsheet or an hourly activity tracker—employees choose whichever suits them best.

5. Regularly Audit and Adapt

Why it matters: Technology evolves rapidly—and so do privacy expectations. Regular reviews ensure the system stays fair.

How to do it:

- **Include privacy in compliance cycles.** When conducting annual IT or HR audits, include steps to verify what data is collected, who has accessed it, and whether retention rules have been followed.
- **Gather emotional feedback.** Use anonymous surveys to gauge the impact of monitoring on stress and morale.
- **Adjust based on findings.** If 40% of staff report feeling "micromanaged," consider scaling back or changing the monitoring approach.

Example:

A quarterly pulse survey reveals 20% of supervisors feel "watched all the time." In response, leadership schedules an independent review and temporarily suspends real-time tracking.

Why These Steps Matter

- **Builds trust:** Employees feel treated as professionals—not suspects.
- **Enhances engagement:** Respectful monitoring supports well-being and collaboration.
- **Reduces risk:** Transparent, consent-based policies lower the chance of legal issues.
- **Improves alignment:** Collecting only meaningful data keeps the focus on performance, not surveillance.

Summary

Excessive monitoring and unnecessary intrusion into personal data do more harm than good. While some oversight is reasonable in a workplace, constant surveillance sends the message that employees aren't trusted—especially when it spills into personal time or private matters. This approach not only erodes morale but also damages the fundamental relationship between supervisors and their teams.

To create a healthier, more productive environment, organizations must start by being clear about **why** they're collecting information, **what** they're collecting, and **how** it will be used. When employees understand the purpose and see that there are real limits and protections in place, they're far more likely to engage and cooperate.

Supervisors play a key role in maintaining this balance. By advocating for transparency, respecting personal boundaries, and using data to support—not judge—employees, they help build a culture rooted in trust and fairness.

Ultimately, organizations need **privacy frameworks** that aren't just about compliance—they should reflect values. A thoughtful approach to privacy doesn't mean giving up accountability; it means shifting the focus from control to collaboration. When people feel respected, they respond with stronger engagement, loyalty, and performance. Trust, not suspicion, should be the foundation of how work gets done.

Chapter 27
Unreasonable Restrictions on the Role of Autonomy

"Micromanagement chains creativity and kills initiative."

When every decision requires approval and every step is second-guessed, your role becomes a scripted performance rather than meaningful work. Unreasonable restrictions strip away your professional autonomy and replace it with frustration. Instead of being a contributor, you become a cog.

Introduction

While supervisors are responsible for guiding teams, it's unhealthy when upper management excessively dictates every decision—from daily tasks to minute operational details. Such excessive control signals a lack of trust, stifles creativity, and erodes job satisfaction. In this chapter, we'll dive into what unreasonable restrictions look like, why they're harmful, and how both supervisors and organizations can shift toward empowerment and autonomy.

What Unreasonable Restrictions Look Like

Unreasonable restrictions in the workplace are excessive controls or rules that limit employees' autonomy, hinder decision-making, and reduce productivity. Here's a breakdown of the specific examples:

1. Micromanaged Workflows

This refers to the situation where managers require constant updates on every step an employee takes during their workday. For example, supervisors may need to log break times, minute-by-minute task updates, and even detailed reports on what is being done and when. This type of micromanagement is often implemented through spreadsheets, time-tracking software, or other systems that require employees to continually input data about their work.

Why it's problematic:

- It undermines employees' confidence and autonomy, as they're constantly monitored.
- It wastes time that could be spent on actual work.
- It leads to stress and burnout, as employees feel they're always under a microscope.

2. Rigid Approval Processes

In some workplaces, even small, routine decisions—like ordering office supplies or making basic schedule adjustments—require approval from multiple levels of management. Instead of being empowered to make decisions independently, employees must submit requests and wait for sign-offs from managers, directors, or even senior leaders, which can take a significant amount of time.

Why it's problematic:

- It slows down decision-making, often causing unnecessary delays.
- It creates inefficiency, where simple tasks become overly complicated.
- Employees may feel that their time and expertise are undervalued, as they can't make decisions without higher-level approval.

3. Overlong Task Approval Chains

This happens when even the most minor tasks or resources (like office supplies, team outings, or promotional items) require approval from a chain of senior leaders or multiple departments. For example, requesting pens or organizing a team lunch may require multiple rounds of approval.

Why it's problematic:

- It creates unnecessary delays for basic tasks.
- It discourages initiative, as employees feel they have to seek approval for things they could handle on their own.
- It wastes time for both the person requesting approval and the managers involved in the process.

4. Uniform Scheduling Rules

When shift schedules are created without considering the specific needs of teams or the personal commitments of workers, it can lead to significant frustration. For instance, a company might implement a strict rule that schedules all shifts without consulting the supervisor or accommodating changes like seasonal demand, special events, or workers' preferences.

Why it's problematic:

- It leads to low morale when employees feel their personal needs are disregarded.
- It can affect team performance if the schedules don't match the demands of the job or the workers' strengths.
- It discourages supervisors from being proactive in managing the schedule based on team input, leading to poor planning and dissatisfaction.

5. Prohibitive Technology Policies

This refers to situations where supervisors or employees need permission to use basic tools or software essential for their work. For example, a supervisor may need to submit a formal request to access a shared drive or analytics dashboards that they need to manage their team or analyze performance.

Why it's problematic:

- It slows down productivity by creating unnecessary barriers to accessing important tools.
- It adds frustration to supervisors who may feel that simple requests are being treated like complex, high-stakes matters.
- It undermines trust, as it gives the impression that management doesn't believe employees can be trusted to use basic tools.

Why These Controls Hurt

1. Kills Initiative and Innovation

When employees are micromanaged, forced to navigate complicated approval processes, or have little room for flexibility, they stop taking initiative. They no longer feel empowered to make decisions or experiment with new ideas. Over time, employees may become disengaged and less creative because they lack the freedom to explore alternative solutions or take ownership of their work.

2. Creates Bottlenecks

The rigid approval processes and the constant need for sign-offs create bottlenecks that slow down work. Teams get stuck in a loop of waiting for approvals or feedback, which delays project timelines and reduces overall productivity. This leads to frustration and low morale, especially when employees feel like they could move forward without the constant delays.

3. Signals Lack of Trust

Excessive control in the form of micromanagement or overly strict processes sends a clear message: "We don't trust you to handle things on your own." When supervisors or employees feel distrusted, their motivation drops. They may stop taking ownership of their work or lose interest in contributing new ideas because they feel like their judgment isn't valued.

4. Increases Turnover Risk

Skilled employees who feel micromanaged or unnecessarily restricted may eventually decide to leave for a job where they have more freedom to make decisions, implement their ideas, and be trusted with greater responsibility. High turnover means losing experienced workers, which can disrupt teams and slow down business operations.

Research from Harvard Business Review

"Research from Harvard Business Review and other studies highlights the significant positive impact of empowerment on employee engagement and performance, suggesting that when employees are trusted and given autonomy, engagement tends to rise, and overall performance improves. Empowerment fosters a positive cycle of trust, innovation, and productivity, while micromanagement often leads to disengagement and inefficiency."

Summary

Unreasonable restrictions, such as micromanagement, rigid approval processes, and overly controlling policies, harm both the individual employee and the organization as a whole. These practices lead to disengagement, bottlenecks, and a lack of trust. By giving employees more autonomy and reducing unnecessary controls, companies can foster a more productive, innovative, and empowered workforce.

Real-World Examples

Example 1: The Over-Engineered Supply Request

A warehouse supervisor needed replacement gloves. The online form required five fields: unit cost justification, manager approval, and finance sign-off—all before purchase. By the time the gloves arrived, several team members had slipped on the floor.

Example 2: Scheduling So Tight It's Unpredictable

A health clinic required physicians and supervisors to confirm roster changes 30 days in advance. When illness struck, substitutes were hard to find. Supervisors lost credibility with both staff and patients.

Strategies for Supervisors

1. **Gather Evidence**
2. Document recurring restrictions, delays caused, and the impact on team morale or productivity.
3. **Propose Leaner Processes**
4. Offer streamlined alternatives—for instance, supervisor-level purchase authority up to a threshold, with monthly audits.
5. **Align with Organizational Goals**
6. Show how trust and agility tie to better outcomes—faster customer service, happier teams, fewer errors.
7. **Pilot Delegation Models**
8. Suggest a small-scale test of lighter approval workflows—track time saved and mistakes averted.
9. **Escalate When Necessary**
10. If blockers persist, take the case to HR or leadership—focus on data and improved efficiency.

What Organizations Can Do

1. Map and Simplify Decision Chains

What it means:

Organizations should create a clear structure that outlines which decisions supervisors can make on their own and which ones need to be escalated. Think of it as a flowchart: if a decision is about X and under Y amount of risk or cost, the supervisor handles it. If it's beyond that, it goes to the next level.

Why it matters:

When decision-making is murky or overly complex, supervisors hesitate to act. Simplifying and mapping these chains reduces delays and empowers people to move confidently within their roles.

2. Set Micro-Authorization Limits

What it means:

Grant supervisors the authority to make routine spending decisions or resource allocations within a defined budget or threshold. For example, they might be allowed to approve purchases under $500 or schedule team coverage without extra sign-off.

Why it matters:

When every small action requires approval from upper management, teams slow down and morale dips. Small, practical decision-making power builds efficiency and shows trust without risking misuse.

3. Train for Trust-Based Leadership

What it means:

Leaders—especially senior ones—should be trained in how to delegate effectively, how to let go of excessive control, and how to support autonomy without losing accountability. This isn't just about soft skills—it's a strategic shift in leadership culture.

Why it matters:

Many senior leaders micromanage not out of malice, but habit. Teaching leaders how to lead through trust rather than control equips them to build stronger, more responsive teams.

4. Solicit Feedback Regularly

What it means:

Conduct short, focused surveys or check-ins (quarterly is ideal) to ask supervisors about any friction they experience in daily processes—especially areas where they feel blocked, overruled, or mistrusted.

Why it matters:

When supervisors are given a voice in identifying barriers, it creates a feedback loop that improves processes in real time. It also signals that leadership is listening and willing to adapt.

5. Measure Outcomes

What it means:

Track key indicators—such as how long it takes to complete projects, how often errors happen, or how frequently staff leave. Then compare those trends against how tightly decisions are controlled at various levels.

Why it matters:

Too much control almost always leads to slower results and lower morale. When companies measure the impact of their control systems on real-world performance, they're better able to adjust policies and create healthier, more effective workflows.

Summary

When supervisors are bogged down by excessive rules and constant approvals, they stop acting like leaders and start functioning like clerks—just passing tasks along and following checklists. That stifles initiative, innovation, and ownership.

The way forward is through **empowered autonomy**: a culture where supervisors are trusted to make thoughtful decisions within clear boundaries. With the right mix of documented processes, honest dialogue, and small, low-risk changes (pilots), organizations can shift toward more agile, human-centered systems.

The result? Better morale, faster performance, and stronger retention of skilled people—because trusted teams don't just follow orders, they lead progress.

Chapter 28
Threats of Unwanted Reassignment

"Threatening to move you isn't about logistics — it's about control."

Suddenly, your role is in flux. You're told you might be reassigned to a less desirable position or location — often with no clear reason. These threats hang over your head, creating stress and uncertainty. They aren't about business needs but about exerting power through fear.

Introduction

Being a supervisor means taking pride in your team and the progress you lead. But when managers threaten sudden or unwanted reassignments—to unfamiliar roles, distant locations, or less desirable shifts—it destabilizes that dedication. These threats become tools of control, sowing uncertainty and undermining both performance and trust. This chapter explores how unwanted reassignment threats surface, their impact, and how supervisors—and organizations—can address them constructively.

How Threats of Reassignment Appear

1. **Stranded After Changes**
2. A manager says, "We might move you to the rural branch next month," without providing a clear reason or timeframe.
3. **Gatekeeping Critical Roles**
4. A supervisor who asks for new responsibilities hears: "We'll shift you out if we need someone more loyal."
5. **Retaliatory Transfer Threats**
6. Speak up or miss a goal? Then senior leadership suggests, "Maybe you'd fit better in another department."
7. **Unspoken Ultimatums**
8. The message is never in writing—but teammates whisper: "If she pushes further, they'll move her elsewhere."
9. **Routine but Coercive Turnover**
10. Each project wrap-up includes a mention of reassignment, creating subtle pressure to remain silent.

Why It's Used

- **Power Maintenance**
- Threatening reassignment keeps supervisors aligned with leadership's will.
- **Cost Savings**
- Shifting people is cheaper than engaging in difficult conversations or performance coaching.

- **Risk Management**
- Move a supervisor before a problem escalates—without directly addressing the issue.
- **Team Scare-Tactics**
- It sends a message that nobody is immune, and dissent or autonomy may lead to displacement.

Real-World Examples

Example 1: The Unannounced Shift

Oliver, a warehouse supervisor, was spearheading a new efficiency program. After raising concerns about outdated equipment, he was told, "We might transfer you to another facility that needs help," and sent a relocation form. Though framed as "an opportunity," Oliver understood it as a veiled punishment.

Example 2: The Cultured Displacement

Harpreet, leading a diverse IT team, requested inclusion in leadership planning meetings. Soon after, she was informed that another manager would oversee the project—she'd be reassigned quietly. No performance issue was ever discussed.

Impact on Supervisors and Teams

- **Alarms and Distrust**
- Trusted supervisors begin to question everything—and who they can rely on.
- **Disrupted Team Continuity**
- Employees lose faith when leadership shifts mid-stream, and combined efforts erode.
- **Reduced Transparency**
- Power moves become hidden through whispers rather than explicit conversation.
- **Weak Cultural Norms**
- Without clear standards, anyone can be reassigned ruthlessly, diminishing loyalty.

Strategies for Supervisors

1. **Ask for Clarifications**
2. When reassignment is hinted:

   > "Could you help me understand the business context or expectations behind a possible move?"

3. **Confirm Temporariness**
4. If it's project-based, ask:

   > "Is this a temporary assignment linked to Project X? What's the expected timeline?"

5. **Document Conversations**
6. Record the dates, who said what, and any relevant context in a private journal or email summary.
7. **Align with Career Goals**
8. Express your preferences:

> "I'm committed to growing this team and appreciate any assignments that match my skills and goals."

9. **Escalate Respectfully**
10. If threats persist without discussion, involve HR or trusted leaders. Focus on your commitment—and the need for stability in leadership for team success.

What Organizations Should Do

1. **Set Clear Reassignment Policies**
2. Define what triggers a reassignment—project needs, personal preference, or performance issues—and how transitions are handled.
3. **Require Formal Dialogue**
4. Every reassignment conversation should include a written rationale, an impact discussion, and a mutually-agreed transition plan.
5. **Link Reassignment to Career Planning**
6. Treat transfers as part of development—not punishment.
7. **Gather Feedback Post-Move**
8. Survey supervisors after reassignment to understand whether it was fair, clearly communicated, and supported.
9. **Audit Patterns Over Time**
10. Analyze reassignment data: frequency, departments, demographics. Look for patterns that suggest bias or misuse of reassignment as retaliation.

Summary

Unwanted reassignments are often framed as "opportunities," but when they are used to pressure or control employees, especially supervisors, they become a tool of fear, not growth. When someone is told they might be "shifted" for asking questions or seeking new challenges, it sends a clear message: stay in line or you are replaceable. Over time, this kind of leverage chips away at trust, discourages initiative, and makes supervisors more cautious than curious.

To restore a sense of safety and fairness, supervisors can take proactive steps, such as asking direct questions about the purpose of potential changes, maintaining a clear record of conversations, and ensuring that any discussion of reassignment is tied back to real development goals, rather than vague warnings.

For organizations, the bigger responsibility is to build **transparent, fair reassignment protocols** that are people-centered. When job changes are communicated with honesty, explained with purpose, and tied to real growth paths, employees experience them as supportive, not punitive.

That kind of clarity reinforces trust, encourages ambition, and turns movement within the organization into something people can look forward to, not fear.

Chapter 29
Pressure to Resign Under Duress

"Being pushed out softly feels just as harsh as a door slammed shut."

Sometimes, the message isn't direct termination but persistent pressure to quit. Excessive workloads, hostile environments, or constant criticism wear you down until resignation feels like the only option. It's a cruel tactic that lets employers avoid accountability while ending your career prematurely.

Introduction

A supervisor's role thrives on purpose, influence, and growth. Yet in some workplaces, subtle or overt pressure can lead talented leaders to feel they have no choice but to resign. Whether through continuous criticism, moral exclusion, or humiliating assignments, this form of coercion is both emotionally damaging and professionally stifling. This chapter examines the phenomenon of forced resignation under pressure, its profound impacts, and strategies for individual resilience and organizational accountability.

How Forced Resignation Can Be Manufactured

1. Microscopic Criticism & Public Blame

When every small error is spotlighted in team meetings—and major wins are barely acknowledged—it creates a clear signal: no matter how hard you work, you'll only be known for your failures.

How it plays out:

- You miss a minor deadline, and it's dissected during a weekly all-hands, while your recent big-project success quietly slips by unnoticed.
- Over time, you start feeling constantly on edge—you're judged in front of peers, but never truly credited. The subtle message becomes, "We won't celebrate your wins—but we will highlight your missteps."

2. Isolation & Withholding Resources

A supervisor is effectively set up to fail when vital tools, information, or access are withheld. Without these, even routine tasks become uphill battles—and quitting starts to look like the only reasonable option.

How it shows:

- Budget requests are repeatedly deferred or left unaddressed.
- Emails about policy updates or staffing changes get sent to everyone—except you.
- You begin to realize you're not being supported in your role—and maybe, they're hoping you'll notice and walk away.

3. Unfair Performance Reviews Leading to "Mutual Separation"

A twist on the exit interview: you are given a poor performance review despite clear evidence of strong results, and then prompted to accept a severance package and leave quietly.

How it plays out:

- You hit your goals. You hear thanks from peers. But the official review paints a different picture.
- The review letter arrives asking you to "sign off" on a separation agreement.
- You're left in a bind: accept the implied guilt and leave, or fight it—and risk a drawn-out, damaging conflict.

4. Overwhelming Workload and No Support

This isn't just a busy season—it's an intentional setup. Projects multiply, your to-do list explodes, but no extra help is offered. When you push back, you're told you're being too sensitive or not handling stress well.

How it plays out:

- Multiple high-priority projects land on your desk—without reassigning any other tasks.
- You bring this up in management meetings, and management turns it against you: you're told to "learn to manage better" or "stop being overwhelmed by a full-time job."
- The result: chronic exhaustion, frustration, and the nagging thought that maybe quitting would bring some relief.

5. Threatened Reassignments or Demotions

A classic unofficial threat: repositioned as an "opportunity" while carrying a clear message—if you don't comply, you'll be reassigned to a less visible or less desirable role.

How it shows:

- You express concern or ask for clarification, and the response is: "We might move you to [new team/location] if things don't improve."
- No written documentation—just implied.
- The subtext becomes loud and clear: stick with the status quo—or leave under your own steam.

Why These Tactics Work—and Why They're Dangerous

- **They erode confidence**: Constant criticism or shifting goalposts make you feel incompetent.
- **They isolate you**: When excluded or unsupported, you lose allies and feel powerless.
- **They get results quietly**: Forced resignation looks like voluntary departure—protecting the organization's reputation.
- **They upset team stability**: Losing a valued supervisor this way demoralizes the entire team.

What You Can Do

1. **Keep Records Daily** — meetings, criticisms, workloads, requests.
2. **Challenge Specifics Politely** — ask, "Can we talk through this particular criticism?"
3. **Push Back on Load** — frame it as a practical concern: "I see a capacity issue—can we discuss priorities?"
4. **Ask for Next Steps in Writing** — if reassigned, clarify expectations and timeframes clearly.
5. **Tap External Advice Early** — HR, mentor, union, or trusted legal counsel can help you understand your rights.

Bottom Line

When you start to notice this pattern—minor missteps amplified, resources withheld, pressure tactics creeping in—it's not a coincidence. Supervisors deserve clarity, fairness, and respect. Recognizing these tactics early gives you the power to respond—and potentially change the outcome before your resignation is "the only option."

Real-World Examples

Example 1: The Exit Email

Rina was a well-regarded operations supervisor. Over months, colleagues noticed increasing negativity from above—her requests were ignored, and blame for minor errors piled up. One day, a stern email clarified: "If you're not fully committed, HR can prepare a mutual separation package." Terrified of damaging her professional record, Rina resigned quietly.

Example 2: The Burnout Ultimatum

Jason was managing two major projects simultaneously. When he requested help, he was told to "figure it out." After months of no support, deteriorating health forced him to resign, not out of desire, but from exhaustion and despair.

The Impact of "Managed Exit" Tactics

- **Loss of Confidence & Trust**

- A supervisor who is forced out this way often loses faith in leadership—and in their own competence.
- **Career Setbacks**
- Having resigned under pressure—especially without a clear reason—can open the door to negative references or closed opportunities.
- **Team Disruption**
- Teams lose stability, and talent flight tends to follow when leadership is seen as manipulative.
- **Toxic Workplace Culture**
- Environments where exit pressure is acceptable breed fear, silence, and moral harm.

Strategies for Supervisors

1. **Understand Your Rights**
2. In Canada, forced resignations due to hostile or intolerable work conditions can be considered wrongful dismissal. Seek legal advice if you sense coercion—this may qualify as "constructive dismissal."
3. **Keep a Paper Trail**
4. Document interactions: excessive criticism, removed resources, formal threats, or repeated emails/joint meeting notes. This evidence is critical for internal complaints or legal claim strength.
5. **Voice Concerns Early**
6. Rather than waiting until burnout, raise your concern with HR or trusted senior leaders:

   > "I'm finding it increasingly difficult to meet expectations with current resources and feedback style. Can we talk about a plan that supports both the team and my ability to perform?"

7. **Seek External Validation**
8. Mentors, professional networks, or peers may confirm whether the pressure you're facing is abnormal. Their perspective can reinforce your understanding of the situation.
9. **Plan an Exit with Strategy**
10. If the pressure becomes untenable, prepare in advance. Line up references, update your resume, and have a professional letter ready—so if you leave, it's on your terms.

What Organizations Should Do

1. **Train Leaders on Ethical Exit Protocols**
2. Ensure managers understand that pressuring employees to resign is unethical—and illegal in many cases.
3. **Conduct Independent Investigations**
4. If resignation hints arise, HR should proactively check in, explore toxic behaviors, and offer mediations or support.
5. **Create Safe Reporting Channels**
6. A neutral, anonymous system must exist so individuals can flag unfair exit pressure without risking retaliation.

7. **Offer Workplace Mediation or Support Plans**
8. Instead of driving exits, offer coaching, role adjustments, or team restructuring to resolve conflicts.
9. **Monitor Turnover Patterns**
10. High resignation rates in one team or under a single manager should prompt audits and leadership review.

Summary

When resignation is subtly framed as the only reasonable path forward—through pressure, isolation, or manipulated evaluations—it creates a quiet but damaging rupture in workplace trust. What looks like a "choice" on the surface is often a forced hand, leaving supervisors feeling cornered, disrespected, and stripped of their dignity. This kind of environment doesn't just push people out; it signals that open dialogue and honest challenges are no longer welcome.

Supervisors can reclaim a sense of control by recognizing the signs early and taking thoughtful steps, such as learning their legal and organizational rights, keeping detailed records of performance and communications, consulting with mentors or legal counsel, and preparing a clear and intentional exit plan if needed. These actions help shift the dynamic from reactive to proactive.

For organizations, the responsibility runs deeper. Rather than creating conditions that quietly force people out, companies must commit to building transparent, fair, and accountable systems. A healthy workplace should allow space for disagreement, growth, and feedback—without fear of retaliation. When challenges are met with respect instead of resistance, exits become rare—and trust, stability, and morale grow stronger.

Chapter 30
Baseless Legal Threats or Implications

"Empty threats are a weapon disguised as law."

You raise concerns or push back, and suddenly legal consequences loom — often with little or no basis. Baseless threats are designed to intimidate and silence, leveraging fear of litigation to suppress voices. It's a coercive move to shut down dialogue, not resolve issues.

Introduction

When supervisors are told they could face lawsuits, fines, or legal consequences without a valid reason, it's more than intimidation—it's a form of emotional and professional coercion. Here's how this tactic often plays out:

1. Vague Accusations of Misconduct

Definition:

Mixed messages suggesting legal wrongdoing with no specifics—for instance, being told you "could be disciplined—or worse—for that error," without any policy reference or actual infraction.

Example:

A supervisor accidentally shared a confidential internal memo with a peer. Instead of being asked to correct the error, their director warned:

"That kind of slip can get you and the company sued. We'll have to look into greater consequences."

Weeks later, nothing happened—but the threat stayed. The supervisor felt constantly watched and fearful of making mistakes.

Why it matters:

- Destroys psychological safety by making every decision feel potentially illegal.
- Encourages a culture of fear rather than learning.
- Lacks fairness, since there's no evidence or established process backing it up.

2. Legal Threats Used as a Retaliation Tool

Definition:

Managerial threats are issued in response to reasonable actions, like taking leave or pointing out wrongdoing, without fulfilling the required legal threshold.

Example:

After raising concerns about safety protocols, a plant supervisor was verbally cautioned by an executive:

"If you keep this up, our lawyers will have your job, and you might find yourself liable for slander."

The message was clear: stop asking questions or risk a legal fight. No policy violation had occurred; it was simply used to shut down dissent.

Why it matters:

- Converts legitimate feedback into a threatening issue.
- Silences important concerns, harming morale.
- Can be illegal if it violates whistleblower protections or employment laws.

3. Disproportionate Threats to Force Compliance

Definition:

Warnings that small issues could escalate into legal crises—when they're clearly within normal managerial scope—used to force immediate obedience.

Example:

A supervisor reported inconsistent time logs on behalf of their team. The director responded:

"I'll have our compliance team look at all your log entries—and they'll be looking for fraud. You're treading dangerous ground."

There were no real accusations, but the supervisor was left wondering if "all he's done wrong" might come back later.

Why it matters:

- Imposes a chilling effect on supervisors exercising normal managerial vigilance.
- Undermines trust in leadership.
- Can have actual legal consequences when used to justify baseless HR actions or future firing.

Why These Tactics Are Harmful

- **Emotional Distress:** Living under threat causes ongoing anxiety.

- **Poor Leadership Culture:** Trust breaks down when legal fears are brandished instead of respectful dialogue.
- **Silenced Feedback:** Supervisors stop raising concerns—dangerous in safety, compliance, or ethics-driven roles.
- **Potential Rights Violations:** Depending on jurisdiction, this could breach labor laws or whistleblower protections.

What Supervisors Can Do

1. **Seek Specifics:**
2. Ask calmly, *"Could you point me to the specific policy or law I might be in violation of?"*
3. **Document Everything:**
4. Keep records of who said what, when, and in what context. Save emails, note dates of conversations.
5. **Request Formal Follow-Up:**
6. Instead of issuing informal threats, request a written policy review or a compliance checklist.
7. **Lean on Appropriate Support:**
8. In Canada, explore resources under **PIPEDA**, provincial employment standards, or union rights. If protected under whistleblower laws, know your rights before escalating.
9. **Consider Legal Advice:**
10. If threats persist without justification—and start affecting your professional record—talk to an employment lawyer or legal counsel.

Cultural Best Practices for Organizations

Organizations should never weaponize legal language. Instead:

- Use factual language about policy, contract terms, or regulatory compliance.
- Refer to issues with documentation, not speculation.
- Offer clarity—"Here's what is required," not "You could be sued."
- Provide fair warnings and remediation—not shock threats.
- Educate managers so they know when legal consultation is necessary—and when it isn't.

Summary

Threats of legal action, especially when there is no valid basis, may seem like an easy way to assert control or silence pushback. But these tactics come at a high cost. They create a chilling effect, where anxiety takes hold, communication shuts down, and mistrust spreads through the team. Even if no lawsuit ever materializes, the fear alone can discourage people from speaking up, asking questions, or flagging real concerns.

Supervisors facing this kind of pressure do not need to respond with panic or confrontation. Instead, they can protect themselves by staying calm, asking thoughtful questions, documenting all interactions and decisions, and escalating concerns to trusted HR contacts or legal counsel when needed. Quiet confidence and clarity often speak louder than fear.

On the organizational side, the most resilient and respected cultures are not built on intimidation. They are built on open, respectful dialogue. Replacing vague threats with clear communication, evidence-based feedback, and fair, transparent processes sends a powerful message: disagreement is not a threat, and accountability is shared. In that kind of environment, trust grows, and so does performance.

Part V: Identity-Based Discrimination

Discriminatory behaviors based on identity, age, beliefs, or culture.

Chapter 31
Racial, Ethnic, or Cultural Discrimination

"Prejudice in the workplace dims the brightest talents."

Discrimination based on race, ethnicity, or culture is more than unfair — it's a barrier that blocks opportunity and stifles potential. When your identity becomes the reason for exclusion or mistreatment, the workplace stops being a place of growth and starts being a place of pain.

1. Microaggressions in Everyday Conversation

These are the kinds of comments people often don't realize are hurtful. They might be intended as compliments or casual small talk, but they reveal unconscious biases—and over time, they leave a lasting impact.

Example:

A South Asian supervisor is constantly asked, *"Where are you really from?"* even though she was born and raised in the country. Or people mispronounce her name again and again, even after she's politely corrected them. She hears, *"You speak English so well,"* as if that's surprising.

Impact:

These moments send a quiet message: *You don't quite belong.* No matter how successful or fluent you are, your identity is being treated as "other." The intention might not be malicious, but the effect is still isolating.

2. Assumptions About Cultural Norms or Behavior

This happens when people judge someone's actions through the lens of a stereotype instead of seeing the person for who they are.

Example:

A Black supervisor who prefers to observe and think before speaking is labeled "disengaged." But a White colleague who behaves the same way is described as "thoughtful" or "measured." It's not about the behavior—it's about how it's being interpreted.

Impact:

These assumptions can hurt a leader's reputation and undermine their influence. When people view your actions through a biased lens, it's harder to be evaluated fairly or recognized for your true strengths.

3. Exclusion from Important Decisions or Meetings

Being left out—whether intentionally or not—can be deeply damaging, especially when the reason is based on assumptions about culture or "fit."

Example:

A Middle Eastern supervisor isn't invited to a leadership retreat because it's described as informal and relaxed, with the implication being: *He might not fit in.* But he's qualified, ready, and fully capable—just not given the chance.

Impact:

Exclusion doesn't just impact that one event. It limits access to networks, leadership conversations, and growth opportunities. It sends a message that certain people are only allowed to go so far.

4. Cultural Tokenism

Being asked to represent your culture can feel flattering at first—but not when that's the only value people see in you.

Example:

A Latina supervisor is asked to bring traditional food for a company event and speak about her heritage. But when it comes to strategic meetings or big decisions, her input is ignored or sidelined.

Impact:

It feels like you're being showcased, not empowered. Like your culture is being used to promote the company's image, but your voice isn't truly respected where it counts.

5. Unequal Expectations or Standards

This happens when people are held to different rules based on where they're from or how they're perceived culturally.

Example:

A Filipino supervisor expresses concern for a struggling employee and is told she's being "too emotional." Yet when a White colleague shows similar concern, it's praised as strong, compassionate leadership.

Impact:

The rules feel like they're always shifting—and not in your favor. It becomes exhausting to constantly monitor how you're coming across, always wondering if you're being judged more harshly than others.

Why This Is Harmful

Bias in the workplace isn't always loud or obvious. Often, it hides in small moments like who gets invited to speak, who's heard in meetings, and who's quietly left out.

But for supervisors from racial or cultural minority backgrounds, these moments add up. Over time, they create an uneven playing field where some leaders are constantly battling to be seen, heard, and taken seriously. It's not just frustrating. It's deeply harmful. These experiences don't just hurt morale; they shape career trajectories, diminish well-being, and quietly push talented leaders out of spaces they worked hard to enter. The damage is real, and it reaches far beyond the individual.

1. Erodes Sense of Belonging

Imagine walking into your workplace each day and feeling like you don't quite fit. You work just as hard, care just as much, but somehow, you're still on the outside. Maybe your contributions are overlooked in meetings. Maybe your cultural references are met with blank stares—or worse, jokes.

When supervisors experience racial or cultural bias, especially in subtle forms, it chips away at their sense of being part of the team. Over time, this leads to what psychologists call *identity threat*—the feeling that who you are isn't truly welcome. It's more than hurt feelings. It's a slow erosion of motivation, security, and connection.

2. Drains Mental and Emotional Energy

Dealing with bias—especially the kind that's indirect or coded—requires constant mental effort. You might second-guess how to phrase things, wonder if a comment was intentional, or replay conversations in your head long after the meeting ends.

This kind of emotional labor doesn't show up on a time sheet, but it's exhausting. It can lead to burnout even when your workload is manageable. Supervisors shouldn't have to carry the hidden cost of constantly managing others' perceptions. That's not leadership—it's survival mode.

3. Reduces Engagement

When you feel like your input doesn't count—or worse, that it's ignored or misattributed—you start to pull back. Not because you don't care, but because you're trying to protect yourself.

You stop volunteering for new projects. You speak less in meetings. You begin to think, "Why bother?" This withdrawal is one of the most damaging effects of workplace bias. It doesn't just affect the individual—it stifles innovation, creativity, and progress. When bright voices go quiet, everyone loses.

4. Weakens Teams

Bias isn't just a personal issue—it's a team issue. When one team member is treated unfairly, everyone sees it. Some people feel anxious, wondering if they're next. Others may feel guilty but unsure how to help. Trust begins to unravel.

Collaboration suffers because people become cautious, territorial, or disengaged. Team morale declines. What once felt like a place of shared goals now feels fragmented and fragile. And over time, that disconnection can spread like a slow leak—undermining everything the team is working to build.

Bottom Line

Racial and cultural bias in leadership doesn't just hurt feelings. It damages relationships, lowers performance, and limits potential. Supervisors need to feel safe, respected, and empowered—just like everyone else. When we fail to address these harms, we lose not only talent but also trust.

What Supervisors Can Do

Facing bias—whether subtle or overt—can be exhausting. However, there are calm and professional ways supervisors can respond while maintaining their dignity and authority. This section provides practical and respectful strategies to help supervisors navigate discrimination without losing their composure in the process.

1. Name It Calmly

"When my name is changed in meetings, I feel overlooked. Could we please correct that?"

Sometimes, the most powerful move is the simplest: naming the behavior. Calling attention to missteps, even minor ones like mispronouncing a name or confusing identities, helps reset the tone and establish respect.

For example, if a manager consistently calls you by the wrong name—even after correction—it sends a signal that your presence isn't fully seen. Calmly but directly addressing it can shift the room's energy. You don't need to shame the person—just clarify what respect looks like.

This isn't about being overly sensitive. It's about ensuring others take the time to treat you with the basic recognition they'd expect for themselves.

2. Educate with Care

"Past leaders have found micro-affirming comments more inclusive than questioning cultural norms."

It's not your job to teach others—but sometimes, sharing a thoughtful insight helps someone course-correct without embarrassment.

Let's say your manager jokes about your cultural dress or questions a holiday you observe. Rather than respond defensively, you could say, "In many organizations, leaders have found it powerful to encourage cultural celebration—not question it." This shifts the conversation from personal to professional and invites learning without confrontation.

Tone matters here. The goal isn't to accuse, but to redirect with purpose and grace.

3. Build Allies

"I noticed X was said—could we talk about ways to include everyone more equitably?"

Sometimes, silence from others hurts more than the bias itself. One of the most effective ways to combat exclusion is to **build a quiet circle of allies**—people who are willing to speak up when something feels off.

It doesn't always need to be a public confrontation. After a meeting where something felt biased, connect with a colleague you trust. Say something like:

"I felt a bit sidelined when my ideas weren't acknowledged. Did you pick up on that?"

If they did, invite them to help elevate inclusive behavior going forward.

Allies don't need to speak *for* you—but they can help ensure your voice isn't lost.

4. Record Examples

This is about **self-protection**, not paranoia. Keeping a simple, private log of incidents gives you clarity—and credibility.

Example:

- April 3: Team lead laughed at my accent during client debrief.
- April 12: My pitch was dismissed, then restated later by another manager and praised.
- April 20: Email about Ramadan accommodations ignored.

You don't need to record everything, just consistent patterns that demonstrate disregard or bias. Should you ever need to bring it up with HR, you'll be armed with dates and context—not just feelings.

5. Use Formal Channels When Needed

HR should be a **resource**, not a **last resort**.

If direct conversations don't lead to change—and if the bias persists or escalates—it's appropriate to engage formal support.

Start with your documentation. Bring specific examples, remain composed, and speak to the **pattern**, not just isolated moments. You could say:

"I've noticed repeated instances where I feel excluded from leadership decisions. Here are a few examples over the past month. I'm hoping we can explore solutions."

In Canada, human rights protections apply at the provincial and federal level. If internal efforts stall, external channels—like a union rep or a human rights tribunal—may be appropriate.

Final Thoughts

Bias in leadership spaces doesn't always show up as open hostility. More often, it's the **small cuts**—overlooked contributions, misattributed work, jokes that aren't funny, or assumptions that sting. When left unaddressed, they add up and wear you down.

But calm, strategic action helps reclaim your voice. You don't need to shout. You just need to stand—and be seen.

Quote

"Respect is not a privilege reserved for a few—it's the foundation every leader deserves to stand on."

— *Anonymous*

Reflection Prompt

Take a moment to ask yourself:

Have I ever stayed silent in moments where someone around me was minimized, misrepresented, or dismissed—simply because it was easier?

What would it look like to be an ally, not just in theory, but in the room where it happens?

How Organizations Can Build Truly Inclusive Cultures

1. Offer Cultural Competency Training

What it means:

This training helps managers and leaders recognize biases that are often difficult to see—such as unintentional favoritism, microaggressions, or unconscious stereotypes.

How to do it well:

- Use real-world examples and role-playing—not just academic theory.
- Encourage honest dialogue. Mistakes happen; what matters is learning from them.
- Focus on actions: How will a manager change how they speak, invite feedback, or thank team members?

Why it helps:

When leaders actively learn to spot and correct biased behaviors, trust grows—and inclusive leadership becomes a habit rather than a checklist.

2. Set Clear, Fair Rules

What it means:

Whether it's running meetings, giving feedback, or making decisions, clear rules level the playing field. Bias has less room to hide when norms exist.

How to do it well:

- Establish meeting protocols: ensure everyone quotes, provides name pronunciation, or explains context briefly before contributing.
- Create feedback guides that encourage clarity and respect—avoid vague comments like "too aggressive" or "not assertive enough."
- Share these rules publicly, so everyone knows what fair communication looks like.

Why it helps:

When we all follow the same playbook, double standards fade. Objective rules make it harder for constant bias to slip in.

3. Ensure Inclusive Decision-Making

What it means:

Don't let important conversations—and the power that comes with them—happen without diverse voices at the table.

How to do it well:

- Keep a simple "room roster" log to check who attends key decision-making meetings.
- Set expectations: aim for at least two people from underrepresented groups in each major forum, including the leadership team, hiring panel, and budget planning.
- Rotate meeting structures or assign facilitators to encourage input from all participants.

Why it helps:

Strategy and resource allocation reflect whoever's in the room. Broader representation means richer ideas—and more fairness.

4. Encourage Peer Networks

What it means:

Support cross-cultural connection through mentorship groups, employee resource networks, or casual peer check-ins.

How to do it well:

- Fund and promote Employee Resource Groups (ERGs) that welcome diverse cultural experiences.
- Organize monthly mentorship circles pairing supervisors from different backgrounds.
- Host informal team lunches where people share culture, work challenges, or leadership tips.

Why it helps:

These communities create safe spaces—supporters, allies, troubleshooters—without isolation or "otherness." They foster belonging and continuous growth.

5. Monitor Outcomes Fairly

What it means:

Data can uncover biased trends before they become systemic. Pay attention not just to feelings, but real results.

How to do it well:

- Track promotion rates, performance reviews, probation outcomes, and turnover segmented by culture or race.
- Schedule quarterly check-ins with HR and managers to explore why differences exist.
- Take swift action: Investigate if one group is rarely promoted, or if another group leaves more often.

Why it helps:

Where bias creeps in, data exposes it. By asking "why," you build accountability—and send a message: everyone gets an equal opportunity here.

Bottom Line

Building inclusion is an ongoing journey, not a one-time effort. By blending **Cultural Competency Training**, **transparent rules**, **diverse decision teams**, **peer networks**, and **data monitoring**, organizations take real steps to dismantle bias—and make every supervisor feel seen, heard, and valued.

Would you like me to create a **Cultural Inclusion Toolkit**—with workshop outlines, policy templates, and measurement dashboards—to support these actions?

Summary

Racial or cultural discrimination may be subtle—but its effects are real and damaging. Supervisors dealing with this need tools, support, and allyship. Organizations must act deliberately—through training, policy, representation, and cultural accountability—to create a truly inclusive environment where all contributions are valued equally.

Chapter 32
Gender-Based Bias or Harassment

"Bias isn't just personal — it's systemic."

Whether it's dismissive comments, unequal expectations, or outright harassment, gender bias creates an uneven playing field. It chips away at confidence, limits opportunity, and undermines professional dignity. When people face disrespect or unfair treatment simply because of their gender — or because they don't conform to traditional gender roles — it has lasting effects on morale and career growth. This chapter explores how gender-based bias and harassment show up, why they're harmful, and how supervisors and organizations can actively challenge and change them.

Sidelining Based on Gender Stereotypes

What it looks like:

Decisions are made based on assumptions about capability tied to gender—not on skill, experience, or potential. These biases often play out subtly but have real consequences for opportunity, development, and inclusion.

Example (Sidelining of a Woman)

Scenario:

Samantha, a transportation supervisor, is ready to contribute to both operational logistics and equipment planning. She formally requested access to the quarterly equipment-budget meetings.

Biased Response:

Her male counterpart was welcomed in immediately. But Samantha was told,

"That's for the equipment guys—you're handling route logistics."

Impact:

- Samantha missed a chance to build expertise, influence budgeting decisions, and expand her leadership scope.
- The team received a clear message: her role is limited by gender, not ability.

Example (Sidelining of a Man)

Scenario:

Aaron, a male healthcare supervisor with a psychology degree, applied to lead a new patient well-being and emotional support initiative. He had top patient engagement scores and a track record of empathetic leadership.

Biased Response:

The department head suggested,

"We really need someone naturally empathetic—let's consider Jasmine."

Impact:

- Aaron was denied the opportunity despite fitting the role.
- The bias reinforced harmful stereotypes—men are less nurturing—even when evidence shows otherwise.

Why Both Matter

When organizations rely on gendered assumptions—whether underestimating women or overlooking men in empathetic roles—they:

- **Undermine trust:** Talent is sidelined, causing frustration and disengagement.
- **Limit diversity:** Teams suffer when selection is based on stereotypes, not skills.
- **Stunt innovation:** Fresh ideas go missing when diverse voices are excluded.

What Organizations Can Do

- **Use competency-based selection:** Define roles by skills and track record—not gendered traits.
- **Standardize opportunity invitations:** Create open application processes for leadership roles or special initiatives.
- **Diversify panels:** Include diverse voices in decision-making to check biases and assumptions.

These two examples highlight how **gender-based sidelining** isn't a one-way street—it's systemic and impacts talent across the gender spectrum. Addressing it means building truly fair processes and holding teams accountable to equitable practices.

2. Dismissal of Professional Feedback

What it looks like:

Feedback or ideas are often overlooked, questioned, or ignored—not because of their content, but because of the identity or perceived authority of the person sharing them. Later, when someone else (often from a more socially "privileged" or favored group) repeats the idea, it is praised, validated, or implemented. This subtle dynamic can happen to anyone—but it often reflects deeper issues of bias tied to gender, power, or perceived hierarchy.

Example 1: Jamie's Overlooked Insight

Jamie, a female logistics coordinator, proposed using real-time traffic data to reconfigure morning delivery routes. Her suggestion was met with polite silence. Later in the same meeting, Alex, a senior male supervisor, made the exact same recommendation.

The manager responded: "That's a brilliant solution—exactly what we need."

Jamie didn't say anything at the time, but privately felt dismissed and undervalued. Her confidence took a hit, and she began holding back on future ideas.

Example 2: Marcus Not Taken Seriously

Marcus, a soft-spoken male supervisor in a predominantly female HR team, recommended a new digital tool to track employee engagement. The room grew quiet, and someone said, "Interesting, but that might be a bit technical for our team."

A week later, his colleague Priya introduced the same tool in a more assertive tone during a leadership roundtable. The department director praised her "initiative" and greenlit a pilot project.

Marcus felt confused. He wondered if his communication style—or even assumptions about his role—had influenced how his input was received.

Why It Matters

- **Undermines Psychological Safety:** When people feel their input is consistently dismissed, they disengage or self-censor—even when they have valuable insights.
- **Reinforces Inequity:** If some voices are routinely ignored while others are elevated for saying the same things, trust in the system erodes.
- **Wastes Talent:** Good ideas get delayed or lost when the messenger matters more than the message.

What Teams Can Do

- **Credit Ideas Publicly:** Leaders should develop the habit of saying, "Great idea, Jamie brought that up earlier—let's explore it further."
- **Use Round-Robin or Anonymous Submissions:** These techniques help eliminate bias in the early stages of idea evaluation.
- **Train on Listening Bias:** Workshops on unconscious bias can help team members recognize these moments in real time and correct course.

Final Thought

Dismissal of feedback based on who shares it—whether intentional or unconscious—isn't just a fairness issue. It stifles creativity, slows progress, and sends the message that visibility matters more than value. When all voices are heard and credited equally, the entire organization benefits.

Reflection:

"True leadership listens—not just to hear, but to understand. When every voice is valued, ideas grow stronger, and teams thrive. Dismissing feedback based on who speaks is not only unfair, it stunts growth and breeds mistrust. By fostering a culture where respect is given before recognition, we create spaces where everyone can contribute fully, regardless of gender or background. This is the foundation of authentic, effective leadership."

3. Harassment in Tone or Language

What it looks like:

Harassment through tone or language often involves comments or jokes that unfairly target someone based on gender. For female supervisors, this might mean being labeled "bossy," "too emotional," or facing intrusive questions about family planning. At the same time, male supervisors can experience similar bias—being mocked for showing vulnerability, accused of lacking leadership "strength," or pressured with personal questions about their family commitments. It's essential to acknowledge that these behaviors can originate from any level, including female managers who may unconsciously or deliberately target male supervisors with unfair remarks or stereotypes.

Example:

In one department, Sarah, a female manager, was called "too harsh" or "micromanaging" by some colleagues simply because she held firm expectations. Meanwhile, a male supervisor under her, David, was repeatedly teased by Sarah about being "too sensitive" and questioned in meetings about whether he planned to take time off for family duties, which undermined his authority in front of the team. Both Sarah and David experienced subtle but harmful language that chipped away at their confidence and credibility.

4. Unequal Evaluation Standards

What it looks like:

Evaluation criteria can be biased by gender stereotypes, where women are often judged on subjective traits like "attitude," "fit," or "likeability." At the same time, men are assessed more directly on skills, results, and leadership qualities. Similarly, men can face biased assessments if they show behaviors considered "too soft" or "unassertive," which might be overlooked or praised differently if exhibited by women. This double standard seeps into performance reviews through gender-coded language, affecting confidence, career growth, and opportunities for both genders.

Example:

In a mid-sized company, Maria received feedback to "be more assertive" in meetings, despite demonstrating strong leadership. Meanwhile, her male peer, Mark, exhibiting a similar communication style, was praised as "confident" and "decisive." Conversely, Mark was later criticized for "not showing enough empathy" during team conflicts—feedback that was less commonly directed at female supervisors. Both Maria and Mark felt the sting of unequal standards that shaped their evaluations and influenced promotion decisions, highlighting how gender bias can operate in multiple directions.

5. Gendered Body Language Expectations

What it looks like:

Penalties for physical gestures or speech patterns—like a woman being told she "talks too much" while men are lauded for being "talkative and engaging."

Example:

Liana received feedback to "smile more" during presentations, while men were encouraged to be "engaging" and "commanding." She felt reduced to appearance standards, not professional skills.

Why This Harms Supervisors and Teams

1. **Erodes Confidence:**
2. Continual bias chips away at belief in one's leadership ability.
3. **Communication Stalls:**
4. Avoiding participation or speaking up becomes a way to avoid pushback.
5. **Costs Inclusion and Culture:**
6. When people feel judged by gender—not capability—team cohesion weakens.
7. **Hinders Talent Pipeline:**
8. High-potential women, men, or non-binary supervisors may walk away, derailing diversity efforts.

What Supervisors Can Do

1. **Name It Respectfully:**

    > "When my suggestions aren't acknowledged—then highlighted elsewhere—I feel undervalued. Could we ensure all ideas are heard in the moment?"

2. **Track Patterns:**
3. Record instances where comments or evaluations show bias. Date, context, and who was present.
4. **Seek Allies:**

5. Partner with a peer who can speak up:

   "Let's make sure all voices are heard—even if the idea was shared earlier."

6. **Ask for Feedback Equity:**
7. Request structured feedback with examples:

   "Could you share one specific instance where I could've strengthened my feedback?"

8. **Elevate Concerns Through Formal Channels:**
9. If comments continue or affect promotion, engage HR with documented patterns:

   "I'd like your support in creating a fair review process that avoids gender-coded language."

What Organizations Should Do

1. **Train on Gender Bias:**
2. Use examples, role-playing, and language review to help leaders spot and correct bias.
3. **Define Fair Evaluation Standards:**
4. Create a rubric focusing on skills, behavior, impact—not subjective traits like "attitude" or "temperament."
5. **Monitor Review Language:**
6. Audit performance reviews regularly for stereotypes, gendered phrases, and unequal feedback.
7. **Encourage Cross-Gender Mentoring:**
8. Pair male allies with female/non-binary supervisors to promote understanding and sponsorship.
9. **Track Equity Outcomes:**
10. Measure promotion rates, turnover, and retention disaggregated by gender identity to spot and correct disparities.

1. Establish Clear, Role-Based Evaluation Criteria

Why it matters:

Subjective impressions like "strong leader" or "good communicator" are vague and can be interpreted through biased lenses.

How to do it:

- Use **predefined rubrics** tied to the actual responsibilities of the role.
- Evaluate based on **output, goals, and behavior** — not personality traits.

Example (Balanced):

Instead of saying:

- "She's too emotional" or "He's not assertive enough,"
- Use:
- "Needs improvement in stakeholder communication during high-pressure scenarios."

2. Train Evaluators to Recognize Gender-Based Double Standards

Why it matters:

Both men and women can be penalized for violating gender expectations:

- A woman being "direct" might be called abrasive.
- A man expressing stress may be told he's "not leadership material."

How to do it:

- Offer bias training focused on **stereotypes that apply to all genders.**
- Include real-world examples like:
    - Male supervisors being denied paternity leave or called "too soft"
    - Female supervisors seen as "aggressive" for leading firmly

Tip: Include exercises that show how identical behaviors get labeled differently.

3. Calibrate Reviews Across Departments

Why it matters:

One manager may be more lenient, while another may unconsciously apply more pressure based on gender or personality.

How to do it:

- HR reviews and "norms" evaluations before they're finalized.
- Ask questions like:

    "Would this feedback be the same if the person were a different gender?"

4. Review Language in Written Feedback

Why it matters:

Words like "nurturing," "bossy," "quiet," or "aggressive" often reflect **personality judgment**, not job performance.

What to do:

- Ask reviewers to support adjectives with **concrete behaviors.**
- Avoid coded terms that disproportionately target one gender.

Balanced Note:

Men are sometimes described as "cold" or "unapproachable" for being quiet; women might be called "emotional" for being expressive. Both can be unfair.

5. Collect Peer and Upward Feedback

Why it matters:

One manager's view may be biased. Broader input can paint a fuller, fairer picture.

How to do it:

- Include 360-degree reviews from team members and collaborators.
- Make sure feedback from both genders is considered equally credible.

6. Track Trends Over Time

Why it matters:

You may not notice bias in one review, but patterns often reveal inequities.

How to do it:

- Track:
    o Frequency of negative or positive keywords by gender
    o Promotion rates across roles and departments
    o Performance scores over time

Example:

If women are often marked down for "not fitting in" and men for "not being team players," it may reveal **subjective norms** harming both.

7. Allow for Feedback Rebuttals

Why it matters:

Sometimes the review is inaccurate or missing context.

How to do it:

- Allow employees to write a **response** before a review is finalized.
- Train managers to consider rebuttals seriously and review the documentation.

8. Audit Promotions and Raises

Why it matters:

Even if reviews are neutral, outcomes may still favor one gender.

How to do it:

- Compare review scores to promotion and pay decisions.
- Ask: "Are people with similar evaluations getting similar opportunities?"

Final Note: Fairness Is for Everyone

Creating evaluation systems that reduce bias **isn't about favoring women or men**—it's about making sure no one is held back for being who they are. Fair evaluation processes benefit:

- Women trying to lead without being called "too much"
- Men who express stress without being seen as "weak"
- Anyone who defies outdated stereotypes and still shows up to lead, grow, and contribute

Summary

Gender-based bias isn't always loud—it can be subtle but unrelenting. Naming it, documenting it, and creating awareness are the first steps toward restoring equality. Organizations can support this by establishing gender-fair practices, promoting transparency in reviews, and implementing advocacy programs that uplift all supervisors—not just some.

Chapter 33
Ageism: Discrimination for Being 'Too Young' or 'Too Old'

"Value isn't measured by years — but too often, it's judged that way."

Being considered "too young" or "too old" is a common, painful experience in many workplaces. Ageism shuts down opportunities and dismisses contributions based on stereotypes rather than skills. It's a subtle exclusion that costs careers and lives of experience.

Introduction

Age discrimination isn't just stereotyping older workers—it can affect younger supervisors too. Whether you're perceived as "too inexperienced" or "past your prime," assumptions about age can erode confidence, block opportunities, and foster a subtle, yet real, form of exclusion. Let's explore how this plays out, the impact it has, and what can help.

How Age Bias Shows Up

1. Being "Too Young"

Example:

Emma, a 27-year-old production supervisor, suggested a shift to automated scheduling software. Her suggestion was dismissed with remarks like "Let's wait until Emma has more leadership experience." Later, a more seasoned peer reiterated the idea and received immediate buy-in.

Why it hurts:

Being older isn't a guarantee of better ideas, and your capabilities shouldn't be underestimated solely based on age.

2. Being "Too Old"

Example:

Robert, a 58-year-old IT supervisor, faced pressure to step aside after proposing new remote-work strategies. He was told, "Maybe it's time for someone less set in their ways to drive this change." This message made him feel sidelined and undervalued.

Why it hurts:

Assuming older leaders resist new ideas can block seasoned perspectives that balance innovation with experience.

The Real Impact

- **Lost Credibility:** Age-related preconceptions overshadow track records and expertise.
- **Lower Aspirations:** Young leaders may stop volunteering; older ones might hesitate to pitch new ideas.
- **Unfair Exclusion:** Projects and promotions slip away—and age, not merit, becomes the deciding factor.
- **Team Fragmentation:** Age bias divides teams, rather than uniting them around shared goals.

What Supervisors Can Do (Explained in Detail)

1. Show Your Skillset

Young Supervisors:

If you're new to leadership or perceived as "too young," it's vital to back up your role with concrete evidence of your capability. Create a working portfolio that includes:

- Examples of successful projects you've led
- Metrics that show growth under your management (e.g., productivity increased 15% in 6 months)
- Any relevant certifications or workshops attended (like conflict resolution or team leadership)

This approach doesn't just prove you're capable—it shifts the conversation from "age" to **achievement**.

Older Supervisors:

If you're perceived as "outdated" or resistant to change, it's important to show that you're not just keeping up—you're **leading** change. You might do this by:

- Taking part in digital training or software updates
- Bringing in modern best practices or hybrid team strategies
- Sharing stories of recent success where your experience helped solve a new problem

This reminds others that learning is a mindset, not a generational trait.

2. Address Assumptions Directly

It takes confidence and emotional intelligence to handle assumptions head-on—but done respectfully, this can reset a damaging narrative.

If you're younger and notice hesitation about your leadership, a calm one-on-one might sound like:

"I know my age might make my role here feel unexpected. But I've already led teams through system upgrades and delivered on tight deadlines. I'm confident I can bring strong results here, too."

If you're older and being nudged out of strategy conversations:

"I've noticed I haven't been looped in on recent planning meetings. I want to make sure my background and insight are still contributing value to the team."

These statements are **assertive without being confrontational**, and they make it harder for others to ignore the underlying bias.

3. Document Successes

When age bias is subtle, **proof matters**.

Keep a private but organized record of:

- Emails thanking you for successful execution
- Data from projects you've led
- Feedback from peers, clients, or upper management

Why? When it comes time for performance reviews, promotions, or defending your credibility, you'll have a trail of evidence that shows your contributions. That's especially useful when age-based assumptions creep into evaluations or decisions.

4. Seek Mentorship or Peer Allies

Younger supervisors:

Reach out to seasoned colleagues who understand the value of fresh thinking. A mentor who's respected in the organization can endorse your ideas, advocate for you in meetings, or simply offer advice on how to navigate hierarchies.

Older supervisors:

Team up with rising stars who are fluent in the latest tools or trends. This shows that you're not afraid to adapt—and more importantly, that **collaboration, not competition**, is your mindset.

Peer allies also provide backup when subtle age bias emerges in meetings or decision-making.

5. Escalate If Necessary

If private conversations and clear results aren't enough, and age-based bias continues to block your advancement, it may be time to seek formal recourse. This can include:

- Filing a concern with Human Resources
- Speaking to a manager outside your department
- Contacting a workplace diversity officer or ombudsperson
- Reviewing internal discrimination policies or codes of conduct

In Canada, the **Canadian Human Rights Act** protects employees from age discrimination. In the U.S., the **Age Discrimination in Employment Act (ADEA)** serves a similar function. If internal options fail, external legal counsel or advocacy organizations may be helpful.

You don't have to suffer in silence or wait until it gets worse.

Final Thought

Whether you're a 28-year-old trying to prove you belong at the table or a 58-year-old being quietly shuffled to the sidelines, **age bias doesn't define your value**—your results do. Utilize tools such as feedback, records, respectful dialogue, and allies to take control of your narrative.

What Organizations Should Do — Tackling Age Discrimination

1. Clarify Policies on Age Equity

Organizations should make it unmistakably clear: **age cannot be a barrier** to opportunity. That starts with codified policies in HR handbooks, leadership guidelines, and job postings.

What this looks like:

- A clear line stating: *"Employees of all ages will be evaluated and assigned based on qualifications, not age-based assumptions."*
- Language in promotion policies that removes vague criteria like "leadership maturity" unless it's tied to specific behaviors or results.

Why it matters:

When expectations are subjective, age-based assumptions creep in. Without strong policy language, managers may unconsciously think:

- "She's too young to lead a cross-functional team."
- "He's too close to retirement to invest in."

Clear policy = accountability.

2. Train for Age Bias Awareness

Just as organizations train for cultural competency or gender sensitivity, **age bias deserves specific attention.**

Include scenarios like:

- A younger supervisor being called "green" and passed over for high-visibility projects, even with a strong track record.
- An experienced team lead being told, "This new tech might be a bit much," despite decades of adaptability.
- Interviewers assuming a younger applicant won't stick around—or that an older one won't adapt to change.

Why it matters:

Most age bias isn't hostile—it's **subtle and rooted in stereotypes.** Training helps managers recognize when they're assuming, rather than assessing.

Tip: Use real-world anonymized examples in training for a stronger impact.

3. Enforce Fair Criteria

Age should never be a proxy for skill, growth potential, or leadership capacity. Instead, roles should be defined based on **core competencies**, not how long someone's been in the workforce.

What this looks like:

- Promotions based on project outcomes, peer feedback, and KPIs.
- Leadership tracks that welcome both early-career and late-career candidates—based on **ability**, not age.

Example:

Instead of saying, *"We're looking for someone seasoned,"* shift to:

"We're looking for someone who has led at least two cross-functional initiatives with measurable results."

Why it matters:

When standards are fair and consistent, they level the playing field. Talent isn't about how many candles were on your last birthday cake—it's about what you bring to the table.

4. Balance Teams Constructively

Intergenerational collaboration can be an organization's secret weapon—**if done intentionally**. Diverse ages bring different insights: energy and fresh thinking from younger leaders; wisdom, pattern recognition, and calm problem-solving from experienced ones.

What this looks like:

- Pairing younger and older managers as co-leads on complex projects.
- Creating reverse mentoring programs where junior staff teach senior leaders about tech trends, and senior leaders mentor on strategy or people management.

Why it matters:

Age diversity improves team performance. According to a 2020 study by Deloitte, organizations with age-diverse teams were more likely to report innovation and strong employee engagement.

But to benefit from that, you must **design for it**—not just hope it happens.

5. Monitor Age-Related Metrics

If organizations aren't tracking age bias, they're likely missing it. Metrics shed light on patterns that might otherwise remain hidden.

Track areas like:

- Age of employees promoted to leadership roles
- Who receives training opportunities (by age group)
- Compensation differences across generations in similar roles
- Exit interview data related to perceived age bias

Why it matters:

If 80% of promotions are going to employees under 35, or if no one over 50 is being offered new project leadership, something's off—even if unintentional. Data gives organizations a reason to pause and ask: *"Are we unintentionally sidelining valuable talent?"*

Final Thought

Age discrimination doesn't always shout—it often whispers. It shows up in assumptions, exclusions, and overlooked potential. But when organizations build structures that prioritize fairness, clear criteria, and intergenerational respect, everyone thrives.

Summary

Age bias can hurt supervisory teams—whether it targets emerging talent or seasoned professionals. Fighting it requires accurate policies, inclusive evaluation, strong mentorship, and awareness built into leadership training. With balanced systems and respect for all generations, organizations unlock their full talent potential—no matter what year someone was born.

Chapter 34
Religious Disrespect or Exclusion

"Faith should be a source of strength — not a cause for exclusion."

When religious beliefs become grounds for disrespect or exclusion, the workplace becomes a hostile and unwelcoming environment. Denying accommodations or mocking beliefs isn't just rude — it violates basic respect and human rights. Inclusion means honoring all faiths, or none.

Introduction:

Why Religious Respect Matters in the Workplace

Religious diversity is a core aspect of human identity, yet it's often mishandled or ignored in professional settings. When supervisors are disrespected or excluded because of their faith—or perceived lack of it—it undermines their authority, silences their voice, and disrupts psychological safety. Religious disrespect in the workplace doesn't always come in overt forms. It often manifests subtly, through exclusion from events, insensitive scheduling, or dismissive attitudes toward expressions of belief.

Supervisors carry a dual burden. They're expected to support diverse teams while managing up—and if their own beliefs are disregarded or minimized, they can feel isolated and powerless to address the imbalance. This chapter explores the ways religious exclusion shows up, how it harms, and what organizations and leaders can do to build a respectful, inclusive environment.

1. What Religious Disrespect Can Look Like

a. Insensitivity to Religious Holidays or Practices

Example: Nadia, a Muslim supervisor, requests time off for Eid. Instead of support, her manager questions, "Is that a real holiday?" The team is quietly frustrated about having to adjust, even though Christian holidays are always respected.

Impact: Nadia feels like her traditions are seen as inconvenient rather than meaningful. This chips away at her sense of belonging.

b. Mocking or Dismissing Beliefs

Example: During lunch, Raj, a Hindu supervisor, mentions that he's fasting. A colleague jokes, "You don't look spiritual." The group laughs. Nobody says anything—including leadership.

Impact: Raj leaves the room feeling humiliated. He avoids bringing up anything personal again and becomes more withdrawn in team spaces.

c. Unequal Accommodation

Example: A company easily approves Christian Bible study groups but hesitates when a Jewish supervisor asks for a prayer room during High Holidays.

Impact: Selective support communicates favoritism and alienates employees of minority faiths.

d. Exclusion from Social Norms or Events

Example: A holiday party is planned around alcohol with no halal or kosher options. A Sikh supervisor quietly declines the invite—but the absence is interpreted as "not a team player."

Impact: Religious supervisors face the impossible choice of violating their values or seeming disengaged.

2. Why This Harms Supervisors and Teams

- **Undermines Psychological Safety**: Supervisors are less likely to express concerns or bring their full selves to work when faith-based identity is ignored or ridiculed.
- **Impacts Leadership Credibility**: Being treated as "different" affects how teams perceive the supervisor's authority and influence.
- **Breeds Resentment and Division**: When some beliefs are honored and others dismissed, team morale suffers—and hidden biases fester.
- **Legal and Reputational Risk**: In countries like Canada, the U.S., and the U.K., failure to accommodate religious practice can lead to human rights complaints or litigation.

3. Real-World Example: Ali's Story

Ali, a department head in a Canadian logistics firm, observed that his colleagues scheduled key meetings during Friday prayers—even though he had requested 30-minute accommodation weeks in advance. When he tried to adjust the meeting time, he was told, "We all have commitments—you're not the only one." Later, his performance review noted that he was "unavailable at critical times." Ali filed an internal complaint and eventually worked with HR to introduce a company-wide inclusive scheduling guide.

4. How Organizations Can Prevent Religious Exclusion

a. Establish Clear Religious Accommodation Policies

- Define protected practices under local laws (e.g., prayer, dietary needs, attire).
- Create simple request forms and fast-track approvals.

b. Offer Interfaith Education and Awareness

- Train leadership on different religious observances and their workplace impact.

268

- Include real-world examples in DEI workshops: fasting, prayer time, holidays, clothing choices, etc.

c. Create Inclusive Scheduling Norms

- Avoid major meetings or deadlines on known holy days (e.g., Yom Kippur, Ramadan, Diwali).
- Rotate office celebrations—e.g., include Eid, Hanukkah, and Lunar New Year in year-end messages.

d. Design Inclusive Social Events

- Offer alcohol-free options, vegetarian/halal/kosher food, and quiet spaces.
- Make participation optional without consequence or judgment.

e. Encourage Faith-Safe Spaces

- Create neutral prayer rooms or reflection spaces open to all.
- Invite employees to share traditions through lunch-and-learns or newsletters—voluntarily, never mandated.

5. What Supervisors Can Do If They Face Exclusion

1. Document Patterns Respectfully

Write down what happened, when, and how it made you feel. Note how it affected your ability to lead.

2. Raise Concerns Early

Use calm language: "I've noticed key meetings sometimes overlap with my religious observance. Can we explore alternative times?"

3. Seek Allies in Leadership or ERGs

Ask others to help normalize practices like holiday leave or dietary accommodations.

4. Know Your Rights

In Canada, for example, religious rights are protected by:

- *Canadian Human Rights Act* (federally)
- *Provincial Human Rights Codes*
- Employers must accommodate up to the point of "undue hardship."

6. Closing Reflection

"Diversity is not about how we differ. Diversity is about embracing one another's uniqueness."

— Ola Joseph

Religious inclusion isn't about special treatment—it's about equal dignity. When organizations make space for all beliefs, everyone feels seen, valued, and empowered to lead. Supervisors shouldn't have to choose between faith and fairness. They deserve both.

Chapter 35
Discriminatory Assignment of Tasks or Projects

"Who gets the hard work — and who gets the credit — often reveals hidden biases."

Task assignments aren't always neutral. When certain employees are consistently given less meaningful, repetitive, or unpleasant tasks, while others receive high-profile projects, it signals bias. These patterns stunt career growth and perpetuate inequality.

Introduction

When supervisors assign tasks, their choices signal who is trusted, valued, and seen as capable. However, when supervisors or managers direct work based on bias—whether conscious or unconscious—they not only waste talent but also undermine morale, equity, and overall performance. This chapter explores how task assignment discrimination happens, why it's harmful, and what supervisors and organizations can do to correct it.

1. What Discriminatory Task Assignment Looks Like

a. Non-Visible Tasks vs. High-Visibility Projects

Promoting routine, low-risk work to certain demographics while assigning others high-profile projects.

Example:

- **Female supervisor Lena** is frequently assigned compliance reports. When a client-facing upgrade project opens, her male peer, Tom, is instantly tapped—even though Lena led similar efforts with success and visibility.

b. Task Creep Through Unpaid Extra Work

Assigning after-hours or menial tasks disproportionately to certain supervisors without recognition.

Example:

- **Young male supervisor Aaron** picks up weekend stock take and after-hours equipment cleaning. His peers, older or female, are rarely asked—even though Aaron wasn't consulted.

c. Stereotypical Skill Mapping

Tasks assigned based on assumptions, not expertise—like giving administrative duty to someone thought to be "naturally organized" or technical roles to "tech-savvy men."

Example:

- **Senior data-savvy supervisor Diana** is overlooked for analytics work and is instead given event coordination. Meanwhile, her male junior counterpart is tasked with developing company dashboards.

2. Why This Happens

• Implicit Bias

Most supervisors believe they are fair, but unconscious mental shortcuts often influence decisions. These biases are automatic, meaning leaders may unknowingly assume someone's skills or reliability based on characteristics such as gender, age, ethnicity, or tenure with the company. For example, a manager might assume a younger supervisor lacks experience and avoid giving them big projects, even if their work record says otherwise. These invisible biases shape who gets opportunities without anyone actively meaning to discriminate.

• Comfort Zones

People naturally gravitate toward others they feel familiar with or can easily relate to. Supervisors often assign tasks to team members they "click" with, share similar backgrounds, or have worked with before. This creates a comfort zone that feels safe and predictable. Unfortunately, this comfort can shut out others who are equally or more capable but less familiar. For instance, a supervisor might repeatedly give important client meetings to someone from their own cultural group while unintentionally sidelining others.

• Performance Anxiety

Assigning high-stakes or visible tasks carries risks: if the project fails, the supervisor's own reputation is affected. Because of this pressure, risk-averse leaders often stick with "safe bets" — employees they know well and believe will succeed. This approach discourages spreading chances around and keeps some talented supervisors stuck in routine or less visible work. It's a way to protect themselves, but it stifles diversity and growth on the team.

• Cultural Stereotyping

Some traits and abilities get unfairly linked to demographic groups rather than individual strengths. For example, patience might be assumed to be a "female" trait, while technical savvy is assumed to be "male." This stereotyping leads to pigeonholing people into certain roles or tasks without considering their real skills or interests. A woman who is excellent with data might be overlooked for analytics work because of these assumptions, while a man might be pushed into technical roles even if his strength lies elsewhere. These stereotypes limit opportunities and reinforce unfair patterns.

3. The Real Impact

• Loss of Growth

When talented supervisors are consistently passed over for challenging assignments or development opportunities, their professional growth stalls. They miss out on chances to build new skills, gain visibility, and prove their abilities in high-impact situations. Over time, this limits not only their career trajectory but also the organization's ability to fully leverage its workforce. Imagine a promising supervisor who consistently receives routine tasks while others take on strategic projects—their potential remains untapped, a loss for everyone.

• Erosion of Trust

When employees notice that opportunities are handed out unfairly or repeatedly to the same people, it damages their trust in leadership. They start to feel the system is rigged or biased, which leads to disengagement and decreased motivation. This isn't just about individual feelings; it affects team morale and can create a culture of suspicion and resentment. When trust breaks down, people stop giving their best effort and may even consider leaving the company.

• Reduced Confidence

Hearing messages like "you're not ready" or being excluded from important projects sends a clear signal that management doubts their capabilities. Over time, these repeated rejections chip away at a supervisor's self-esteem and confidence. This internal impact can become a self-fulfilling prophecy—feeling undervalued, they might hesitate to speak up or take initiative, further reducing their chances of advancement. Confidence is key to leadership, and when it's undermined, both the individual and the team suffer.

• Inequitable Outcomes

Because promotions, raises, and recognition often go to those handling the most visible and critical work, the uneven assignment of tasks creates a cycle of inequality. Those who get repeated chances to shine are rewarded accordingly, while others remain stuck without the credentials or track record needed to move forward. This imbalance reinforces existing biases and creates systemic barriers that are hard to break. Ultimately, it means the organization loses out on diverse leadership and the innovation that comes with it.

4. What Supervisors Can Do

1. Rotate Project Assignments

Supervisors should keep track of who has recently led important projects or taken on high-visibility roles. This could be as simple as maintaining a matrix or spreadsheet that records each person's assignments. By doing so, supervisors can ensure these opportunities don't always go to the same few individuals. Rotating projects encourages fairness and helps develop a broader range of skills within the team. It also signals to employees that everyone has a chance to grow, which boosts motivation and engagement.

Example: If John led the last three major projects, the supervisor might intentionally assign the next key project to someone like Priya, who has been ready but overlooked.

2. Assign by Strength—Not Gender or Tenure

Rather than assigning tasks based on outdated stereotypes—such as assuming women should handle communication, or younger employees can only do "basic" work—supervisors should match tasks to real skills and strengths. This requires knowing each team member's capabilities and past performance. Experience and job length shouldn't be the default deciding factors; a newer employee with a knack for data analysis should get challenging analytical tasks regardless of how long they've been on the job.

Example: Maria is great at explaining complex technical details clearly to clients, so she's assigned the client presentations, even though she's newer than some colleagues.

3. Ask for Preferences and Development Goals

Engage your team members in conversations about what projects they want to take on and where they want to grow. During regular one-on-one check-ins, supervisors can ask questions like, "What types of projects excite you?" or "Are there skills you want to develop?" This approach helps uncover individual ambitions and ensures that supervisors don't overlook employees by default. When preferences are ignored repeatedly, it can highlight unconscious bias or unfair practices.

Example: During a check-in, Ahmed expresses interest in leading a marketing campaign, so the supervisor ensures he gets the next opportunity to lead one.

4. Challenge Your Own Assumptions

We all have unconscious biases. When supervisors think something like, "She's not technical enough for this project," it's essential to pause and reflect. Instead of relying on gut feelings or stereotypes, supervisors should ask for concrete evidence of skills and review past work. This helps avoid unfairly dismissing someone's abilities based on assumptions. Over time, challenging these biases will lead to more objective and inclusive decision-making.

Example: Before deciding not to assign a software upgrade task to Emily because "she's not technical," the supervisor reviews Emily's recent successful handling of a related data migration project.

5. Provide Transparency

Transparency builds trust. Supervisors can maintain a shared log or dashboard that is regularly updated to show who is working on which projects, who has led which initiatives, and upcoming opportunities. When everyone has visibility into assignments, it's harder for favoritism or bias to go unnoticed. Employees feel more confident that chances are distributed fairly, and supervisors hold themselves accountable.

Example: The team's project log is reviewed monthly in a team meeting, allowing members to see who has had leadership roles and prompting discussions about fair rotation.

Summary:

By rotating assignments, focusing on strengths, engaging employees in their development goals, reflecting on biases, and being transparent, supervisors create a fairer and more empowering work environment. These steps don't just improve fairness—they also enhance team performance and individual growth.

5. What Organizations Should Do

1. Standardize Role Rotation Policies

Organizations should create clear policies that require departments to regularly rotate key roles and responsibilities among supervisors. This means that important functions—such as being the client lead, managing budgets, or heading special projects—shouldn't always fall to the same individuals. By institutionalizing rotation, organizations ensure broader exposure and development opportunities for more employees, which helps prevent favoritism and unconscious exclusion. It also supports a culture where everyone feels they have a fair shot at high-impact experiences.

Example: The finance department might set a rule that every quarter, the "budget owner" role shifts to a different team member, ensuring everyone develops budget management skills over time.

2. Train on Task Assignment Bias

Training programs should actively address biases in how tasks are assigned. Instead of theoretical discussions, training should include practical exercises. For example, participants might review case scenarios and ask themselves, "Would I assign this project to Maria or John? Why?" This self-reflection reveals hidden biases and assumptions. These exercises help leaders become aware of patterns where they might unconsciously favor some employees over others based on factors such as gender, age, or other characteristics, rather than ability or interest. Over time, this awareness can lead to more deliberate and equitable decisions.

Example: In a workshop, managers role-play assigning projects and receive feedback on whether their choices are fair or influenced by stereotypes.

3. Monitor Assignments

Organizations should systematically track who is given which types of work, including high-visibility projects, routine or "grunt" tasks, and opportunities to collaborate across departments. Data should be analyzed to spot trends based on gender, age, race, or other demographics. If certain groups are consistently passed over for challenging assignments or only given less visible work, that's a red flag. Regular monitoring creates accountability and enables early intervention to correct imbalances.

Example: HR collects quarterly reports showing how many cross-department projects were led by women versus men, or how many complex assignments were given to younger versus older supervisors.

4. Reward Equitable Leadership

Fair delegation and inclusive task assignment should be recognized and rewarded as important leadership qualities. When evaluating manager performance, organizations can include criteria that assess how well supervisors distribute opportunities among their team members. Rewarding equitable leadership incentivizes managers to be mindful about sharing projects broadly and fairly, rather than concentrating work among favorites. This also signals organizational commitment to fairness beyond just policies.

Example: A manager who consistently rotates key tasks and mentors diverse team members might be acknowledged in performance reviews or considered for leadership awards.

5. Pipeline Preparation

When selecting participants for leadership development programs or promotions, organizations should prioritize individuals who have demonstrated experience with a variety of projects and responsibilities. This means valuing breadth of experience and exposure over just tenure or fitting a "comfort zone." Preparing future leaders with diverse, challenging experiences helps create a stronger, more adaptable leadership pipeline and reduces bias toward those who only had opportunities because they were "safe" choices.

Example: A leadership program might require applicants to submit examples of different types of projects they've led, ensuring selection is based on proven versatility.

Summary:

By establishing formal policies for rotation, training managers on bias, carefully monitoring assignments, rewarding fairness, and preparing leaders through diverse experiences, organizations can create a more just workplace where talent can thrive regardless of identity or background.

6. Case Study: Equal Opportunity in Action

At a mid-size marketing firm, the head of HR noticed that their senior female marketing supervisor, Nina, hadn't led a campaign in two years. Projects kept going to her junior male counterparts—even though Nina had previous successes. The firm introduced a requirement: "Campaign lead must shift annually." In one year's time, Nina led a multi-channel campaign that achieved record results—and her influence in the leadership team grew immediately.

7. Summary

When tasks are assigned unfairly, talent is wasted and potential is blocked. By deliberately matching skills to opportunities, rotating visible roles, and monitoring fairness, supervisors and organizations create a culture of trust, equity, and growth.

Chapter 36
Pressure to Conform to Cultural Norms

"Diversity isn't just about who's in the room — it's about allowing everyone to be themselves."

When you're nudged—or shoved—to fit a workplace culture that doesn't respect your identity or values, it's more than uncomfortable. It's a subtle form of erasure. Pressure to conform stifles individuality and creativity, turning a mosaic of perspectives into a dull, uniform gray.

Introduction

Workplaces often pride themselves on being team-oriented and collaborative—but when "team culture" becomes a uniform standard everyone must mold themselves into, it can be deeply exclusionary. Cultural pressure to "fit in" may not be explicitly stated in policy, but it's felt in subtle, daily expectations: dress like the group, speak like the group, socialize in the "right" way, and avoid bringing too much of your authentic self to work.

For supervisors, especially those from underrepresented backgrounds, this pressure creates a constant tension between performing their roles and masking parts of their identity. The workplace becomes less about thriving and more about surviving without standing out "too much."

What Cultural Pressure Looks Like

Cultural conformity can appear deceptively harmless. In practice, it manifests through unspoken codes, workplace rituals, or informal norms that signal whether someone is seen as a "good fit."

Examples include:

- **Dress and appearance codes** that are not formal policy but strongly implied—like discouraging natural hairstyles, traditional clothing, or religious attire.
- **Communication styles** that favor assertiveness over collaboration, or humor over clarity—pressuring individuals to speak differently to be taken seriously.
- **Social expectations,** such as happy hours, sports talk, or alcohol-centered events, where supervisors who abstain feel alienated or judged.
- **Punishing difference** through comments like "You're so intense," "You don't seem like one of us," or "You'd go further here if you loosened up."

Real-World Example:

Ahmed, a first-generation Canadian supervisor, often brought his own lunch and avoided team pub nights due to religious restrictions around alcohol. Though he consistently met deadlines and led his team effectively, he was repeatedly passed over for strategic projects. When he asked for feedback, a senior leader told him he "wasn't as visible or social as others." Despite a strong performance, the unwritten requirement was to assimilate into a dominant social culture, which cost him advancement.

Julia, on the other hand, was a younger supervisor in a male-dominated utilities company. She avoided sports banter, didn't drink, and kept to herself after work hours to care for aging parents. She was once told during a performance review, "You're competent, but we don't see you building a strong rapport with leadership." The subtext? She wasn't blending into the informal cultural mold.

Why This Happens

- **Dominant Culture Norms**: Even in diverse workplaces, there is often a default to one "acceptable" way of dressing, speaking, and behaving—usually aligned with the majority group's values.
- **Affinity Bias**: Leaders tend to support those who resemble their own experience—leading to a sameness in who's seen as promotable or "easy to work with."
- **Avoidance of Discomfort**: Cultural differences can make some leaders uncomfortable, so they unconsciously favor those who conform.
- **Unwritten Rules**: Things like how to act in meetings, what tone to use with executives, or how casual to be are never explained but always judged.

The Harm It Causes

1. **Identity Suppression**
2. Supervisors feel they must filter or hide aspects of their identity—religious, cultural, linguistic, or personal—to feel safe or accepted.
3. **Burnout and Emotional Fatigue**
4. Constantly code-switching or masking your real self takes a toll. It drains emotional reserves that could otherwise be used to lead teams or innovate.
5. **Undermined Engagement**
6. When individuals feel excluded or unseen, they stop sharing ideas, voicing concerns, or volunteering for initiatives—robbing the organization of diverse input.
7. **Unfair Evaluation and Advancement**
8. Leaders may unconsciously equate cultural conformity with leadership readiness, pushing out talented supervisors who simply don't mimic the dominant mold.

What Supervisors Can Do

1. **Name It with Nuance**
2. Use respectful language to raise awareness. For example:
3. *"I've noticed our team tends to socialize around activities I can't fully participate in. Could we find other ways to connect that include more voices?"*
4. **Bring Authenticity in Gradual Steps**
5. Share small, personal insights or traditions over time to normalize differences. When done consistently, this expands the cultural range of what's accepted.

6. **Find Allies**
7. Look for other team members who also feel like "outsiders." Together, you can suggest inclusive practices or act as sounding boards for each other.
8. **Document Exclusion**
9. If you notice a pattern where cultural non-conformity affects assignments, visibility, or reviews, track these incidents. It can help identify bias and justify conversations with HR.

What Organizations Should Do

1. **Clarify "Cultural Fit" in Hiring and Promotion**
2. Ban vague language like "not a culture fit" unless clearly defined. Replace with skill-based criteria and diversity-minded evaluation.
3. **Offer Cultural Intelligence Training**
4. Go beyond "diversity awareness." Teach leaders how to respect and manage across cultural norms—including different ways of expressing leadership, disagreement, or formality.
5. **Redesign Social Norms**
6. Rotate team bonding around inclusive options (e.g., volunteering, team learning days, coffee chats). Don't rely solely on after-hours, alcohol-based events.
7. **Celebrate Difference, Not Just Tolerance**
8. Normalize and highlight diverse traditions and leadership styles. Let employees lead cultural initiatives, share experiences, or display symbolic items at their desks.
9. **Monitor Career Progression by Demographics**
10. If those from certain backgrounds consistently stall in middle management, investigate where bias or assimilation pressure may be operating.

Closing Reflection

"True belonging doesn't require us to change who we are; it requires us to be who we are."

— Brené Brown

The strength of an organization lies not in how well everyone blends in—but in how bravely and respectfully they show up as their full selves. Cultural conformity can seem harmless, but over time, it shrinks the voices, creativity, and morale of those who lead from a place of difference. When organizations value contribution over conformity, they unlock true inclusion—and that's where innovation begins.

Chapter 37
Stereotyping and Labeling

"Labels simplify people — and destroy potential."

"Discrimination doesn't always come in loud, obvious ways. Sometimes, it's a quiet box someone puts you in — based on your background, accent, appearance, or age. Once inside, you're expected to stay there. These biased labels reduce you to a stereotype, ignoring your complexity and turning your identity into a liability. Breaking free means reclaiming your story — on your own terms."

What It Looks Like

Stereotyping in the workplace happens when assumptions replace curiosity. Instead of asking what someone brings to the table, people rely on preconceived ideas—and those ideas shape how opportunities, feedback, and respect are distributed.

Real Examples:

- **Fatima**, a Middle Eastern woman in a municipal logistics department, was constantly told she was "too soft-spoken" to lead. Colleagues assumed she wouldn't want to manage tough contract negotiations—despite having previously done so successfully at a private firm.
- **Nathan**, a tall, athletic Black supervisor, was frequently asked to "deal with warehouse conflicts," despite his expertise being in operational data. He joked about it at first, but the pattern wore him down: "They see muscle before they see skill."
- **Priya**, a South Asian woman in IT, was repeatedly asked if she'd like to help plan cultural potlucks—but never invited to join innovation projects. The assumption? She was "great with people" but not "technical."

These may seem minor on their own. But over time, labeling people—even through seemingly "positive" stereotypes—restricts what roles they're allowed to take, how they're evaluated, and whether they're seen as leadership material.

Common Workplace Labels

Stereotype Label	Real Impact
"Too emotional"	Dismisses passion or valid pushback
"Aggressive"	Often used for assertive women or minorities
"Quiet = not leadership"	Overlooks introverts who lead with strategy
"The tech guy"	Limits broader leadership involvement
"Mom first"	Suggests a woman isn't serious about work
"Old school"	Used to sideline older workers from projects

Labels become shorthand. And shorthand denies depth.

Why It Happens

Stereotyping isn't always malicious. Often, it comes from:

1. **Cognitive Shortcuts**
2. The brain uses past patterns to categorize people quickly. In fast-moving work environments, this becomes a default—especially when leaders don't pause to challenge their assumptions.
3. **Cultural Conditioning**
4. Societal narratives shape how we view others. For instance, the media often portrays younger workers as impatient or older workers as out of touch.
5. **Lack of Exposure**
6. If someone hasn't worked closely with diverse colleagues, they may rely on stereotypes to "fill in the blanks."

The Harmful Impact

- **Loss of Talent**: People labeled as "not leadership material" may never be offered the chance to prove otherwise.
- **Mental Exhaustion**: Constantly battling assumptions is draining. It forces people to perform emotional labor just to be seen clearly.
- **Silenced Innovation**: When people don't feel free to show their full selves, they hold back—especially on bold or creative ideas.
- **Turnover and Disengagement**: Those who feel boxed in are more likely to check out—or leave entirely.

How Supervisors Can Respond

1. **Speak Up When You See It**
2. If someone gets labeled unfairly, interrupt the moment.
3. Example: "Actually, I've seen her lead under pressure—let's give her a shot."
4. **Define People by Performance, Not Profile**
5. Instead of "She's not really the type," ask: "What have they delivered? What do they want to do next?"
6. **Ask About Hidden Talents**
7. During check-ins: "Is there a part of your skill set you don't get to use here?" You'll often be surprised.
8. **Reject Compliments That Reinforce Stereotypes**
9. "You're so articulate" or "You're surprisingly technical"—these can carry unconscious bias. Aim for respectful, specific feedback.
10. **Model Curiosity, Not Assumption**
11. Instead of "You probably wouldn't want this," ask: "Would you be interested in leading this next time?"

What Organizations Should Do

- **Provide Bias Interruption Training**
- Teach teams to spot labeling in meetings, hiring, and feedback sessions.
- **Use Behavior-Based Evaluations**
- Performance reviews should measure outcomes and actions—not vague terms like "fit" or "style."
- **Diversify Project Leads**
- Track who gets chosen for high-visibility assignments—and intervene when patterns emerge.
- **Encourage Identity Awareness**
- Invite self-identification in optional staff surveys to better understand representation and inclusion gaps.
- **Recognize Subtle Bias in Recognition**
- Audit who gets credit, spotlighted, or celebrated. Does it reflect everyone's contribution—or just a few favored types?

Final Thought

"Labels are for filing. Labels are for clothing. Labels are not for people."

— Martina Navratilova

In a high-performance workplace, stereotypes don't just hurt feelings—they hurt results. When we let go of shortcuts and see people clearly, we create space for everyone to contribute fully.

Workshop Case Study: *Labels in Action*

Scenario

At Summit Solutions, a mid-sized consulting firm, leadership has identified a repeating issue: certain staff are being sidelined from key projects due to unspoken assumptions.

Scenario Description:

- **Elena**, a quiet and thoughtful team supervisor, often has her ideas ignored in meetings. When she finally speaks, a louder colleague repeats the same point and gets the credit.
- **Ravi**, a young Black supervisor, is repeatedly asked to organize social events or internal communications—tasks seen as "fitting his personality." Leadership assumes he isn't interested in client-facing roles.
- **Marcus**, an older white supervisor, is passed over for new technology projects because managers describe him as "one of the more seasoned folks who might prefer stability."

Despite talent and interest across the board, project assignments keep reinforcing these labels.

Discussion Questions

1. **Identify the Labels**
    - What stereotypes are being applied to Elena, Ravi, and Marcus?
    - Are they "positive" labels, negative, or mixed—and why does it still hurt?
2. **Explore the Impact**
    - How might each person feel in this scenario?
    - What risks does the team face when opportunities are restricted this way?
3. **Take Perspective**
    - Swap roles: If you were Elena, Ravi, or Marcus, what would you do?
    - As a colleague or peer, how could you notice and intervene?
4. **Brainstorm Solutions**
    - What could supervisors at Summit Solutions do differently to stop labeling from influencing assignments?
    - How could leadership create safeguards against unconscious stereotyping? (e.g., anonymous proposal feedback, rotation policies, etc.)
5. **Reflect on Personal Experience**
    - Have you noticed a similar situation in your workplace—either for yourself or a colleague?
    - What's one action you can take today to challenge stereotypes in your team?

Action Steps

- **Create a "Label Log":** Encourage participants to write down when they observe labeling in real time, followed by follow-up questions like "Would I say this about anyone else?"
- **Role-Play Exercise:** Practice stepping in as an ally by saying, "I've noticed something; let's focus on the idea, not the person."
- **Commitment Round:** End the session by each person naming one step they'll take in the next two weeks to call out—or prevent—labeling.

Chapter 38
Mockery of Accent, Appearance, or Beliefs

"Mockery is a weapon disguised as humor."

In workplaces that claim to celebrate diversity, mocking how someone speaks, dresses, or what they believe still happens far too often. These aren't harmless jokes — they're subtle attacks that isolate and demean. Whether delivered as banter, side comments, or raised eyebrows, mockery chips away at confidence and belonging, making people feel ashamed of who they are.

This chapter examines how these behaviors manifest in the workplace, their detrimental effects, and how supervisors and organizations can address them respectfully and constructively.

What It Looks Like

1. Mockery of Accent

Comments that mimic or exaggerate a person's accent—even in jest—signal that their way of speaking is inferior or comical.

- *Example*: A supervisor from Eastern Europe presents during a cross-functional meeting. Afterward, someone remarks, "That was a thick accent—you sure we caught all that?" The room laughs. The supervisor remains silent, unsure whether to defend or ignore it.

2. Dismissal of Dress

Cultural or religious attire is viewed as "unprofessional," "too ethnic," or "distracting," even when it aligns with company dress codes.

- *Example*: A Sikh team leader wears a turban to a company-wide event and is told quietly, "You'd look more relatable without the headgear." Though framed as feedback, the message implies that he must erase a part of his identity to be accepted.

3. Ridicule of Beliefs

Whether it's prayer routines, fasting, or ethical stances, mocking someone's belief system—through jokes or dismissive comments—creates division and discomfort.

- *Example*: During Ramadan, a Muslim supervisor declines lunch meetings. A peer jokes, "You're starving yourself for a month? That's extreme!" Others chuckle. The supervisor forces a smile but feels ridiculed for their spiritual practice.

These behaviors often come masked as humor or "harmless observations," but the underlying message is clear: "You're different—and we're not okay with that."

Why It's Harmful

1. It Undermines Professionalism and Authority

When supervisors are mocked or dismissed because of how they speak, what they wear, or their personal beliefs, it weakens their standing within the team. This kind of behavior shifts focus away from their skills and achievements, instead spotlighting superficial differences that create a sense of "otherness." For example, a supervisor who speaks with an accent might find colleagues less willing to trust their decisions—not because of the quality of their work, but simply because their manner of speaking is unfamiliar or stigmatized. This unfair skepticism erodes the natural respect that supervisors need to lead effectively, making it harder for them to command authority or influence team outcomes.

2. It Erodes Belonging

Belonging is a vital part of feeling safe and valued at work. When leaders face mockery about their identity—whether for cultural dress, language, or religious practices—they often feel pressured to conceal these parts of themselves to avoid ridicule. This need to "fit in" can cause them to withdraw, participate less actively, or avoid expressing unique perspectives. For instance, a supervisor who is teased for wearing traditional attire might start dressing more conservatively or avoid conversations about their culture. This loss of authentic presence not only diminishes their own job satisfaction but also deprives the team of diversity in thought and creativity.

3. It Reinforces Bias for Others

Allowing mockery to go unchallenged sets a harmful precedent. When team members witness disrespectful behavior towards one person's accent or beliefs and see no consequences, it implicitly signals that such conduct is acceptable. This can embolden others to engage in similar behavior, creating a workplace culture where exclusion and bias thrive. For example, if a supervisor hears a colleague mocked for their faith and no one intervenes, they may fear becoming the next target and hesitate to share their true self. Over time, this perpetuates division, undermines unity, and stalls efforts toward inclusivity.

4. It Fuels Attrition

The emotional burden of being "othered" or ridiculed wears heavily on individuals. Over time, supervisors who face ongoing mockery or dismissal may become disengaged, demoralized, and ultimately decide to leave their roles. This departure isn't driven by workload or career dissatisfaction alone, but by the invisible, cumulative stress of not feeling accepted or respected. For example, a highly skilled supervisor who is repeatedly teased about their cultural background might start seeking a workplace where their identity is embraced. This loss of talent is costly for organizations, which not only lose leadership but also the valuable perspectives that promote innovation and growth.

What Supervisors Can Do

1. Address Disrespect Calmly and Clearly

When you're the target of disrespectful comments, responding calmly and clearly can set a strong example and help shift the conversation back to professionalism. For instance, if someone mocks your accent or pronunciation, saying something like, "I'd appreciate it if we focused on the content of my ideas, not how I pronounce them," gently but firmly redirects attention to what truly matters—your work and expertise.

If you witness a colleague being mocked, stepping in with a respectful reminder like, "Let's steer away from comments about appearance or accent—they don't belong in a professional space," signals that such behavior isn't acceptable. This kind of intervention helps create a safer environment for everyone and shows that respect is expected.

2. Educate Without Shame

Sometimes, mockery comes from a lack of understanding rather than malice. Supervisors can use moments of curiosity or questions as opportunities to educate colleagues without making them feel judged or defensive. For example, explaining that "This attire is important in my culture—it's part of how I show respect and focus at work," invites others to learn and appreciate different cultural practices.

This approach fosters empathy and broadens perspectives, helping colleagues see beyond stereotypes or assumptions. It also empowers supervisors to take ownership of their identity without feeling the need to apologize or hide it.

3. Find Allies or Mentors

Repeated experiences of mockery or dismissal can be isolating and emotionally draining. It's important for supervisors to seek out support systems such as trusted peers, mentors, or affinity groups who share or understand their experiences. These allies provide emotional validation, practical advice, and can amplify concerns when institutional change is needed.

For example, joining a workplace diversity group can connect you with others who've faced similar challenges and work collectively to promote respect and inclusion. Mentors can also offer guidance on how to navigate difficult conversations or escalate issues constructively.

4. Document and Escalate When Needed

If disrespectful behavior persists despite efforts to address it directly or through education, it's crucial to keep a record of incidents. Documenting what was said, when, and in what context provides clear evidence that can support formal complaints or discussions with HR or workplace mediators.

This documentation helps ensure that concerns are taken seriously and enables organizations to identify patterns of behavior that need addressing. Remember, involving HR or neutral mediators isn't about escalating conflict unnecessarily—it's about ensuring a respectful and safe work environment for everyone.

What Organizations Should Do

1. Set Clear Boundaries in Conduct Policies

Organizations need to make it absolutely clear that mocking or belittling someone's personal identity—whether that's their accent, the way they dress, or their religious or spiritual beliefs—is unacceptable. This means updating workplace behavior guidelines to explicitly state these protections. Clear rules help everyone understand the line between friendly banter and disrespect, making it easier for supervisors and employees to hold one another accountable. For example, a policy might specifically mention that jokes or comments about language differences or cultural dress are prohibited. This clarity prevents ambiguity and fosters a respectful atmosphere.

2. Offer Cross-Cultural Training

Many workplaces have diversity programs, but meaningful change requires more than just surface-level efforts. Cross-cultural training should dive deep into unconscious bias—those subtle, often unnoticed assumptions that influence how people perceive others. Training should teach cultural humility, encouraging employees to recognize what they don't know and approach differences with curiosity rather than judgment. It should also equip staff with practical skills to respond constructively if they witness or experience mockery or exclusion. For example, role-playing scenarios can help employees practice intervening in a respectful, effective way.

3. Celebrate Diverse Expression

To truly embrace inclusion, organizations must celebrate the full range of identities and expressions within their teams. Highlighting supervisors and leaders who bring their authentic selves to work sends a powerful message that difference is valued, not just tolerated. This can be done through newsletters that share personal stories, hosting speaker events featuring diverse voices, or having leadership openly discuss the importance of inclusivity. When employees see role models confidently expressing their culture or beliefs, it helps normalize differences and encourages others to feel safe doing the same.

4. Create Safe Reporting Channels

Employees need to know exactly where to turn if they feel mocked, belittled, or excluded—and they must trust that their concerns will be handled seriously and confidentially. Organizations should provide multiple reporting options—such as anonymous hotlines, dedicated HR contacts, or diversity officers—and clearly communicate these channels to all staff. Importantly, the process should be supportive rather than punitive, aiming to resolve issues constructively while protecting those who speak up from retaliation. When people feel safe reporting problems, the workplace culture improves for everyone.

5. Promote and Protect Diverse Leaders

Finally, it's crucial that diverse supervisors feel empowered to bring their whole selves to work without fear of needing to "fit in" or hide their roots. Leadership development and promotion pipelines should intentionally include and support individuals from diverse backgrounds. This might mean mentoring programs tailored to underrepresented groups or ensuring hiring committees are trained to recognize and counteract bias. When diverse leaders are visible and protected, it signals to the entire organization that inclusion isn't just a policy—it's a priority.

Examples of Successful Implementation

1. Clear Boundaries in Conduct Policies

Example: A multinational tech company revised its code of conduct to specifically include language about respecting cultural dress and accents. They included a zero-tolerance statement for mocking or exclusionary jokes tied to personal identity. After the update, managers received training to reinforce this policy and learned how to address infractions quickly. This clarity helped reduce incidents and increased reporting of concerns.

2. Cross-Cultural Training

Example: A large financial firm introduced immersive workshops focusing on unconscious bias and cultural humility. Instead of just lectures, the training included interactive role-plays where employees practiced stepping in when they witnessed exclusionary behavior. Surveys after the training showed a 40% increase in staff confidence to intervene respectfully.

3. Celebrating Diverse Expression

Example: A healthcare organization started a monthly "Culture Spotlight" newsletter featuring stories from employees about their heritage, dress, or spiritual practices. They also hosted lunchtime talks by diverse leaders who shared how embracing their identity impacted their leadership. This fostered curiosity and normalized cultural differences across the team.

4. Safe Reporting Channels

Example: A retail company set up an anonymous reporting hotline staffed by trained diversity officers, alongside a dedicated email address and in-person ombudsperson. They publicized these channels widely and ensured prompt follow-up. Employees reported feeling more comfortable raising concerns, and overall reported incidents dropped by 25% within a year.

5. Promoting and Protecting Diverse Leaders

Example: An engineering firm created a leadership mentorship program targeting underrepresented groups, pairing emerging supervisors with senior leaders committed to inclusion. They also reviewed promotion criteria to eliminate bias and provided unconscious bias training for promotion panels. As a result, diversity in leadership roles increased by 15% over two years.

Sample Policy Language for Conduct Guidelines

Respect for Personal Identity

Our organization is committed to fostering a workplace where everyone is valued and respected. Mockery, ridicule, or exclusion based on a person's accent, attire, cultural or religious beliefs, or any other aspect of personal identity is strictly prohibited. Comments or behaviors that demean, belittle, or stereotype others will be treated as serious violations of this policy.

All employees, supervisors, and leaders share responsibility for creating an inclusive environment where diversity is celebrated, and everyone can contribute fully without fear of discrimination or harassment.

Real-World Example

Daniela, a Spanish-speaking operations supervisor in Toronto, often received teasing remarks about her "passion" and accent. During a client pitch, a peer offered to speak in her place "so they understand us better." Daniela brought this to her regional director, who invited her to co-lead a cultural fluency workshop. After the workshop, comments shifted, and more diverse supervisors were tapped for visible roles.

Closing Reflection

"When people feel they must leave their identity at the door, the workplace loses far more than authenticity—it loses trust, engagement, and heart."

Part VI: Protecting Yourself and Pushing for Change

How to respond, recover, and drive accountability.

Chapter 39
Know Your Legal Rights (Canada + Global Context)

"Knowledge is the first line of defense against injustice."

Understanding your legal rights is empowering. It gives you tools to protect yourself, speak up safely, and hold employers accountable. Whether in Canada or abroad, knowing what's legally unacceptable at work turns confusion into clarity — and vulnerability into strength.

1. Legal Protections in Canada

a. Canadian Human Rights Act (CHRA)

Applies federally (e.g., banks, airlines). It bans discrimination—including harassment—based on protected grounds like race, religion, gender, age, or creed en.wikipedia.org+3chrc-ccdp.gc.ca+3albertahumanrights.ab.ca+3. Harassing remarks or actions—even casual jokes—are illegal if they create an intimidating or hostile environment.

b. Provincial Human Rights Codes

For provincially employed supervisors, acts like Ontario's Human Rights Code (OHRC) protect the same grounds—including accent, dress, and creed—and cover employment decisions like assignment, discipline, and promotion. These codes also require **duty to accommodate** religious practices or dress unless doing so causes undue hardship. time.com+15thehayneslawfirm.com+15htwlaw.ca+15.

c. Canadian Charter of Rights and Freedoms

Section 15 ensures equality before the law for all Canadians, safeguarding against stereotyping and systemic bias that harm dignity. canada.ca+3en.wikipedia.org+3en.wikipedia.org+3.

Key Points for Supervisors:

- Discrimination and harassment based on personal identity are legally prohibited.
- Employers must accommodate protected characteristics—like religious dress or languages—unless there is genuine undue hardship.
- You can file a complaint through provincial human rights commissions or the Canadian Human Rights Commission.

2. Global Overview

a. International Law

Countries that ratified the International Labour Organization's Convention 111 must outlaw workplace discrimination based on race, religion, age, etc. This creates a foundation for national laws. albertahumanrights.ab.ca+2ccohs.ca+2chrc-ccdp.gc.ca+2chrc-ccdp.gc.caen.wikipedia.org.

b. European Union

Under the EU's Equality Directive 2000/78/EC, member states must enforce anti-discrimination protections for religion, age, disability, and sexual orientation. en.wikipedia.org.

c. United States

Title VII (Civil Rights Act), ADEA (Age), and ADA (Disability) protect against workplace discrimination. High-profile Supreme Court rulings like Faragher v. City of Boca Raton and Burlington Industries v. Ellerth establish employer liability when internal complaints aren't addressed. time.com.

d. Other Jurisdictions

Most modern democracies—like the UK, Australia, and South Africa—have strong legal frameworks protecting workers from discrimination and harassment, with reporting mechanisms and enforcement through labor tribunals or courts.

3. Examples of How These Protections Work

a. Language and Accent

Ontario case: An Arabic-speaking supervisor was told to "speak Canadian" at work. The OHRC ruled that English-only rules are discriminatory unless legally necessary. reddit.com.

b. Religious Dress

Case of a Sikh employee fired for not wearing a safety helmet over his turban. The Canadian Human Rights Tribunal found the termination discriminatory and ordered loss-of-income compensation. htwlaw.ca.

c. Creed-Based Policies

In Ontario, failing to accommodate religious days off or prayer time without undue hardship is discriminatory. albertahumanrights.ab.ca+2thehayneslawfirm.com+2sultanlawyers.com+2.

4. What Supervisors Should Do

Even if you're in a leadership role, you are still protected by law. You don't give up your rights just because you're responsible for others. If you're experiencing bias, discrimination, or unfair treatment based on your identity, here's how to respond:

1. Know Your Rights

Before you can advocate for yourself, it's important to understand what protections are already in place. In Canada, supervisors are protected under the **Canadian Human Rights Act** (for federally regulated workplaces) or **provincial human rights codes** like those in Ontario, Alberta, or British Columbia. These laws protect against discrimination based on gender, race, religion, age, sexual orientation, disability, and more. They also provide a right to **reasonable accommodation**, which is especially relevant for religious practices or health-related needs.

Example: If you are being denied a promotion and suspect it's due to age or ethnicity, knowing that your province's human rights code prohibits this kind of bias gives you a legal foundation to raise your concern.

2. Use Employer Procedures First

Before escalating issues externally, it's often best (and sometimes legally required) to use the formal steps within your organization—like filing a report with **Human Resources (HR)**, requesting a **mediation**, or following a **respectful workplace policy**. Courts and tribunals often look favorably on employees who first tried internal solutions.

Example: In a case like *Burlington Industries v. Ellerth* (U.S.), the court ruled that employers are only liable for harassment if they didn't have—or didn't enforce—internal reporting mechanisms. In Canada, similar principles apply: document that you made a reasonable effort to resolve issues internally.

Tip: Request a written copy of the workplace harassment or anti-discrimination policy from HR. It's your right.

3. Document Everything

In any case involving discrimination, bias, or harassment, **contemporaneous records** (notes taken soon after an incident) are invaluable. Keep a detailed, factual record of:

- What happened
- What was said or done
- Who witnessed it
- The impact it had on your work or well-being

Use your personal device or notebook, and save copies of relevant emails or chat messages (as long as it doesn't breach policy).

Example: A supervisor kept notes over several months of being repeatedly excluded from meetings after disclosing her pregnancy. When she later filed a complaint, those notes strengthened her case and led to a policy review.

4. Seek External Help When Needed

If internal procedures don't resolve the issue—or if you feel the process itself is biased—you can file a complaint with:

- **Your provincial human rights commission** (e.g., Ontario Human Rights Tribunal)
- **The Canadian Human Rights Commission** (for federally regulated workplaces)
- **A union representative** (if applicable)
- **A legal clinic or employment lawyer** (many offer free consultations)

Timelines for filing complaints vary by jurisdiction, but can be as short as 12 months, so don't delay.

Example: A Sikh supervisor was denied accommodation to wear his turban in a factory role. After internal complaints went nowhere, he filed with the Canadian Human Rights Commission. The tribunal found in his favor and awarded damages.

5. Ask for Accommodation

If your concern relates to religion, disability, family status, or cultural needs, you have a right to **request accommodation**. This means asking your employer to make reasonable adjustments so you can participate fully in the workplace.

Approach the conversation respectfully and clearly. Explain what you need and how it supports your ability to work—not as a demand, but as a partnership.

Example:

"As part of my faith, I observe Friday afternoon prayer. I'd like to request an adjusted schedule on Fridays, and I'm happy to start earlier on those days to meet expectations."

Employers must accommodate such requests unless doing so would cause "undue hardship"— usually related to safety, cost, or operational feasibility.

Final Thought

Taking action doesn't make you difficult—it shows you value fairness, professionalism, and dignity. Supervisors set the tone not just through performance, but through the courage to advocate for themselves and others when something isn't right.

5. Why This Matters

Understanding and upholding workplace rights isn't just about avoiding lawsuits. It's about shaping a stronger, fairer environment—especially for those in supervisory roles. Here's why it matters on multiple levels:

• Legal Accountability

Why it's important:

Organizations have a legal duty to prevent discrimination and harassment under Canadian laws like the *Canadian Human Rights Act*, the *Employment Equity Act*, and provincial human rights codes. When employers ignore or mishandle complaints, they expose themselves to **financial liability**, **public scrutiny**, and **reputational damage**.

Example:

In 2020, a BC Human Rights Tribunal awarded over **$50,000** in damages to a worker who was racially harassed and then punished for speaking up. The employer's failure to act swiftly and fairly was a key factor in the judgment.

Takeaway:

Ignoring discrimination isn't neutral—it's costly, and legally negligent. Proactively addressing issues protects the organization and the people who lead within it.

• Cultural Integrity

Why it's important:

A respectful workplace culture isn't just "nice to have"—it's essential to retaining strong, ethical supervisors. When leaders feel safe bringing their full selves to work, they lead with **authenticity**, **clarity**, and **trust**.

Real-World Insight:

When employees—especially supervisors—see discriminatory behavior go unchallenged, they either disengage or feel complicit. That undermines the entire leadership structure.

Example:

A female Muslim supervisor in Alberta felt pressure to remove her headscarf during a company photoshoot to "look more relatable." HR later apologized, but the damage to her sense of dignity lingered. Her effectiveness as a team lead dropped—not because of skill, but because her identity wasn't respected.

Takeaway:

Protecting rights means protecting the integrity of the leadership pipeline. No one can lead effectively while feeling diminished.

• Operational Strength

Why it's important:

Research consistently shows that **diverse leadership teams** outperform homogenous ones in terms of decision-making, creativity, and risk management. When supervisors from different backgrounds are supported—not stereotyped—they bring richer perspectives that strengthen the business.

Data Point:

McKinsey's 2023 report found that companies in the top quartile for **ethnic and gender diversity** on executive teams were **36% more likely** to outperform their peers in profitability.

Example:

A logistics company in Ontario saw a spike in client satisfaction after promoting bilingual supervisors who could better serve multicultural clients. Diversity wasn't a checkbox—it was a competitive edge.

Takeaway:

Inclusion isn't just a social goal. It's a business advantage. When supervisors from all walks of life thrive, teams thrive.

• Reputation Guard

Why it's important:

How an organization handles rights and discrimination issues speaks volumes—not just internally, but to customers, regulators, job seekers, and the broader community. Today's workforce is watching how companies walk their talk.

Example:

After mishandling a discrimination claim involving an Indigenous employee, a government agency in Canada faced not only legal backlash but also community protests and media coverage. Public trust dropped, recruitment slowed, and employee turnover rose.

Takeaway:

Trust takes years to build and seconds to break. An organization that respects human rights signals strength, responsibility, and credibility to everyone it interacts with.

Final Thought

When supervisors understand why these rights matter—and when organizations commit to upholding them—everyone benefits. It's not just about checking legal boxes. It's about creating workplaces where leadership is accessible, diverse, and grounded in dignity.

Summary

Supervisors in Canada are protected under comprehensive human rights legislation that defends against discrimination and harassment through internal policy, provincial codes, federal law, and constitutional rights. Globally, similar protections exist in almost all modern legal systems, combined with mechanisms for reporting and recourse. Knowing and using your rights helps ensure respectful, inclusive, and equitable leadership—setting a strong example and safeguarding your professional integrity.

Chapter 40
How to Document, Report, and Rebuild with Confidence

"What you write down can save you — but only if you keep writing."

Clear documentation is your armor. It captures facts, patterns, and incidents that might otherwise be dismissed. Reporting is daunting but essential. And rebuilding after harm requires patience, support, and self-compassion. With the right steps, recovery is possible.

For supervisors facing bias, exclusion, or retaliation, the impact is both personal and professionally disruptive. But how you respond — how you document, report, and rebuild — can be a turning point in your leadership journey. This chapter offers actionable strategies to help you take back control with integrity and confidence.

1. Why Documentation Matters

Documentation is not about revenge—it's about clarity and protection.

When issues escalate, memory alone isn't enough. The moment you feel something is "off," start recording specifics. Patterns of discrimination, exclusion, or misconduct often reveal themselves over time.

Example:

Nadia, a logistics supervisor, noticed that her assignments were suddenly reduced after she filed a complaint. She kept a daily log of changes in workload, emails received, and meetings excluded from. Six weeks later, this pattern formed a strong basis for her HR case.

What to Record:

- **Date, time, location**
- **Who was involved (including witnesses)**
- **What exactly was said or done**
- **Impact on your work or well-being**
- **Any response from management or HR**

Keep this log secure—on your personal device or physical notebook—not your work computer.

2. How to Report It Effectively

Reporting misconduct or unfair treatment isn't just about naming the harm—it's about creating space for change.

A. Start Internally (If Safe)

- Use your company's formal grievance process (HR, ethics line, union, etc.).
- Bring your documentation.
- State facts calmly, avoiding emotional labels like "toxic" or "vindictive." Focus on impact.

Example Statement:

"I want to raise a concern that I believe reflects a pattern of exclusion. I've documented five meetings in the last month that all other team leads attended, and I was excluded without explanation. It's affecting my role clarity and morale."

B. Escalate Externally (If Needed)

If internal processes fail or feel biased, escalate to:

- **Human Rights Commissions** (e.g., Canadian Human Rights Commission or your provincial body)
- **Labor Board or Employment Standards Office**
- **Legal support**: Consider an employment lawyer for confidential advice

Tip: Keep copies of all correspondence, especially if filing externally.

3. Protect Your Well-Being in the Process

Reporting injustice can be emotionally draining. Don't try to go it alone.

A. Find Allies

Look for internal or external supporters—peers, mentors, or advocacy groups. Many organizations also have Employee Resource Groups (ERGs) for support.

B. Set Boundaries

Protect your emotional space. Step back from triggering environments when needed, take short leaves if offered, and disconnect from team chats after hours if they feel unsafe.

C. Access Mental Health Support

Many leaders carry emotional burdens in silence. EAPs (Employee Assistance Programs), therapists, or culturally aware counselors can help you process what's happening.

4. Rebuild Your Confidence

It's easy to internalize mistreatment. But what happened to you says more about the environment than your worth. Rebuilding begins with small, intentional steps.

A. Reconnect with Purpose

Why did you enter this role? Revisit your early wins, affirmations from colleagues, and the communities you serve.

Exercise:

Write down three professional moments where you made a real impact. Keep them visible.

B. Reframe the Narrative

Don't let mistreatment define your story. Instead of "They pushed me out," say:

"I chose to step away from a system that didn't align with my values. And I'm building something better."

C. Invest in Growth

Use this as a pivot: take a course, start a mentorship circle, speak up at a conference. Turn your lived experience into leadership insight.

5. Leave a Trail for Others

Every time you document unfairness, push back respectfully, or report with clarity—you make it easier for the next person to do the same.

Ways to Do That:

- Mentor someone newer who might face similar bias
- Join or build advocacy networks in your industry
- Speak (anonymously if needed) at staff meetings about a respectful culture
- Recommend better practices to HR or leadership

Closing Reflection

You may never get the apology you deserve. But you can still own your story, assert your rights, and emerge with more strength, not less.

"The strongest leaders aren't those who've never been shaken—but those who refused to break."

Chapter 41
When to Speak Up and When to Walk Away

"Knowing your limits is as important as knowing your rights."

There's courage in speaking out — and wisdom in choosing when silence or departure is the healthiest choice. Not every battle is yours to fight, and sometimes walking away is a powerful act of self-preservation. Your well-being comes first, always.

How Supervisors Can Protect Themselves, Assert Their Rights, and Seek Justice

In the complex world of workplace dynamics, supervisors often find themselves in a unique and precarious position. Tasked with enforcing rules, managing teams, and meeting performance targets, they walk a fine line between leadership and vulnerability. While much has been written about the rights of employees, supervisors—especially those in middle management—can be overlooked when it comes to workplace protections and advocacy.

One of the most important yet rarely discussed survival skills for supervisors is learning **when to speak up and when to walk away**. This isn't about ego, fear, or aggression—it's about wisdom, timing, and strategic self-preservation.

Speaking Up: Protecting Your Principles and Position

Speaking up is often seen as a sign of strength—but for supervisors, it's also a matter of **professional responsibility**. Whether it's defending your team from unfair treatment or challenging upper management decisions that violate ethical standards, knowing how to voice concern appropriately is essential.

1. When Policies or Ethics Are Violated

Supervisors are often the first to witness violations of labor laws, harassment policies, or unethical directives. In such cases, silence can make you complicit—and potentially liable.

Example:

A warehouse supervisor, Melissa, noticed her regional manager regularly falsifying shift logs to avoid paying overtime. Instead of confronting the manager directly, she documented the inconsistencies and filed an internal ethics report. Her action not only protected her team but also protected herself from future retaliation by showing she had followed proper reporting protocols.

2. When You're Being Undermined or Targeted

It's not uncommon for supervisors to face retaliation, micromanagement, or being set up to fail by toxic leadership. Speaking up early—professionally and factually—can stop the spiral.

Strategy:

- Request a private meeting.
- Use neutral, fact-based language: "I've noticed some changes in task delegation that are affecting my team's clarity. I'd like to better understand expectations."
- Document everything in follow-up emails.

If no action follows, your paper trail becomes critical later if legal or HR intervention is needed.

3. When Advocating for Your Team

Many supervisors feel caught between frontline employees and upper management. Advocating for fair treatment, better tools, or reasonable deadlines shows leadership.

Tip:

- Present concerns with solutions: "We've had three equipment failures this month. Approving new parts could reduce downtime by 30%."

Walking Away: When Staying Becomes Self-Destructive

As much as speaking up is vital, **knowing when to walk away** is equally critical—especially when your well-being, credibility, or career is on the line. Walking away doesn't always mean quitting. Sometimes, it means stepping back from a confrontation, avoiding retaliation, or planning a strategic exit.

1. When Speaking Up Won't Change Anything

Some workplaces are entrenched in a toxic culture. If your feedback is consistently ignored or punished, continuing to speak up may become futile.

Example:

Jamal, a call center supervisor, raised concerns about unrealistic call quotas and mental health issues among staff. After three HR meetings with no action—and increased hostility—he began documenting everything while discreetly seeking employment elsewhere. When he left, he submitted a final exit memo and later joined a class action for wage and hour violations.

2. When Your Mental or Physical Health is Declining

No job is worth chronic stress, anxiety, or burnout. Supervisors often endure high-pressure environments, and the expectation to "be strong" can lead to silence.

Walk-away markers include:

- Dread every morning
- Physical symptoms (headaches, insomnia)
- Isolation from peers or being cut out of decision-making

Strategy:

Consult a therapist, document your symptoms, and consult a labor attorney or HR before resigning. Protect your health—and your paper trail.

3. When Legal or Professional Liability is Possible

If upper management is engaging in fraud, safety violations, or discrimination—and you're being asked to enforce or ignore it—staying silent could make you legally vulnerable.

Case Law Reference:

In *Digital Realty Trust, Inc. v. Somers*, 583 U.S. ___ (2018), the U.S. Supreme Court held that whistleblower protections under the Dodd-Frank Act apply only when employees report directly to the SEC. This ruling highlights the importance of knowing **how** and **where** to speak up legally—sometimes, walking away and reporting externally is safer than internal protest.

How to Make the Call: Speak or Walk?

Ask Yourself:

- Is this a one-time issue or a pattern?
- Am I safe to speak up? Physically, legally, reputationally?
- Have I documented enough?
- If I speak up, is there a reasonable chance of change?
- If I walk away, do I have support, savings, or a plan?

Decision Matrix:

Situation	Speak Up	Walk Away
Policy violation	✓	✗
Repeated retaliation	✓ (with evidence)	✓
Unsafe work environment	✗ (immediate)	✓
Disagreement in style	✓ (openly)	✗
Systemic abuse of power	✓ (strategic)	✓ (eventually)

Conclusion: Quiet Courage or Strategic Silence

The power of a supervisor isn't just in issuing orders or meeting quotas—it's in knowing when to **defend their values**, and when to **defend their peace**. Speaking up can change a workplace. Walking away can change your life.

Justice doesn't always come through confrontation. Sometimes, it comes from choosing to take your skills, integrity, and leadership where they'll be respected—and protected.

Chapter 42
Finding Allies: HR, Unions, Legal Support, and Unions

"You don't have to face the storm alone."

Finding the right allies can change everything. Whether it's HR, legal counsel, or unions, allies offer protection, guidance, and solidarity. Together, you stand stronger against workplace injustice — and open the door to real change.

How Supervisors Can Navigate Workplace Challenges through Strategic Support Networks

Supervisors are expected to be the problem-solvers, the intermediaries, and the leaders. But what happens when they themselves face unfair treatment, retaliation, or legal gray areas? Many supervisors find themselves in a difficult position—caught between the expectations of upper management and the needs of their team. In such cases, **finding the right support** isn't optional—it's essential for survival, self-protection, and justice.

While supervisors are often assumed to be "in the know," many are not trained or empowered to handle serious workplace disputes involving harassment, discrimination, retaliation, or unethical conduct. That's why understanding how to approach Human Resources, engage with unions, consult legal counsel, and lean on trusted allies can mean the difference between career collapse and recovery.

1. Human Resources: Internal but Not Always Impartial

Many believe HR is there to "help employees," but the reality is more complex. HR serves the **company first**, which means their support may be limited—especially when a supervisor's complaint involves senior leadership or systemic problems.

When to Go to HR

- **To document official complaints** (harassment, discrimination, retaliation)
- **To request formal mediation**
- **To clarify workplace policies**

Example:

Sofia, a department supervisor, noticed that despite strong performance reviews, she was being sidelined from key projects after reporting sexist remarks from a senior executive. She brought her concerns to HR, documenting dates, emails, and prior reviews. Though HR did not act decisively at first, her formal documentation helped her build a legal case when she later filed a claim with the EEOC.

Tips:

- Always follow up verbal conversations with emails.
- Ask for copies of your complaint or any HR response.
- Avoid overly emotional language; stick to facts and timelines.

Caution:

HR is **not** legally obligated to protect you personally. If your issue involves illegal conduct or if HR is dismissive, it's time to look elsewhere.

2. Labor Unions: A Shield for Supervisors—Sometimes

Union protection varies by industry and region, but if you're a supervisor in a **unionized environment**, your rights and protections may already be spelled out in a collective bargaining agreement (CBA). However, many unions don't extend protections to supervisory staff, especially those with hiring or firing authority.

When to Engage with Your Union

- If you are a **union-represented supervisor**, your union can help with:
  - Unjust discipline or demotion
  - Violations of the CBA
  - Retaliation for whistleblowing or grievances

Example:

Chris, a lead supervisor at a public transportation agency, was written up for "insubordination" after he reported unsafe equipment. Because he was in a supervisory union, his rep filed a grievance, and the write-up was later rescinded. The union also helped negotiate an agreement that kept Chris in his position while removing him from the hostile environment.

If You're Not in a Union:

- Some professional associations act similarly to unions, offering legal support or advocacy.
- Consider organizing with peers if your sector has union potential.

3. Legal Counsel: When the Stakes Are High

Sometimes the best move is to stop talking to internal actors and start talking to a lawyer. **Employment attorneys** specialize in workplace disputes involving discrimination, retaliation, wage theft, and wrongful termination. Consulting a lawyer does not mean you're suing—it means you're getting a **reality check** from someone who works for you, not your employer.

When to Get Legal Advice

- After being demoted, fired, or disciplined unfairly
- When reporting a serious legal violation (discrimination, harassment)
- If you're asked to sign something that seems suspicious (e.g., NDAs, severance)

Example:

After 10 years as a supervisor in a nonprofit, Jamila was abruptly terminated and offered a small severance package—on the condition that she sign a non-disclosure agreement. Sensing something wasn't right, she contacted an employment lawyer who discovered potential grounds for a retaliation claim based on prior whistleblowing. The lawyer helped her negotiate a larger settlement and a neutral reference.

Finding the Right Lawyer

- Look for attorneys who specialize in **employment law**, not general practice.
- Free consultations are often available.
- Some lawyers work on contingency if the case is strong.

Resources:

- National Employment Lawyers Association (NELA): www.nela.org
- Your state labor board or bar association

4. Allies: The Quiet Power of Trusted Colleagues

Never underestimate the importance of **interpersonal support**—especially from peers who understand the unique pressure of leadership roles. While HR or legal channels are formal, your **informal allies** may be just as critical.

Who Are Your Allies?

- Other supervisors who've faced similar treatment
- Former employees who've left under suspicious circumstances
- Mentors, advocates, or trusted professionals inside or outside your organization

Example:

Carlos was facing increasing pressure from his director, who regularly berated him in front of staff. Though HR brushed off his concerns, another supervisor privately shared her own similar experience—and later corroborated his story in a formal statement. Together, they brought concerns to the company's ombudsman, triggering a wider investigation.

How Allies Help:

- **Validate** your experience ("You're not imagining it.")
- **Share documentation** or patterns of behavior
- **Strengthen your case** when you decide to report or escalate

Practical Strategy: Build a Web, Not a Line

Don't rely on one channel alone. The smartest move is to **build a web of support**, combining formal and informal allies. Here's a strategic order of escalation:

1. **Start with documentation**—email trails, meeting notes, timelines.
2. **Consult trusted peers** to check your perception.
3. **Go to HR or internal channels** only with clear, factual information.
4. **Contact your union (if applicable)** for specific guidance.
5. **Seek legal advice** before signing or filing anything major.

Conclusion: You Are Not Alone

Too often, supervisors feel like they're supposed to handle everything alone—solve every conflict, smooth over every tension, and suppress their own struggles. But no one, regardless of title, is beyond the need for support.

Whether you're facing injustice, retaliation, or ethical conflict, knowing **where to turn and when to speak** can protect your career, your reputation, and your well-being. HR, unions, attorneys, and peers each offer part of the puzzle. The key is knowing how to use them—not out of fear, but from a position of strength, clarity, and purpose.

Chapter 43
Mental Health Recovery After Workplace Harm

"Healing isn't linear — but it's possible."

Workplace harm leaves invisible scars. Recovering your mental health requires time, support, and often professional help. It means rebuilding confidence, setting boundaries, and reclaiming joy. Recovery is a journey — and every step forward matters.

A Guide for Supervisors Seeking Recovery, Dignity, and Long-Term Resilience

Harassment in the workplace doesn't just leave bruises on reputations or career paths—it can leave deep emotional scars. For supervisors, the impact of harassment is often compounded by isolation. They're expected to lead, maintain composure, and protect others—so when they are harassed, the pain is not only personal, but also political and professional.

Whether the harassment comes from a superior, a peer, or even subordinates, the aftermath can shake your confidence, disrupt your focus, and erode your trust in the system. Healing is not a straight path. It is layered, non-linear, and deeply personal. But it is possible—with the right awareness, support, and self-compassion.

Understanding the Psychological Impact

Being harassed at work—especially when you're in a supervisory role—can trigger a range of emotional and physiological responses. Some supervisors report feelings of shame or confusion, questioning whether they "should have done more" to stop it. Others internalize the abuse, especially if retaliation follows an attempt to speak up.

Common responses include:

- **Anxiety or hyper-vigilance** (especially in meetings or around the harasser)
- **Depression or burnout**
- **Anger or irritability**
- **Isolation or withdrawal from peers**
- **Trouble sleeping or chronic fatigue**
- **Self-doubt and imposter syndrome**

Example:

Monica, a mid-level manager in a marketing firm, was frequently subjected to inappropriate jokes and physical proximity from her regional director. After reporting it to HR, she was slowly removed from high-visibility projects and eventually transferred to a less strategic department. Although the harassment stopped, the retaliation severely damaged her confidence. She began to question her ability to lead. Only after seeking therapy did she begin to reframe the experience—not as a reflection of her worth, but of the organization's failure.

Steps to Begin Healing

Healing after harassment is a complex and multifaceted process, involving both emotional and strategic components. It involves recognizing what happened, honoring your response, and reclaiming your mental and professional space.

1. Validate Your Experience

One of the most damaging outcomes of workplace harassment is gaslighting—being told it wasn't "a big deal," or that you "misread" the situation. Whether it was verbal, psychological, or physical, your discomfort is real.

- **Keep a private journal** of what happened and how it affected you.
- **Speak to a therapist** or counselor, preferably one with experience in trauma or workplace issues.
- **Avoid minimizing** the event ("It wasn't that bad") as a coping mechanism. Healing starts with naming what hurts.

2. Seek Mental Health Support

Supervisors may hesitate to seek counseling for fear of looking weak. But therapy isn't weakness—it's strategic recovery.

Types of help available:

- **Cognitive Behavioral Therapy (CBT):** Focuses on reframing negative thought patterns.
- **Trauma-informed therapy:** Helps process events that may have left psychological wounds.
- **Support groups:** Local or online groups where others share similar experiences.

Example:

After being harassed by a senior executive, Daniel, a shift supervisor, started experiencing panic attacks. He initially thought he was "just tired," but after seeing a counselor, he realized he had developed workplace-related PTSD. Six months of therapy helped him regain control over his emotions and rebuild his leadership confidence.

3. Reclaim Your Narrative

You are more than what happened to you. Reclaiming your sense of self is essential to moving forward—not just emotionally, but professionally.

Tips:

- **Update your resume** to reflect your strengths, not just job titles.
- **Take a course, mentorship, or leadership training** to reinvest in your growth.
- **Speak or write** (even privately) about your journey—not for others, but to remember your resilience.

Reframing Example:

"I was targeted because I spoke up for fairness" rather than "I caused trouble."

"I was removed from projects, but I never compromised my ethics."

4. Evaluate Whether to Stay or Leave

Sometimes healing means staying—and reclaiming your space. Other times, it means walking away from a toxic environment to protect your peace. Neither choice is weak.

Ask yourself:

- Has the workplace genuinely addressed the issue?
- Do I feel safe returning to my role?
- Am I being supported or sidelined?
- Is staying helping or hurting my healing?

If you choose to leave, **leave with intention**, not shame. The workplace failed you, not the other way around.

5. Find Community and Purpose

Being harassed can feel deeply isolating. Rebuilding trust—especially in people or institutions—takes time. Surrounding yourself with trusted colleagues, mentors, or support groups can accelerate the healing process.

Practical steps:

- Attend industry events or professional networks unrelated to your current employer.
- Mentor younger professionals—giving back can be healing.
- Join LinkedIn groups or online forums focused on workplace dignity or leadership recovery.

Resilience Is Not About Suppressing Pain

There is a myth in many workplace cultures—especially among supervisors—that being "resilient" means pushing through, ignoring pain, and never showing vulnerability. In reality, **resilience means facing what happened, learning from it, and refusing to let it define your future.**

Healing doesn't always mean "getting over it." Sometimes, it means **living with it**, but no longer letting it control your decisions, your worth, or your voice.

Conclusion: Moving Forward with Power and Peace

Healing after workplace harassment is a deeply personal journey—but it doesn't have to be a lonely one. Supervisors, more than anyone, need to remember that they are not immune to harm—and not above seeking help. Recovery isn't weakness. It's leadership in its most courageous form.

By recognizing your pain, accessing professional help, rebuilding your sense of self, and making empowered decisions, you are not just healing—you are **reclaiming your dignity** and opening a path for others to do the same.

Chapter 44
What Organizations Must Do to Prevent Abuse

"Prevention is better than cure — especially when it comes to workplace harm."

Systemic change starts with leadership commitment, clear policies, and a culture of respect. Organizations must actively prevent abuse, listen to employees, and hold wrongdoers accountable. A healthy workplace is not a luxury — it's a necessity.

Building Workplaces That Foster Respect, Accountability, and Equity

Workplace harassment, discrimination, and systemic injustices don't arise in a vacuum. They thrive in environments where policies are weak, leadership is complacent, and culture tolerates silence or complicity. To protect supervisors—and all employees—organizations must do more than react to incidents. They must **proactively change the system** to build safer, fairer, and more empowering workplaces.

This means shifting from a mindset of compliance to one of genuine commitment. It requires structural changes, leadership accountability, transparent communication, and inclusive culture building. Let's explore what organizations must do to enact meaningful systemic change.

1. Establish Clear, Enforced Policies with Real Consequences

Many organizations have harassment and discrimination policies in place, but they often lack effective enforcement. To change the system, policies must be:

- **Comprehensive and updated regularly:** Cover all forms of misconduct, including subtle power abuses and retaliation.
- **Easily accessible and communicated:** Employees and supervisors should know their rights and obligations.
- **Enforced consistently:** No exceptions for senior leaders or high performers.

Example:

A multinational tech company revamped its anti-harassment policy to include mandatory annual training, an anonymous reporting hotline, and transparent disciplinary procedures. After a high-profile case of sexual harassment, the CEO publicly confirmed the termination of the offender, sending a clear message that no one is above the rules.

2. Train Leadership to Model and Enforce Ethical Behavior

Organizational culture starts at the top. Leaders—especially supervisors—must be trained not only to recognize and prevent harassment but to **actively foster inclusivity and respect**. Training should go beyond legal compliance to include:

- **Empathy and active listening skills**
- **Conflict resolution techniques**
- **Bias awareness and mitigation**

Example:

A hospital system introduced "Leadership Accountability Workshops," where executives learned how their decisions impact workplace culture. Supervisors were coached on how to intervene in bullying situations and support victims. The program correlated with a 40% drop in harassment complaints over two years.

3. Create Safe and Confidential Reporting Mechanisms

Employees and supervisors alike need safe channels to report wrongdoing without fear of retaliation. Effective mechanisms include:

- **Anonymous hotlines managed by third parties**
- **Designated ombudspersons**
- **Clear anti-retaliation protections**

Reference:

According to the U.S. Equal Employment Opportunity Commission (EEOC), organizations with confidential reporting options see higher reporting rates and earlier intervention, reducing long-term damage (EEOC Compliance Manual, 2021).

4. Foster a Culture of Transparency and Accountability

Changing the system means moving away from secrecy and denial. Organizations must:

- **Communicate openly about complaints and resolutions** (while respecting confidentiality)
- **Regularly report on workplace culture and diversity metrics**
- **Hold all employees, including leadership, accountable**

Example:

A financial services firm began publishing an annual "Workplace Culture Report," which included data on harassment claims, resolutions, and diversity benchmarks. This transparency helped rebuild trust with employees and stakeholders.

5. Empower Employees and Supervisors Through Education and Support

Prevention requires equipping everyone with tools to recognize and respond to misconduct.

- **Regular, scenario-based training for all levels**
- **Clear guidance on bystander intervention**
- **Mental health resources and counseling**

Example:

After a surge in workplace conflict, a manufacturing company launched a peer-support program where trained employees help colleagues navigate difficult situations, promoting early conflict resolution and reducing formal complaints.

6. Address Systemic Inequities Beyond Harassment

True systemic change involves addressing broader issues, such as wage gaps, promotion biases, and a lack of diversity in leadership.

Reference:

Research by McKinsey & Company (2020) shows that companies with diverse leadership teams outperform peers by 25% in profitability. Inclusive policies and equitable practices reduce the root causes of workplace dissatisfaction and misconduct.

Conclusion: Commitment Over Compliance

Systemic change demands more than policies or training—it requires an organizational commitment to justice, dignity, and respect. When companies invest in culture transformation, transparent accountability, and empowerment, they don't just reduce harassment—they build workplaces where supervisors and all employees can thrive.

Chapter 45
Creating a Healthier Future for Supervisors and Leaders

"Better leaders build better workplaces."

Leadership isn't just about managing tasks — it's about nurturing people. Training, empathy, and accountability equip supervisors to lead with integrity and respect. When leaders model health and fairness, the entire workplace thrives.

Cultivating Resilience, Empathy, and Ethical Strength in Tomorrow's Leaders

Leadership today faces unprecedented challenges—rapid technological change, shifting workforce expectations, and increased scrutiny over workplace culture. For supervisors and leaders to thrive—not just survive—they need to build a healthier future that prioritizes mental well-being, emotional intelligence, ethical decision-making, and inclusive practices.

This chapter explores the foundation for a healthier leadership model that benefits individuals, teams, and organizations alike. By embracing new paradigms and fostering holistic development, organizations can prepare leaders who inspire, innovate, and sustain positive cultures over time.

1. Prioritizing Mental and Emotional Well-being

The traditional image of leadership often celebrates toughness and endurance, but this approach can lead to burnout, isolation, and poor decision-making. Healthier leadership starts with recognizing that mental and emotional well-being is not a luxury—it's a necessity.

- **Regular mental health check-ins** and wellness programs for leaders help normalize self-care.
- Organizations should provide **access to counseling, stress management tools, and flexible work options**.
- Leaders must be trained to **recognize signs of burnout** in themselves and their teams.

Example:

At a global consulting firm, the leadership development program includes mandatory resilience workshops and access to confidential mental health coaching. As a result, turnover rates among managers decreased by 30%, and employee engagement scores improved significantly.

2. Developing Empathy and Emotional Intelligence

Effective leaders understand that success depends on people, not just processes or profits. Emotional intelligence—the ability to understand and manage one's own emotions and those of others—is critical.

- Training in **active listening**, **compassionate communication**, and **conflict resolution** fosters trust.
- Leaders who practice empathy create environments where employees feel valued and safe to express ideas and concerns.

Example:

Maria, a department head, transformed a toxic team culture by prioritizing empathy. She held regular one-on-one check-ins, encouraged open dialogue, and addressed conflicts promptly and fairly. Employee satisfaction within her department increased by 45% over an 18-month period.

3. Embedding Ethical Leadership and Accountability

The healthiest future for leadership demands a recommitment to ethics and integrity. Leaders set the tone for organizational values and behaviors.

- Ethical training should cover **transparency, fairness, and responsible decision-making**.
- Leaders must be held accountable—not just for business outcomes but for how they treat people.
- Creating **whistleblower protections and clear channels for reporting misconduct** encourages ethical vigilance.

Example:

A nonprofit organization implemented a "Leadership Integrity Charter" signed by all managers, outlining commitments to honesty, respect, and equity. Leadership evaluations now include assessments of ethical behavior, and breaches result in consequences regardless of rank.

4. Championing Diversity, Equity, and Inclusion (DEI)

A healthy leadership future is inclusive. Diversity isn't just a metric; it's a source of innovation, empathy, and resilience.

- Leaders should be trained to recognize and challenge their biases.
- Leadership pipelines must be intentionally broadened to include underrepresented groups.
- Inclusive leadership practices include **amplifying diverse voices**, **promoting equitable opportunities**, and **cultivating belonging**.

Example:

Tech giant "Innovatech" revamped its leadership development program to prioritize diversity. They implemented mentorship programs pairing senior leaders with employees from underrepresented backgrounds. Over five years, the percentage of women and minorities in leadership roles doubled.

5. Embracing Continuous Learning and Adaptability

The business environment will continue to evolve rapidly. Leaders who commit to continuous learning—not just about their industry but about leadership itself—are better equipped for long-term success.

- Encouraging leaders to seek feedback and reflect on their growth areas.
- Investing in leadership development programs that include **coaching, peer learning, and experiential opportunities**.
- Promoting adaptability by exposing leaders to diverse perspectives and challenges.

Example:

A healthcare organization created a "Leadership Lab" where supervisors participate in simulations addressing crisis management, ethical dilemmas, and cultural competence. This experiential approach led to improved problem-solving and collaboration skills across leadership tiers.

6. Building Supportive Networks and Communities

No leader succeeds alone. Fostering peer support, mentorship, and community helps leaders sustain their energy and vision.

- Formal mentoring programs connect emerging leaders with experienced mentors.
- Peer support groups allow the sharing of challenges and strategies.
- Leadership retreats and forums build camaraderie and shared purpose.

Example:

A regional manufacturing company launched a quarterly leadership forum where managers across departments exchange experiences, challenges, and best practices. This initiative reduced feelings of isolation and increased cross-department collaboration.

Conclusion: Towards a Leadership Paradigm Rooted in Health

Building a healthier future for leadership means redefining what it means to lead—with heart, humility, and purpose. Leaders who invest in their own well-being, cultivate empathy, uphold high ethical standards, and embrace diversity are better equipped to inspire their teams, drive innovation, and achieve sustainable success.

Organizations that commit to this vision will not only develop stronger leaders but will also foster workplaces where everyone can thrive—today and into the future.

Conclusion

From Silence to Strength — A Path Forward for Supervisors and Leadership

A call for cultural change, accountability, and restoring dignity in leadership.

This book has journeyed through the complex and often painful realities faced by supervisors caught in the crosshairs of power, manipulation, and discrimination within organizations. From the earliest pages describing the subtle and overt **power plays** by upper management, through the emotional and psychological toll exacted by manipulation and isolation, to the systemic barriers denying recognition, fair advancement, and respect, the narrative has been unflinching and comprehensive.

It is a story that many supervisors live, but few feel empowered to share openly. Yet silence, as we have learned, perpetuates the very systems that erode confidence, dignity, and professional fulfillment.

Acknowledging the Struggle

The experiences detailed—from micromanagement that stifles autonomy, to gaslighting that distorts reality; from unfair reviews that sabotage careers, to personal boundary invasions and identity-based discrimination—are not isolated incidents. They are symptoms of deeply rooted organizational cultures that prioritize control over collaboration, fear over trust, and appearance over authenticity.

For supervisors, these conditions can feel like a relentless storm. The mental exhaustion of constant scrutiny, the heartbreak of exclusion, the frustration of seeing hard work ignored—these challenges chip away at both professional identity and personal well-being.

From Victimhood to Agency

Yet this book does not leave readers in despair. The latter sections emphasize **recovery, rights, and resistance**, offering practical pathways for reclaiming power and rebuilding strength. Knowing your legal rights, documenting experiences, finding allies in HR, unions, or legal counsel, and choosing when to speak up or walk away—these are essential tools for navigating toxic environments.

Moreover, healing after harassment and discrimination is a crucial step. Mental health is not ancillary to professional success—it is foundational. Leaders who care for their emotional well-being are more resilient and better equipped to foster positive change.

The Call for Systemic Change

But true transformation requires more than individual resilience. Organizations must **change the system**—not just manage symptoms. This means enacting clear policies, enforcing accountability regardless of rank, cultivating inclusive cultures, and investing in the development of ethical and empathetic leadership.

A healthier future for leadership is one where respect, fairness, and dignity are non-negotiable; where supervisors are valued partners in decision-making rather than pawns in control games, where diversity is celebrated as a strength, not a challenge to be managed.

Restoring Dignity and Building Strength

At its core, this book is a call to restore dignity—both to those who lead and those who are led. Leadership is not about wielding unchecked authority; it is about **serving with integrity, inspiring with empathy, and acting with accountability**.

Moving **from silence to strength** means breaking through fear and stigma to voice truths. It means creating workplaces where supervisors no longer have to sacrifice their mental health, values, or sense of self to succeed.

A Collective Responsibility

The journey forward requires collective commitment. Supervisors must find and nurture their voices. Organizations must listen deeply and act boldly. Societies must uphold principles of fairness and justice in workplace laws and norms.

When all these elements align, the toxic patterns of the past can be dismantled, and workplaces can become thriving communities where everyone—regardless of role or background—can contribute meaningfully and be treated with respect.

Final Reflection

This book is more than an exposé of workplace dysfunction; it is a blueprint for hope and action. It honors the struggles of supervisors everywhere and champions a future where leadership is healthier, fairer, and more human.

The strength to speak out, the courage to resist injustice, and the wisdom to rebuild are within reach. Together, we can move from silence to strength—and build workplaces that reflect the best of what leadership and humanity can be.

Endnote

May this book empower you to reclaim your voice, assert your rights, and inspire change—not only for yourself but for every supervisor and leader who deserves to work with dignity and respect.

Appendices

Appendix A: Signs of a Toxic Power Structure

Use this checklist to identify whether your workplace displays patterns of systemic control and manipulation by upper management.

- ✅ Micromanagement and lack of autonomy

- ✅ Sudden changes to responsibilities without explanation

- ✅ Exclusion from key meetings or decisions

- ✅ Public criticism, private praise (or none at all)

- ✅ Denied access to resources or training

- ✅ Withheld information necessary to do your job

- ✅ Retaliation for raising concerns

- ✅ Frequent fear-based communication ("You should be grateful you have a job")

- ✅ Recognition given selectively to favorites

- ✅ Patterns of discrimination or bias

If you experience three or more of these regularly, it may indicate a toxic leadership environment.

Appendix B: How to Document Workplace Abuse or Harassment

Proper documentation can be critical in protecting your rights. Here's what to record and how:

1. Keep a timeline:

Track incidents by date, time, and people involved.

2. Be factual and specific:

Note what was said or done, how it made you feel, and any witnesses.

3. Save physical or digital evidence:

Emails, performance reviews, text messages, call logs, memos, or meeting notes.

4. Record impact:

Was your work delayed, your mental health affected, or your credibility damaged?

5. Store securely:

Use a personal device or encrypted cloud storage to keep private copies.

Tip: Keep personal notes separate from official HR files.

Appendix C: Sample Email – Reporting to HR

Subject: Request for Support and Review of Workplace Concerns

Dear [HR Representative Name],

I'm writing to formally request a confidential meeting regarding several concerns I've experienced in my role as a supervisor. These involve recurring incidents of [e.g., micromanagement, exclusion from decisions, or behavior that feels discriminatory].

I have documented these events and would appreciate the opportunity to discuss how they have impacted my performance and mental well-being. I am requesting this meeting in good faith, in the interest of finding a constructive and respectful path forward.

Please let me know a convenient time to meet.

Sincerely,

[Your Name]

[Your Job Title]

[Your Contact Information]

Appendix D: Legal Resources (Canada + Global)

Canada:

- **Canadian Human Rights Commission**
- www.chrc-ccdp.gc.ca
- Handles workplace discrimination and harassment complaints across federal industries.
- **Employment Standards Offices** (provincial)
- Varies by province — provides protections for wages, hours, and termination.
- **Occupational Health and Safety Act (OHSA)**

- Includes psychological safety as a component of workplace safety.
- **Legal Aid Services**
- Free or low-cost legal assistance depending on income and region.

Global:

- **International Labour Organization (ILO)**
- www.ilo.org
- Provides global standards on workplace rights and protections.
- **EU: Directive on Transparent and Predictable Working Conditions**
- Offers labor protections, including fair treatment for supervisors in EU states.
- **United States Equal Employment Opportunity Commission (EEOC)**
- www.eeoc.gov
- Protects against discrimination and retaliation in the workplace.

Appendix E: Mental Health and Support Services

National (Canada):

- **Wellness Together Canada**
- www.wellnesstogether.ca
- Free online mental health and substance use support.
- **CAMH (Centre for Addiction and Mental Health)**
- www.camh.ca
- Resources for workplace mental health, trauma, and recovery.

International:

- **Mind (UK)** — www.mind.org.uk
- **Lifeline (Australia)** — www.lifeline.org.au
- **Crisis Text Line** — Text "HELLO" to 741741 (USA & Canada)

Appendix F: Leadership Values Self-Assessment

Reflect on these questions to evaluate your personal leadership integrity and alignment:

1. Do I listen more than I speak when team members raise concerns?
2. Have I ever stayed silent when witnessing mistreatment?
3. Am I actively creating opportunities for others to grow?
4. Do I manage from a place of fear or trust?
5. How do I handle feedback, especially when it's critical?
6. Am I modeling the culture I want others to embody?

Use your answers to guide personal leadership growth or team discussions.

Appendix G: Glossary of Terms

Gaslighting:

A form of psychological manipulation that causes someone to doubt their perceptions or memories.

Retaliation:

Any negative action taken against someone for reporting misconduct.

Power Hoarding:

When leadership intentionally withholds decision-making, access, or credit to maintain dominance.

Ethical Dilemma:

A situation where a person is forced to choose between professional expectations and moral principles.

Psychological Safety:

The belief that one can speak up, take risks, or express concerns at work without fear of punishment.

Thematic Index

Abuse of Power

Accountability & Resistance

Boundaries & Privacy

Career Suppression

Discrimination & Identity Bias

- Legal references – Appx D
- Glossary of terms – Appx G

- Legal references – Appx D
- Glossary of terms – Appx G

Glossary of Terms

Accountability

The obligation of individuals and organizations to take responsibility for actions, decisions, or policies, especially when those cause harm. True accountability includes transparency, consequences, and a commitment to repair.

Age Discrimination

Unfair treatment based on a person's age, often manifesting as assumptions about capability, leadership style, or relevance—commonly affecting both younger and older supervisors.

Boundary Violations

When personal, emotional, or professional limits are disregarded in a workplace setting, such as excessive surveillance, intrusive questions, or pressure to sacrifice personal life for work.

Burnout

A state of emotional, mental, and physical exhaustion caused by prolonged workplace stress, often intensified by unrealistic workloads and constant pressure without support.

Constructive Dismissal

A legal term describing a situation where an employee is forced to resign due to hostile or intolerable work conditions, rather than choosing to leave voluntarily.

Cultural Fit Pressure

The implicit or explicit expectation to conform to a dominant workplace culture—often privileging certain identities, behaviors, or communication styles while marginalizing others.

Discrimination

Unjust or prejudicial treatment based on personal characteristics such as race, gender, age, religion, or disability. It may be overt or subtle, and can occur at both individual and systemic levels.

Emotional Abuse (Workplace)

Non-physical behaviors used to control, intimidate, or devalue an employee—such as gaslighting, shaming, exclusion, or constant criticism. Over time, it can significantly damage self-worth and mental health.

Silent Struggles

Ethical Dilemma

A situation where an employee is pressured to choose between following unethical directives or risking retaliation. Common in workplaces where compliance is valued over integrity.

Favoritism

When managers or leadership show preferential treatment to specific individuals, it is often unrelated to merit. This undermines fairness, morale, and team cohesion.

Gaslighting

A manipulative tactic where someone causes another person to doubt their own perceptions, memory, or sanity. In the workplace, this can involve denying abusive actions, rewriting events, or invalidating concerns.

Harassment

Unwanted, hostile behavior—verbal, physical, or psychological—that creates an intimidating or offensive work environment. It can be based on personal identity or power imbalance.

Imposter Syndrome

The persistent belief that one's success is undeserved or due to luck is often experienced by competent individuals who are regularly undermined or unrecognized.

Invisible Labor

Unacknowledged and uncompensated tasks, such as providing emotional support, mentorship, or extra administrative duties, are often expected of supervisors without formal recognition.

Micromanagement

Excessive control over minor details of an employee's work, often signaling mistrust and stripping the individual of autonomy, decision-making power, and creativity.

Nepotism

Favoritism granted to relatives or close associates in employment or promotions, regardless of qualification. It undermines merit-based advancement.

Occupational Stress

Chronic stress related to job demands, control imbalance, and lack of support which can lead to serious health issues if unaddressed.

Psychological Safety

A work environment where individuals feel safe to speak up, share ideas, or report issues without fear of humiliation, punishment, or retaliation.

Retaliation

Negative actions taken against an employee for reporting misconduct, raising concerns, or exercising legal rights. Examples include demotion, exclusion, or job threats.

Stereotyping

Assigning generalized traits or behaviors to an individual based on their identity (e.g., race, gender, age) often leads to unfair treatment or assumptions.

Surveillance Culture

A workplace norm in which employees are excessively monitored—through cameras, keystroke tracking, or software—creating stress, distrust, and a lack of privacy.

Systemic Abuse

Harmful practices that are not isolated incidents but embedded in the structure, culture, or leadership of an organization. These patterns are often normalized or go unchallenged.

Tokenism

The practice of making only a symbolic effort to include individuals from marginalized groups while maintaining unequal structures of power and privilege.

Trauma (Workplace)

Emotional and psychological harm resulting from prolonged exposure to toxic environments, including abuse, discrimination, and dehumanization. May lead to anxiety, depression, or PTSD.

Whistleblower

An employee who exposes unethical or illegal practices within an organization. Whistleblowers often face retaliation despite legal protections.

References for Further Reading

1. French, J.R.P., & Raven, B. (1959). *The Bases of Social Power*. Studies in Social Power.
2. Kipnis, D., Schmidt, S.M., & Wilkinson, I. (1980). Intraorganizational Influence Tactics: Explorations in Getting One's Way. *Journal of Applied Psychology, 65*(4), 440–452.
3. Northouse, P.G. (2018). *Leadership: Theory and Practice* (8th ed.). Sage Publications.
4. SHRM. (2021). *Managing Difficult Supervisors*. Society for Human Resource Management.
5. Mayo Clinic Staff. (2020). *Job Burnout: How to Spot It and Take Action*. Mayo Clinic.
6. Edmondson, A.C. (2019). *The Fearless Organization: Creating Psychological Safety in the Workplace for Learning, Innovation, and Growth*. Wiley.
7. Gallup. (2021). *State of the Global Workplace: 2021 Report*. Gallup Press.
8. Harvard Business Review. (2020). *Toxic Leadership: How It's Created and How to Fix It*. HBR.
9. Liu, D., Liao, H., & Loi, R. (2019). The Dark Side of Leadership: A Three-Level Investigation of the Cascading Effect of Abusive Supervision on Employee Creativity. *Journal of Occupational Health Psychology, 24*(1), 52–65.
10. Maxwell, J.C. (2013). *Developing the Leader Within You 2.0*. HarperCollins.
11. Brown, B. (2018). *Dare to Lead: Brave Work. Tough Conversations. Whole Hearts*. Random House.
12. American Psychological Association. (2020). *Workplace Stress and Social Support*. APA.
13. Kouzes, J.M., & Posner, B.Z. (2017). *The Leadership Challenge: How to Make Extraordinary Things Happen in Organizations* (6th ed.). Wiley.
14. Patterson, K., Grenny, J., McMillan, R., & Switzler, A. (2012). *Crucial Conversations: Tools for Talking When Stakes Are High*. McGraw-Hill.
15. Society for Human Resource Management. (2022). *Managing Conflict in the Workplace*. SHRM.
16. Benioff, M., & Adler, C. (2019). *Trailblazer: The Power of Business as the Greatest Platform for Change*. Currency.
17. Chouinard, Y., & Stanley, V. (2012). *The Responsible Company: What We've Learned from Patagonia's First 40 Years*. Patagonia Books.
18. Fisher, C.D., & Cortina, L.M. (2021). Using Technology to Detect and Address Workplace Mistreatment. *Journal of Organizational Behavior, 42*(6), 673–689.
19. Garvin, D.A. (2013). How Google Sold Its Engineers on Management. *Harvard Business Review*.
20. Nadella, S., & Shaw, G. (2017). *Hit Refresh: The Quest to Rediscover Microsoft's Soul and Imagine a Better Future for Everyone*. Harper Business.
21. Robertson, B.J. (2015). *Holacracy: The New Management System for a Rapidly Changing World*. Henry Holt and Co.
22. Kotter, J.P., & Heskett, J.L. (2008). *Corporate Culture and Performance*. Free Press.
23. Senge, P.M. (1990). *The Fifth Discipline: The Art & Practice of the Learning Organization*. Doubleday.
24. Pink, D. (2009). *Drive: The Surprising Truth About What Motivates Us*. Riverhead Books.
25. Drucker, P.F. (1999). *Management Challenges for the 21st Century*. Harper Business.

26. Gallup. (2020). *State of the American Manager: Analytics and Advice for Leaders*. Gallup, Inc.

27. Harvard Business Review. (2018). *What Great Managers Do to Engage Their Teams*. Harvard Business Review.

28. Men, L.R. (2015). The Impact of Leadership Communication on Employees' Attitudes and Behaviors. *Journal of Business Communication, 52*(3), 341–363.

29. Smith, P., et al. (2018). The Psychological Impact of Workplace Humiliation: A Study of Employees' Mental Health Outcomes. *Journal of Occupational Health Psychology, 23*(2), 243–255.

30. Goleman, D. (1998). *Emotional Intelligence*. Bantam Books.

31. Einarsen, S., Hoel, H., Zapf, D., & Cooper, C. (2011). *Bullying and Harassment in the Workplace*. CRC Press.

32. American Psychological Association. (2017). *Workplace Bullying and Mental Health. APA Monitor on Psychology*.

33. Sweet, P.L. (2019). The Sociology of Gaslighting. *American Sociological Review, 84*(5), 851–875.

34. Zapf, D., & Einarsen, S. (2005). Mobbing at Work: Escalated Conflicts in Organizations. *European Journal of Work and Organizational Psychology, 14*(4), 445–460.

35. Cummings, T.G., & Worley, C.G. (2014). *Organization Development and Change*. Cengage Learning.

36. Carter, E. (2019). *Leadership and Accountability in the Workplace*. Organizational Psychology Press.

37. Smith, J. (2018). *Managing Up: Building Effective Communication*. Business Leadership Quarterly.

38. Jacobs, F. (2018). *Everyday Leadership Ethics*. Ethical Leadership Press.

39. Bandura, A. (1999). Moral Disengagement in the Perpetration of Inhumanities. *Personality and Social Psychology Review, 3*(3), 193–209.

40. Banks, S. (2016). *Ethics and Values in Social Work*. Macmillan International Higher Education.

41. Cortina, L.M., & Berdahl, J.L. (2008). Sexual Harassment in Organizations: A Decade of Research in Review. In *The SAGE Handbook of Organizational Behavior* (pp. 469–497).

42. DeNisi, A.S., & Williams, K.J. (2018). Performance Appraisal and Performance Management: 100 Years of Progress? *Journal of Applied Psychology, 103*(3), 294–314.

43. Moss-Racusin, C.A., et al. (2012). Science Faculty's Subtle Gender Biases Favor Male Students. *Proceedings of the National Academy of Sciences, 109*(41), 16474–16479.

44. Raver, J.L., & Nishii, L.H. (2010). Once, Twice, or Three Times as Harmful? Ethnic Harassment, Gender Harassment, and Generalized Workplace Harassment. *Journal of Applied Psychology, 95*(2), 236–254.

45. Blau, F.D., & Kahn, L.M. (2000). Gender Differences in Pay. *Journal of Economic Perspectives, 14*(4), 75–99.

46. Castilla, E.J. (2015). Accounting for the Gap: A Firm Study Manipulating Organizational Accountability and Transparency in Pay Decisions. *Organization Science, 26*(2), 311–333.

47. Milkovich, G.T., Newman, J.M., & Gerhart, B. (2014). *Compensation*. McGraw-Hill.

48. Anderson, C., & Brown, C.E. (2010). The Functions and Dysfunctions of Hierarchy in Organizations. *Research in Organizational Behavior, 30*, 55–89. https://doi.org/10.1016/j.riob.2010.08.002

www.ingramcontent.com/pod-product-compliance
Lightning Source LLC
Chambersburg PA
CBHW081653120626
46550CB00010B/2881